PLYMOUTH STATION
THE SHIP-(DERRIFORD)
DARTMOOR
ROLAND LEVINSKI BUILDING - UNIVERSITY OF PLYMOUTH
CIVIC CENTRE
DRAKE CIRCUS SHOPPING CENTRE
HALL
D SPA-
LYMPTON)
ANDREW THE FISHERMAN
CKLEY
OINT
THE MINSTER CHURCH OF ST ANDREW
THEATRE ROYAL & MESSENGER
THE BARCODE
BURNT OUT CHURCH
PLYMOUTH COLLEGE OF ART
ETHODIST CENTRAL HALL
SYNAGOGUE
DRAKE
CROWNE PLAZA
GIN DISTILLERY
SUTTON HARBOUR
THE BARBICAN
LLIOT TERRACE
SENSORY GARDEN
WAR MEMORIAL
MAYFLOWER STEPS
PLYMOUTH FISH MARKET EST. 1892
VUE CINEMA
VUE CINEMA
THE DOME
VIKING STONE
NANCY ASTOR
SMEATON'S TOWER
ROYAL CITADEL
NATIONAL MARINE AQUARIUM
SOUTH WEST COAST PATH
TINSIDE LIDO
ANNUAL FIREWORK CHAMPIONSHIPS
1650
MOUNTBATTEN ACTIVITY CENTRE
MOUNTBATTEN SPIT
MOUNTBATTEN TOWER
N
W
E
S
BOVISAND

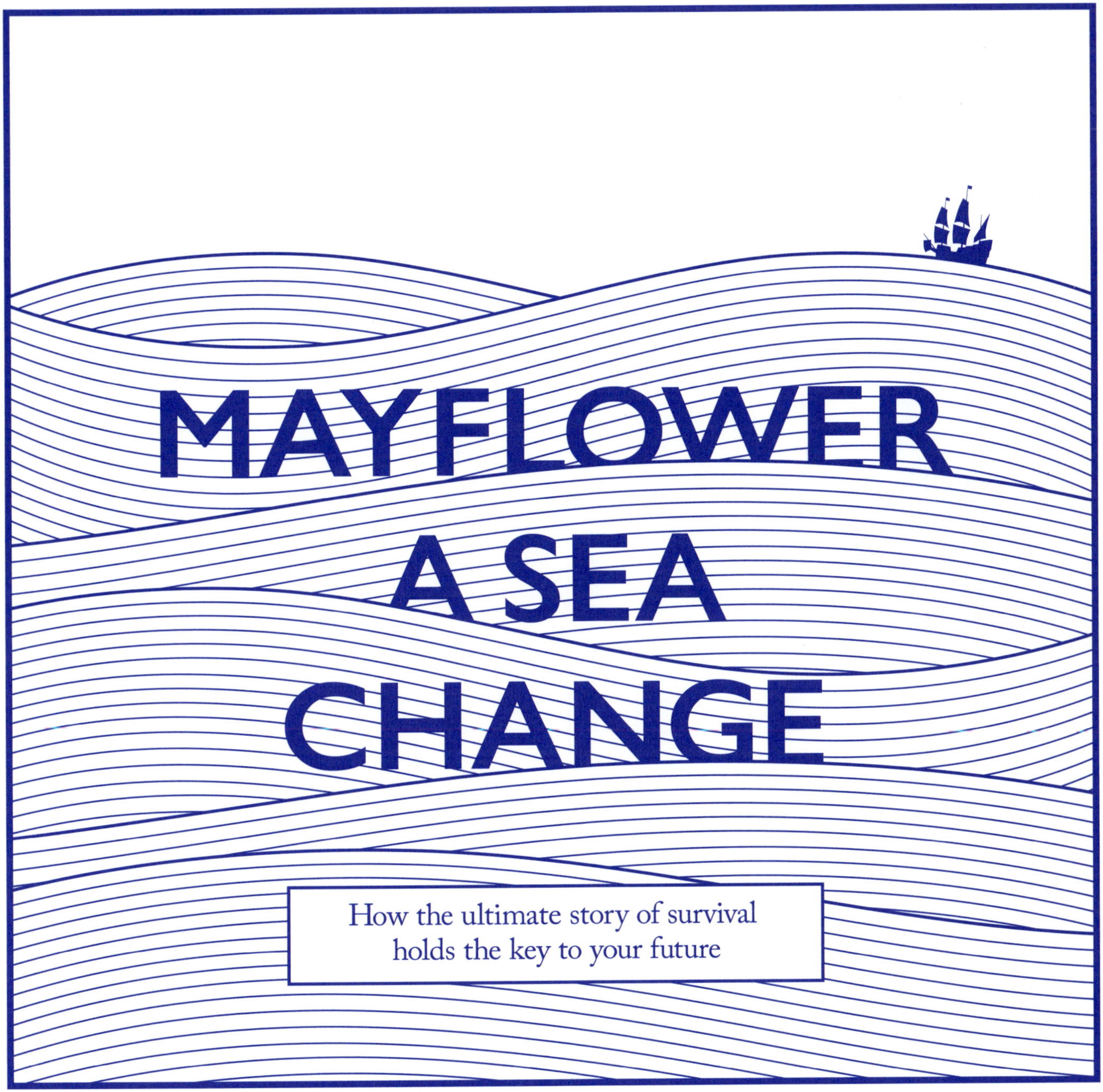

MAYFLOWER A SEA CHANGE

How the ultimate story of survival
holds the key to your future

Bookfluential
Office 1, Residence 2
Royal William Yard
Plymouth PL1 3RP
wordfluential.com

ISBN 978–1–9993493–2–5

Typeset in Adobe Caslon Pro and Gill Sans Nova.
Design by James Edgar Studio. Printed by Deltor.

First Edition. May 9th, 2020. Edited by Charlie Keeler.

Contents

Preface

It's 400 years, 20 generations, 35 million Americans and a mass of cultural and technological changes, since a small ship called the Mayflower, carrying 102 brave souls and 30 crew, set out on an epic odyssey that was not only destined to change its passengers' lives irrevocably, but the very course of world history.

We're a team of writers, publishers, designers and artists, living in Plymouth, Britain's Ocean City, who think there's an even bigger story yet to be told about this most famous of global voyages, and now is the time to tell it. We want people to come on a journey with us: to learn more about the Mayflower story, the story of its people and what led up to it casting off from the Mayflower Steps on Sept 16, 1620 into the dark forbidding seas of the Atlantic, during the hurricane season. We also want to tell the story of its launchpad: Plymouth. A city that's often under-rated – sometimes even ridiculed – in modern times, but a city that has a place in history as the starting point of many of the world's most important and fabulous voyages of discovery and naval campaigns.

We also want you to understand the Wampanoag's story and what happened to the world within which they had existed for 25,000 years and how the Mayflower's arrival and subsequent ships, affected them long term. And, as we continue through the uncharted waters of the 21st century, like in 1620, there's a sea change ahead, owing to: the environmental impact of humanity, immigration, trade, greed, globalisation, pandemics, and challenges to our freedom. The earth can live without us, but we can't live without it. With you, we want to explore some of the themes that face our world, and, by inspiring discussion and debate, invite you to become part of delivering the solutions.

With a pandemic, the equivalent of a modern day plague shutting the entire world down, it has never been more important to look at the past for answers and come up with solutions for a better future, so that both the planet and we survive for the next four hundred years.

Foreword
Wampanoags

Before the arrival, in 1620, of the Mayflower ship that changed the world, Patuxet, in what is now called New England, in the USA, had been part of the Great Wampanoag Nation's territory for 25,000 years.

"The Mayflower 400th anniversary Commemoration in 2020 has great potential. However, the question is whether it will be fulfilled or not," says Cheryl Andrews-Maltais, Chairwoman of The Wampanoag Tribe of Gay Head, Aquinnah. "From the English side, the colonial side, it was a tremendous thing; the people were intrepid, they were brave, bold, and adventurous. They endured incredible hardships and overcame challenges unlike any others in their community. They were able to grow and build for themselves, with our assistance of course, what you see today, and it could and should be celebrated from that perspective. However, on the Wampanoag Indian side, it was devastating to us. Because that which was built, was built on our backs, on our lands, with our resources, using germ warfare, early forms of concentration camp, with forced acculturation, forced Christianity, the forced dispossession of our lands, our traditions, our language, our culture, our speech and our dress; essentially our identity. They have the potential at this 400 year anniversary to bring that truth to the forefront, to balance the story by saying what really happened to us, so we can begin to heal from the atrocities perpetrated against us."

> We can't move forward without healing, We can't heal without the acknowledgement.
>
> *Cheryl Andrews-Maltais, Chairwoman of the Wampanoag Tribe of Gay Head, Aquinnah*

Cheryl, currently serving her fourth term as chairwoman, was the first Tribal Leader to receive a Presidential appointment in Washington DC by the Obama Administration, as a Senior Advisor to the Assistant Secretary – Indian Affairs. She was also named the 2019, 24th Annual National Indian Women's Supporting Each Other, Woman of The Year. She is a Descendant of the Talknot, Ooccooch (or Aucooch) and Haskins Family. Cheryl and many leading members of the Wampanoag community have helped us tell their version of the story in this book.

Cheryl Andrews-Maltais, Chairwoman of the Wampanoag Tribe of Gay Head, Aquinnah

As the Wampanoags were wary of European raiders, who had been pillaging along their shores for centuries, and latterly almost certainly bringing European diseases with them that decimated their numbers between 1616 and 1619, in what become known as the 'Great Dying', and because they had moved into the forests for the winter hunting, they did not make contact with the Mayflower passengers for four months. Instead, scouts kept a watchful eye on them from a distance. "But the Mayflower's passengers were different," says Cheryl. "There were women and children on board and half of them died that first terrible winter, so we decided to help the remainder of them, according to our tribal teachings to preserve all life," Cheryl explains. "Had we made a different choice, Mayflower 400 most likely wouldn't be happening."

Before the Mayflower passengers were able to establish the first settlement in America, whereby governors were elected, not appointed by the Crown, they drew up, with the Wampanoags, the Great Treaty of Peace in 1621, signed by Massasoit (Great Chief) Ousemaquin (Yellow Feather), with his wolf insignia and John Carver, the first elected Governor of the colony. The treaty was to provide mutual protection, and the English military expertise, guns and bullets were a powerful deterrent against advancing hostile tribes, and other European invaders like the French, Dutch and Spanish. Additional to providing strategic knowledge and short range quick fire fighting capabilities, the Wampanoag people shared their deep knowledge of the land with the English, in a sometimes uneasy cultural mix. Archaeology now reveals Wampanoag artefacts of the same period found next to European style homes in Plymouth colony's oldest street, Leiden, showing how they co-existed in the early years after the Pilgrims arrival.

The Wampanoags had for 25,000 years lived in close harmony with the land and natural environment, and were led by male or female Sachems (chiefs) through inheritance, if fit to rule, or elected by the elders and mothers of the tribe, otherwise.

They traditionally worked together, growing food and collecting herbs for medicines. As highly sophisticated growers of corn (maize), squashes and beans, the Native Peoples of America were responsible for the development of corn, into being the most highly nutritious, widely grown, tropical plant in the world today. Grown in the centre of mounds, with climbing beans and soil protecting squashes around their bases, and fertilised with marine compost, they were able to feed two people per acre, in stark contrast to the Mayflower 'newcomers', as the Wampanoags called them, who could only support one person per 10 acres with crops grown in rows, which were maladapted to the soils of Massachusetts. The secrets of this staggering twentyfold difference in yield were taught to the newcomers by the Wampanoags, and were essential to their survival. They were also accomplished traders of seeds for volcanic stone, from which they made their arrowheads.

The Wampanoags lived with the seasons, building wooden dome wetus (homes), which were much better suited for cold weather than the colonial houses, which needed a lot more heating. Wetus were made from layers of large cedar bark panels laid over a sapling framework, tied together using bull rushes, which, being water absorbent, also kept the air inside cool in hot weather. Outside were cat-tails, which, when wet, created a barrier against adverse weather. The wetus could be dismantled and rebuilt in different places, making them not only sustainable, but also environmentally friendly.

The Wampanoag tribal women were bemused by the strange female 'newcomers' who wore thick layers of restrictive European clothing, that caused them to swelter in the summer months. Even on a blisteringly hot day,

working the land, they weren't allowed to discard them, to cool off in the river, like the Wampanoag women. Also, Englishmen struggled to accept tribal women as chiefs, in control of land, and refused to negotiate with them, instead trying to enforce change on them, to fit English forms of government.

What started out as being a merchant adventurer's initial investment in the Mayflower enterprise, of £7,000 (a fortune in its day), returned less than £1,800, but, after seeing how Bradford and half his group survived the harsh winter to form a successful colony, in great part owing to the adoption of the Wampanoags' farming methods and good seedstocks, and the peace treaty with them, others were inspired to emigrate from England. The numbers of ships arriving increased dramatically a decade later, "like the waves on the ocean, they kept rolling in and would not stop, eventually outnumbering the Wampanoags," says Cheryl. These new arrivals, some coming in warships, had a very different attitude: hungry for land, dominion and profit. The treaty finally collapsed in 1675 after the horrific land grabbing of the Massachusetts Bay Colony, settled by Royal Charter with quite different objectives than Plymouth.

> Thanksgiving is celebrated at the expense of native peoples, who had to give up their lands and culture for America to become what it is today.
>
> *Linda Coombs, author and historian from the Wampanoag Tribe of Gay Head*

This led to Sachem Metacom's War (King Phillip's War) with terrifyingly barbaric results; his severed head was displayed for 20 years in the Plymouth colony, while the 8 year old grandson of the deceased Massasoit Ousamequin, who made the original treaty to collaborate and help the 'newcomers', was ironically and appallingly sold into slavery in 1676.

The Native People were forced to adopt the newcomers' religion and a legislative style that didn't match their ancient ways of balancing the land as a gift from the Creator. Instead this great civilisation was totally marginalised and they were treated as foreigners in their own homelands. In truth, "New England" had become no more free than England, "Yes, as your governor, I am free from King James to practice my religion and you, too, are free from King James to practice my religion. But if I don't see you in church on Sunday, I will see you in Church on Monday for a fine," explains Christopher Messier, Visitors' Services Supervisor, Pilgrim Memorial State Park, standing next to where the newcomers first settled. Wampanoags say, ultimately, the English took more with the pen, than with the gun and essentially outlawed their way of life, reducing their population to 5,000 from 67,000 in 1620. But, against all odds, it has continued in pockets like Aquinnah, Mashpee and Pokanoket. Cheryl, like her peers, is deeply conflicted about the Mayflower Commemorations, having been forced, like her ancestors, to lead two lives, which is symbolised by the wampum jewellery she wears at the interview; a combination of white and purple shells representing the duality of the world she lives in. She does not want an empty apology, she wants the Wampanoag's rich cultural wisdom correctly taught in schools and, most important of all, the return of the pieces of the Great Wampum Belt (the equivalent of the crown jewels), ripped off the butchered body of Sachem Metacom, which were given away as war trophies.

In the 1970s, Frank James, 'Wamsutta', then the Wampanoag leader, first revealed these brutal truths on Thanksgiving day, which the authorities tried to suppress. This led to the National Day Of Mourning on Burial Hill, with a plaque condemning the stealing of their land and the brutal ignoring of their culture. Ultimately, it's not about just saying sorry; the trauma of what happened needs to be emotionally addressed. "We need to get back to a fundamental respect for all things living. Everything has spirit energy, even the rocks," says Cheryl. Until the truth is acknowledged, how can we all move forward from this mythologised version of events? We know where we are going, we have been here before, as the ancient cultural wisdom teaches us, we will survive and start again, as we get nearer the 28,000 year change."

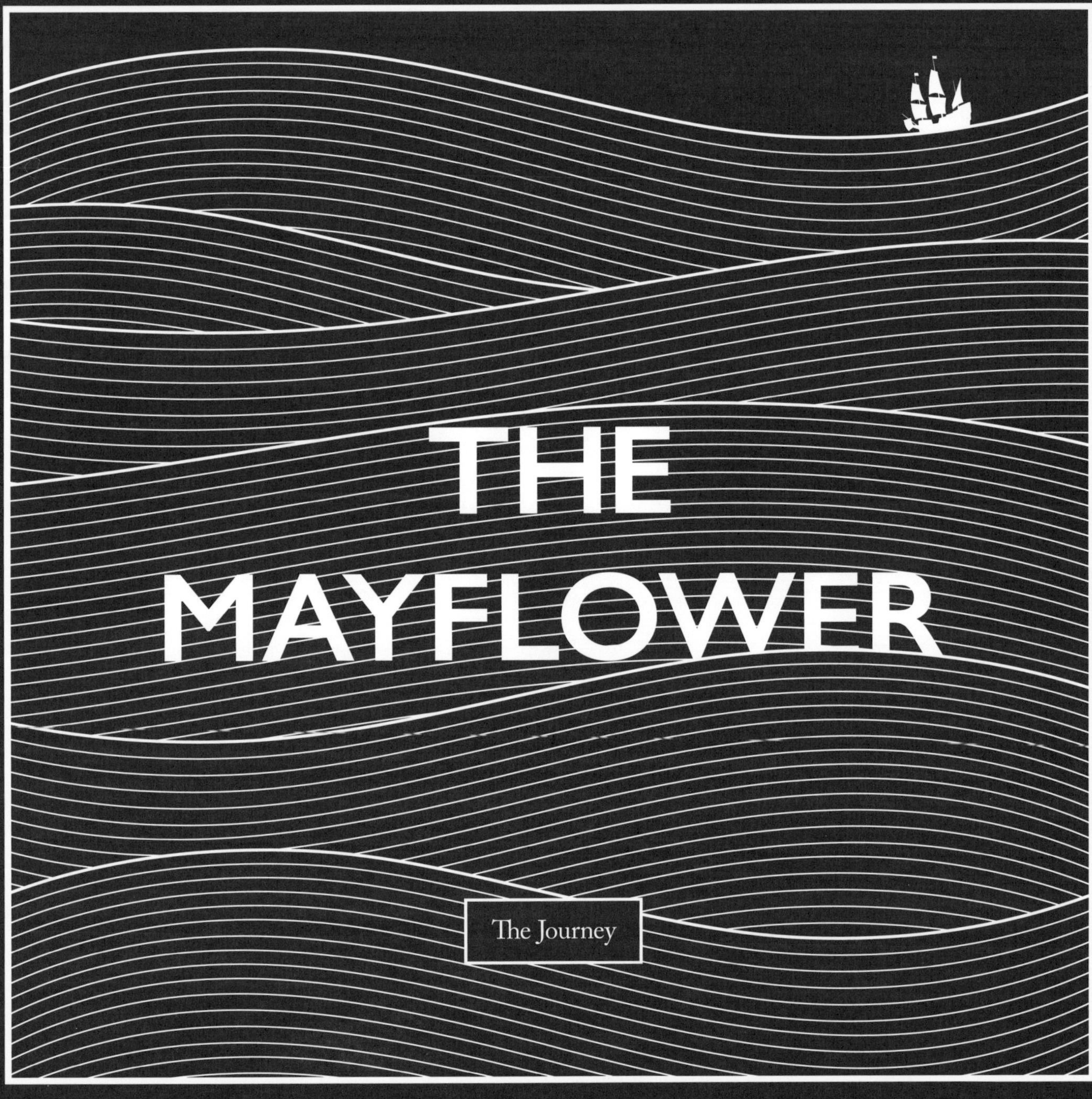

THE MAYFLOWER

The Journey

The Mayflower Introduction

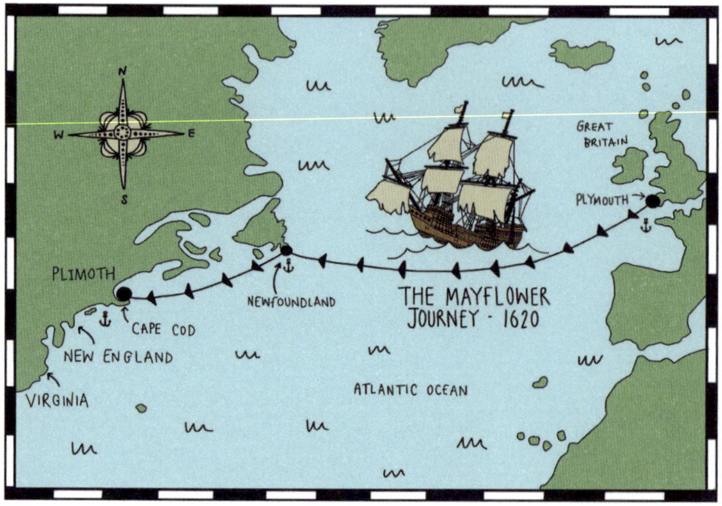

In some ways, the story of a small timber ship, crammed with an assortment of passengers that crossed the Atlantic in 1620, to start a new settlement on the east coast of North America, is a tale that could have faded into history, like ink fading on a sun-bleached page. But, the journey of the Mayflower is a story that has captured the popular imagination for centuries and resonates as much today – as we face political fallout in Europe in 2020 over trade, debt, monopolies, regulations, pandemics, health scares, and immigration – as it did 400 years ago.

The issues that drove the passengers to get on the boat in search of a better life reflect many of the global tensions that still threaten to tear our world apart, today. The search for greater freedoms, land, trade, clear boundaries, power, economic independence and sustainability, all helped propel that ship across the Sea of Darkness.

Our book is the story of that journey and its people from 400 years ago. But it's also an exploration of the city that launched the Mayflower and the people who live in Plymouth today. Through their stories, and looking at their 17th century equivalents, we hope to learn about the past as much as the present. And what do the people who live and work in Britain's Ocean City think life will be like, 400 years from now?

It's a fascinating journey. Come with us, find out what resonates with you, and explore how you, too, can be part of building a sustainable and balanced future for the next 400 years. Be part of the next sea change!

The solutions are not out there, but within all of us, working together, to discover the truths within.

Why
The Mayflower?

"The first to colonise as whole families, they signed a compact agreeing to civil and religious freedoms that influenced the Constitution; created a 54 year peace treaty with the Wampanoags in 1621; and had a 3-day harvest festival with them, that became Thanksgiving."

Lea Sinclair Filson, Mayflower President, Meetinghouse Trust, Director of Tourism, Massachusetts USA

The Mayflower was not the first ship to sail to North America. The Plymouth colonists were a small part of a wider, loosely planned, effort to colonise the continent, following as they did in the footsteps of the Jamestown colony. The Mayflower Compact and the first treaty with the Wampanoags were perhaps the first steps towards the establishment of American democracy and, it's thought, many of its successful ancestral families, including nine presidents. It was also the start of 'the great migration' that changed the lives of the Native Peoples beyond recognition. Later boats brought in draconian land laws, dictated what people could wear and destroyed their culture, as cover for a massive land-grab.

"The 400th anniversary of the Mayflower voyage is referred to as a commemoration, and not a celebration, by both sets of descendants. The Wampanoags, while acknowledging the half century of peace with the Pilgrims, are commemorating the devastating loss of their way of life in the aftermath of colonial settlements, when peace was torn to pieces and waves of other colonists arrived with very different motives. Mayflower descendants are commemorating the loss of over half the pilgrims in the first winter, while stressing the important contribution they made to America as founding families," says Lea Filson. And, while some argue that the real impact of the story has been wildly exaggerated by 19th Century Americans, it still provides a grass roots picture of larger, politically expedient efforts to colonise North America and the forces shaping the West at the time.

The Great Voyage

If infant American democracy was brought to life by the so-called 'Pilgrim Fathers' and their Mayflower Compact, it was born out of one of the most hellish journeys of all time, aboard the Mayflower and through the first winter.

Of the original 102 passengers and at least 30 crew members, who boarded the small wooden ship on 16th September, 1620 in Plymouth, England, 45 of them would be dead within six months; weakened by the terrible crossing of the Atlantic and finished off by a harsh first winter in their new world.

Known by many as 'the boat of nobility', the Mayflower carried a fascinating mix of passengers: 74 were male and 28 female, of which 19 were servants and around 30 were children. And, while 46 of them were religious Pilgrim Separatists from Leiden, who were travelling to set up a new colony where they could live more freely, according to their conscience, more than half of the passengers, though likely to be religious, were not Separatists. These were a mix of commercial prospectors from the London and Plymouth companies, who were sent to establish settlements chiefly for trade and to satisfy the English Crown.

Notable pilgrims included William Brewster, a Separatist leader, elder, teacher and most educated amongst them, who had worked under the Queen's Secretary, William Davison, while he travelled to France to negotiate peace with Spain in 1576, and later, to ally with William of Orange to prevent a Catholic alliance from invading England, (Brewster also had a chair and four islands named after him). Also on board was William Bradford, who became the great governor, cataloguer and writer of On Plimoth Plantation, that charted their adventures and progress, as a small group of Separatists seeking some corner of the globe to live peaceably. Elizabeth Tillie was a thirteen year old, soon to be orphaned girl, who, full of spirit, went on to mother 10 children and become the grandmother of 88 children; Elizabeth Hopkins, gave birth to the first Mayflower born baby, Oceanus; and Susannah White gave birth to the first American born pilgrim, Peregrine.

This unusual assortment of humanity left behind forever their comfortable beds, familiar smells of home-cooking, stargazy pie, morgy broth, Sunday roasts, and the relative safety of England and Holland.

They set off two months late, after endless delays, owing to the Speedwell, the smaller boat they bought in Holland, taking on water, and eventually being declared unseaworthy. Despite strong advice not to depart during the stormy season, the passengers were beyond impatient to leave, feeling the voyage would never happen if delayed for a moment longer. After a reasonable start, poor weather set in and high winds caused them to slow down to snail's pace across a massive body of unforgiving water, into the highest of seas and winds.

They crawled at an average of two miles per hour on a 66 day voyage in a basic damp wooden boat, designed for cargo, with damaged caulking. Living conditions must have been terrible. There were no windows, limited space, nowhere to wash and no toilets, except chamber pots that would regularly have been knocked over in stormy weather.

Imagine being with a hundred other people in the dark, damp, stinking and low ceilinged cargo space, normally reserved for wine caskets and barrels and without natural light. This was further compounded by the increasingly long nights as stormy winter weather slowly wrapped its icy fingers around them.

Supplies were somewhat diminished as a result of the length of the journey and at this time of year the seas were at their most turbulent with annual storms, so chronic seasickness was rampant.

The terrible effects of scurvy, abominable smells and non-existent hygiene battered away at exhausted immune systems. Sufferers would have looked like characters out of Dawn of the Dead; badly bruised all over, gums bleeding and swollen, teeth starting to fall out, skin deathly pale where not darkly bruised, and falling about like paralytics from general weakness – all for a lack of citrus fruit, containing the critical vitamin C that would have prevented all these symptoms of scurvy.

The threat from the angel of death lurked in the shadows and atop each giant wave. The rough and unforgiving crew could sense it; one of their youngest (depicted in Chapter 9 of William Bradford's On Plimoth Plantation) revelled in the fears and degradation of the pious passengers, persecuting them mercilessly.

The pilgrims were only momentarily relieved, through 'God's providence', when the sea claimed their tormentor, after being stricken with a sudden fatal illness. The other fatality was one poor soul, William Butten, a servant who was sick the entire trip, only to die a few days before arriving at Cape Cod. It must have been living hell for the pregnant women, who were on board, unable to wash for 66 days, weighed down in heavy wet clothing.

The signing of the Mayflower Compact

The Arrival of the Mayflower in North America

While arriving at Cape Cod must have been a huge relief, had they but known it, their troubles had only just begun.

They intended to land on the mouth of the Hudson River but, thanks to storms, arrived at Provincetown, Cape Cod, hundreds of miles further up the coast than intended, into an early harsh winter that had months still to run. There was no known place to shelter ashore and no certain way of growing or obtaining food in this territory.

While the pilgrims aboard the ship had different motives for being there, they all accepted the need for a way of governing their new community.

The Mayflower pilgrims had no Crown patent to settle in this land, so before they left the ship, they drew up a document that gave them some sort of legal standing and basis for governing themselves. The Mayflower Compact was a document designed to establish the rules and values of their new community. Signed by 41 of them, it was based very much on religious values and the influence of Magna Carta; an agreement to cooperate for the general good of the colony. They would deal with issues by voting, establishing constitutional law and ruling by the majority.

The Mayflower Compact:

In the name of God, Amen. We, whose names are underwritten, the loyal subjects of our dread Sovereigne Lord, King James, by the grace of God, of Great Britaine, France and Ireland king, defender of the faith, etc. having undertaken, for the glory of God, and advancement of the Christian faith, and honour of our king and country, a voyage to plant the first colony in the Northerne parts of Virginia, doe by these presents solemnly and mutually in the presence of God and one of another, covenant and combine ourselves together into a civill body politick, for our better ordering and preservation, and furtherance of the ends aforesaid; and by virtue hereof to enacte, constitute, and frame such just and equall laws, ordinances, acts, constitutions and offices, from time to time, as shall be thought most meete and convenient for the generall good of the Colonie unto which we promise all due submission and obedience. In witness whereof we have hereunder subscribed our names at Cape-Codd the 11. of November, in the year of the raigne of our sovereigne lord, King James, of England, France and Ireland, the eighteenth, and of Scotland the fiftie-fourth. Anno Dom. 1620.

> The Pilgrims had come to America not to conquer a continent but to re-create their modest communities in Scrooby and in Leiden. When they arrived at Plymouth in December 1620 and found it emptied of people, it seemed as if God had given them exactly what they were looking for.
>
> *Nathaniel Philbrick, Mayflower: A Story of Courage, Community, and War (2006).*

That first winter was fierce: "…for the ground was now covered with snow, and so hard frozen, that we were fain with our cutlasses and short swords, to hew and carve the ground a foot deep, and then wrest it up with levers," Mourts Relation.

The threat of starvation drove the pilgrims to borrow, without permission, corn and other foods from the neighbouring tribes, intending to make good when they later met with them: "and got aboard that night, intending to have brought some beads, and other things to have left in the houses, in sign of peace, and that we meant to truck with them, but it was not done, by means of our hasty coming away from Cape Cod, but so soon as we can meet conveniently with them, we will give them full satisfaction," Mourts Relation.

Looking for food stores, they also dug up some of the tribal graves where food offerings and seed for the next year's crop had been left. While, in some cases, they were guilty of taking 'the prettiest things', before covering the graves up again, we find them also showing respect as written in Mourt's Relation: "we musing what it might be, digged and found a bow, and, as we thought, arrows, but they were rotten; we supposed there were many other things, but because we deemed them graves, we put in the bow again and made it up as it was, and left the rest untouched, because we thought it would be odious unto them to ransack their sepulchers."

The settlers were not expecting a warm welcome from the local indigenous tribe, the Wampanoags, who were rightly still incensed by their people being illegally sold by a rogue Captain Thomas Hunt: "These people are ill affected towards the English, by reason of one Hunt, a master of a ship, who deceived the people, and got them under color of trucking with them, twenty out of this very place where we inhabit, and seven men from Nauset, and carried them away, and sold them for slaves, like a wretched man (for 20 pound a man) that cares not what mischief he doth for his profit." Mourts Relation.

Having lived in Massachusetts for around 25,000 years, the Wampanoags have a rich understanding of the land and cycles of nature. The immediate area around where the pilgrims landed belonged to the Patuxet, a subtribe of the Wampanoags, which had been completely annihilated by a European disease, except for Squanto, later the Pilgrims' interpreter and friend, who had been carried off into slavery, by the treacherous Hunt, years before.

The Wampanoags are accomplished farmers and strongly spiritual. They believe in thanking the earth, the plants, the animals, and any living thing, knowing that without them they would be unable to live; they know the importance of being connected to the land and the living. They were also expert sustainable home builders.

The Wampanoags were once very much in the ascendancy, numbering around 67,000, until some European ships had visited them between 1615 and 1619, and with them a 'virgin soil epidemic' of one or a combination of smallpox, plague, leptospirosis, or diphtheria. Their numbers had subsequently shrunk dramatically, leading to the growth of other rival tribes looking to protect and expand their territories.

However, first contact with the Wampanoags wasn't made until four months after the pilgrims' arrival, and relations with the tribe only really began on March 16, 1621, when a brave Wampanoag called Samoset, who knew a little English from previous fishermen's visits, walked into their camp, and said 'Welcome Englishmen', much to the settlers surprise. Samoset then introduced Miles Standish and the learned William Bradford to the Wampanoag tribal leaders. Subsequent contacts with the Wampanoags were peaceful.

An alliance was set up, after some hand kissing and exchanging of gifts, between Massasoit Ousamequin and John Carver, then Governor of Plimoth, on 22nd March, who then declared:

01 *That neither he nor any of his should injure or do hurt to any of our people.*

02 *And if any of his did hurt to any of ours, he should send the offender, that we might punish him.*

03 *That if any of our tools were taken away when our people are at work, he should cause them to be restored, and if ours did any harm to any of his, we would do the like to them.*

04 *If any did unjustly war against him, we would aid him; if any did war against us, he should aid us.*

05 *He should send to his neighbour confederates, to certify them of this, that they might not wrong us, but might be likewise comprised in the conditions of peace.*

06 *That when their men came to us, they should leave their bows and arrows behind them, as we should do our pieces when we came to them.*

As documented in Mourts Relation,1622.

The Wampanoags and Mayflower Pilgrims stood by their words and all was well with the Plimoth Plantation and the Wampanoags, especially owing to the skills of Squanto, the fluent English speaking Wamapanoag interpreter, who many say, was crucial to the success of building this first treaty and initial good relations.

In November 1621, they all assembled for the first Thanksgiving feast to celebrate the harvest, thanking God for His graciousness and thanking the Wampanoags, who taught the English about the environment and how to hunt and grow food on their land.

Many gifts went to and fro between the Wampanoags and Pilgrims and they collaborated successfully during the early years, often fighting alongside each other, defending each other against other tribes, other European settlers and occasionally other rogue English elements.

William Bradford, in his book *On Plimoth Plantation*, writes of Mayflower pilgrims purchasing land from, and trading furs with, the Native Peoples at the beginning, which suggests that the original intentions were honourable and the trouble arose at a later time, which tragically shaped the darker side of America's history.

Despite the Mayflower pilgrims' promising start at the Plimoth colony, relations between subsequent settlers and the Native Peoples dramatically soured as cultural differences became accentuated and many more ships arrived of passengers with different motives and sensibilities.

A bag was delivered to the pilgrims containing a bucket of arrowheads. The Wampanoags, explained that this was a symbol of what another tribe intended to do to the pilgrims if they stayed. The bag was duly returned to the tribe, filled with lead shot. All went very quiet.

Inevitably, tensions grew over trade, land, the later puritans' increasing religious intolerance and attempts to force acceptance of the settler culture, language and rules.

Many of these settlers were sanctimonious and felt that the Wampanoags should practice the Puritans' form of Christianity, and observe their rules of conduct; ironic since these were the same people who were escaping religious persecution in England.

There was also a drive to profit from the surrounding forests and trade in beaver skins, leading to disagreements between the settlers and the local populations, who enjoyed trading, too, but equally valued balance in nature.

The Next Grim Chapter

What happened next was a grim chapter in America's history. Other ships arrived from Europe over the next decade, but immigration really took off from 1630 to 1640, when around 80,000 Puritans settled in Massachusetts, carrying a form of religious zealotry, and others with only selfish intentions, which brought them into conflict with each other and the Native Peoples, thereby introducing a strange mix of intolerant, criminal and barbaric behaviours to this more peaceful old world culture.

A one-sided history was created as part of the propaganda.

The new colonists were faced with tribes of Native Peoples, who were now in conflict with each other, concerned at uncontrolled immigration and who had been rightly embittered by the previous actions of some unscrupulous Europeans, the seizing of their lands and marginalisation of their culture.

The result was brutal and bloody, and the special relationship with the spiritually wise Wampanoag, without whose friendship and support, most of the original Mayflower pilgrims would never have survived, was inevitably destroyed in 1675 when Metacomet (King Philip, as named by his proselytised father, Massasoit Ousamequin) assembled the Wampanoags and other tribes to attack the now rapidly expanding colonies, only to be decimated in the ensuing war that some say was the worst in US domestic history. It's interesting to consider that the underlying drive behind the settlers' engagement in subjugation and violence was the thirst for land and global trade, as it is today, and when the later colonists felt threatened, their reaction was often brutal and bloody leaving a trail of distrust, injustice and devastation in their wake.

And, as we look at the European Union in 2020, seemingly on the brink of collapse, the incendiary issues seem similar: debt, racism, greed, the dishonest dealings of companies who wish to avoid paying tax while trading on a vast, global scale and the fight for land and finite resources, under pressure from uncontrolled immigration.

> "We are getting near the 28,000 year cycle. I watch more for that time and those impacts, and what our ancient teachings say, than the scary state that the planet is in now."

Cheryl Andrews-Maltais, Chairwoman of The Wampanoag Tribe of Gay Head, Aquinnah

Plymouth, England in 1620

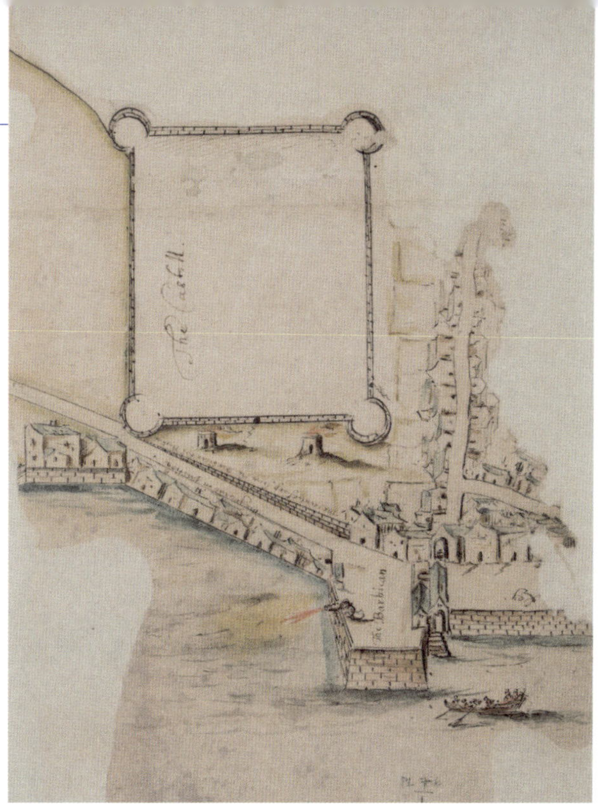

Plymouth Castle by the Barbican

But, what of Plymouth and the land they came from? What did the Mayflower passengers leave behind?

For the settlers arriving in a New England devoid of shelter and food, and travelling into the great unknown, life in Plymouth, from where they sailed, must have seemed much simpler.

In 1620, a typical day in Plymouth would have seemed, by comparison, positively bucolic: one would have been mostly absorbed in sourcing and producing food, household chores and keeping the home fires burning. Dinner by candlelight and stories by the hearth. A nice, relatively easy way to live, if not for the forced attendance at Church and connected persecutions of the Church and Crown for money and control.

Plymouth numbered over 6,000 people, amongst a total population in England of 4 million. Most people were involved in agrarian practices, one way or another, with nearly 50% of the total population being directly involved in farming, compared to around 1% now. This was 140 years before the Industrial Revolution, with its world changing technological advances that mechanised agriculture, and so farming was still hard graft, using horses, oxen and substantial manual labour.

At the top of society were the nobility, followed by the gentry, who were rich enough to lead a life of leisure, then yeomanry who both owned and worked the land, followed by tenant farmers, craftspeople and labourers at the bottom.There were no banks, as we know them, at that time and usury had been in practice for a hundred years after a 1,500 year ban. The equivalent of £10 would buy you five cows, 200 days of labour, a horse, or extraordinarily, only 5 quarts / nearly 5 kgs of wheat. The price of bread was high, as was meat: a poor family might eat meat only once or twice a week - considered a real treat back then. It could take a year of hard labour to earn enough to buy eight cows. But, if you did have money, it could be deposited with goldsmiths, when not commandeered by the Crown in taxes.

As for the range of foods available, the eating of bananas and pineapples was considered novel, and a luxury of the rich, as they were imported at great expense – a pineapple famously cost the equivalent of £1,000 in those days – which was reflective of a narrow range of different food products available from England's limiting climate and our ability to grow different seeds.

> We believe that Peace and Harmony are the will of the Creator and the ultimate spiritual and natural order among all His people.
>
> *All DC Tribes.*

Salt, dried goods, dried leaves, etc would have been put into sacks, wicker baskets and food carts instead of individually shrink-wrapped, plastic or paper bags, and cardboard boxes from supermarkets today. There would have been little to no waste as recycling was as natural a process as any other.

Many more people knew which plants had medicinal value, and how to grow and prepare them, while an apothecary would have made potions from leaves and roots for healing the whole body in a wholesome way, rather than the highly processed, regulated medicines of today, sold by big pharmaceutical industries. That said, many of the life-threatening diseases facing the Mayflower passengers and Native Peoples back then are instantly curable with the advanced modern medicine of today, while refrigeration has revolutionised food production and long term storage.

According to the first hand account, Mourt's Relation, the words "we loosed from Plymouth, having been kindly entertained and courteously used by divers friends there dwelling," suggest that the pilgrims spent some time enjoying Plymouth before finally setting off in the Mayflower. As their victuals would have been severely depleted, having been 6 weeks into the journey already, with almost no progress, it's thought the Mayflower passengers would have supplemented their stocks in Plymouth; probably at the farmer's markets and what was then Fownes, but is now Jacka's bakery, for its famous Captain's Biscuits.

It is likely that they would have taken livestock such as chickens and cows, which they would have killed along the way to include fresh meat in their diets. They also took alcohol to keep their water barrels free from bacteria.

Religion in 1620

The Pilgrims' quest to find a place they could live free of persecution, was as a direct result of the conflict between ideals and values, old and new, at the time.

1620 was 87 years before Scotland united politically with Wales and England to form Great Britain, and religion was at the heart of the country but took a multitude of different forms, with all bowing to the authority of the King, the supreme head of the Church. Religion was highly restrictive: it was a fineable offence to miss church on Sunday, with the threat of imprisonment for repeated offences, in England; and elitist, with services and the bible still in Latin. Witch hunting had reached its peak in Europe, with executions centring around the Holy Roman Empire, that later became Germany.

The seeds had been sown when Henry VIII decided to annul his marriage to Catherine of Aragon, his Catholic wife, in 1533, in his doomed quest for a surviving male line. This resulted in a split with the Pope and the creation of the Church of England, which continued to rule humanity's conscience with a rod of iron, but was being increasingly challenged by reformers keen to take advantage of the split with Rome.

Hitherto indecipherable Latin texts and bibles of the religious institutions were being translated into common languages, opening the world up to alternative interpretations, much like the internet is doing now, challenging political propaganda, the exposing of government corruption and fake news.

Pilgrims lives in Holland

It is not a great jump to understand that religion was often used, in a hypocritical and cherry-picking fashion, to exercise power over people and situations rather than operating in the spirit of the religion to do good by one's neighbour.

Wolves in sheep's clothing were everywhere and often the name of Christianity was used to enslave souls rather than save them. It was against this backdrop of religious intolerance, persecution and posturing that a number of different movements emerged. Although Puritanism was acceptable in England, and even encouraged, it still had to accept that the Church of England was its head, with the Crown being the ultimate authority.

A few rose up against the authority and abuses of the Crown – seeing no real differences to the papacy – who were named Brownists. They could be imprisoned for their beliefs and, if sufficiently militant and insistent in their views, risked martyrdom. But, before their requests were addressed, three of their four main leaders were executed for sedition, while the fourth was imprisoned a number of times.

Blind Justice

Of all their demands, they only managed to force through an agreement for the first widely available English translation of the bible, which made religious understanding and debate among the wider population more widespread.

At the turn of the century, in 1607/08, a congregation of English Protestant separatists, who lived near Scrooby, at the border of South Yorkshire, Lincolnshire and Nottinghamshire, wanted independence from the mainstream church, as they fundamentally disagreed with the retention of certain Catholic practices, including the worship of icons and the extensive tithing of the people. They believed the abuse of alcohol to be a very destructive force and made a number of demands of the Crown. Realising, with their growing numbers that they would not be able to continue under the tyranny of King James I, they emigrated to the Netherlands in search of the freedom to worship as they chose.

The Scrooby Separatists, or Brownists as they were known back then, were betrayed to the authorities on their first attempt to escape to Holland, by the captain of the ship on which they thought they would sail. Their belongings were confiscated and their leaders jailed but, later, reached Amsterdam on their second attempt.

The leader of the Scrooby congregation was John Robinson, who took around 100 souls with him to Holland from England, including William Bradford and William Brewster. Holland played a significant role in the story of the Mayflower Pilgrims.

It was primarily a safe haven to follow their beliefs, on condition they follow the laws of the land and live peacefully among their Dutch neighbours in Amsterdam, then Leiden. There, the Separatists also learnt a lot about the structured process of running a country ethically and with empathy for other religious beliefs, from the Union of Utrecht of 1579, a treaty where seven Dutch provinces had united in their agreement to tolerate the private practice of religion.

The Dutch created the annual thanksgiving celebration that the pilgrims were to imitate after the first year of surviving the new world, Charles Vanreij, the resident historian at Pieterskirk, Leiden, will tell you. And, while the Americans celebrate Thanksgiving during the last long weekend in November, the anniversary of their arrival in America, the Dutch in Leiden celebrate Thanksgiving on October 31st each year, to celebrate their deliverance from the Spanish in 1574, making it a well established festival and prominent example to the Separatists of how to celebrate their blessings by sharing food with everyone, much like the harvest festival at the end of summer.

John Robinson and his following were highly respected in the Leiden community for their lifestyle and wisdom, and were given much credit in the disputes of the day, such as that of 'predestination', and whether the concept of 'salvation by faith not works,' should give way to 'salvation by fate or faith'; something some believe had a significant bearing on proceedings in the new world.

John Robinson's congregation had grown to around 300, so, given that only 46 Separatists left on the Speedwell, most of them remained in Leiden to travel in later years or be absorbed into Dutch culture, going Dutch in a big way.

Ground breaking events in the early 1600s

The early 1600s were exciting times of discovery and new ideas. The Golden Age of the Dutch East India Company saw the development of trade, science, art and military prowess, which were reshaping European people's horizons and opening up opportunities all over the world.

1616 was a particularly seismic year: apart from being the last year the Separatists lived contentedly in Holland before resolving to find a new home, Galileo discovered, with the help of amazing new telescopes, that the Sun is at the centre of our solar system, not the Earth – a heretical idea to the Catholic Church for which he was convicted of heresy, and had to deny, to avoid death.

Meanwhile, the great bard, William Shakespeare died the same year, leaving an extraordinary legacy of provocative literary works from the famous pound of flesh in The Merchant of Venice, to the doomed love and class wars of Romeo and Juliet, to the cursed play, also known as the Scottish play, Macbeth, whose three witches, brought about tragedies with every production, as real witches allegedly cursed the play. Also in 1616, Pocahontas had arrived in Plymouth, after saving the life of Captain John Smith, according to his testimony, in the colony of Virginia.

Accredited as a key figure in building relations between the English and her tribe, the Algonquin Indians, she was introduced to English society as a 'civilised savage' with her husband John Rolfe, but tragically died in 1616 on her way back to her homeland.

In this year also, Sir Walter Raleigh was beheaded, so bringing to a close the Golden Age of those intrepid Elizabethan pirates, privateers and arch enemies of Spain that also included Francis Drake, John Hawkins, William Parker and Richard Grenville, amongst others.

In the same period, while Rembrandt was growing up in Leiden, Flemish artist Rubens was at the height of his powers and, as one of the world's most famous painters, treated the world to 'The Fall of the Damned', completed in 1620. Rubens' focus was centred on the six heady perennial themes of Violence, Power, Lust, Compassion, Elegance, and Poetry; as relevant to today as ever. Later, and no less importantly, his diplomatic skills came to bear, when he was invited to help build peace between England and Spain over the Spanish Netherlands, described as an attempt to "smother the flames which threaten to devastate Europe".

In 1618, the Thirty Years War embroiled Europe, which proved to be the bloodiest the region had ever seen with the loss of 8 million souls from a total of 45 million, proportionately as horrific as WWII.

It was against this backdrop of change in Europe that the Mayflower passengers played their part in the jigsaw of history.

Image left of Sir Walter Raleigh depicted on the Grand Hotel, Plymouth

Earlier Legendary Expeditions to North America

While there had been many recorded expeditions to North America, none of them went expressly to set up a new culture based on new values and principles, as the Separatists on the Mayflower had done.

Legend has it that the very first Europeans to discover North America were Saint Brennan and his merry men, who allegedly discovered Newfoundland in the 6th century AD, as detailed in ancient manuscripts describing a land of luxuriant vegetation, but this was a fleeting visit with no more detail left behind for us to study.

At the end of the first millennium, a Viking called Leif Erikkson had heard that some Viking sailors had spotted a country to the west but not stopped, and decided to check out the legends of these lush lands and set sail westwards from Greenland. It is thought that Leif finally arrived at a place called Baffin Island that he rather unimaginatively named 'stone slab land' before making a temporary archaeologically proven settlement around 1000 AD, finally, on Newfoundland Island, for a winter. He then hurried back to Greenland after realising that, despite his good fighting genes, he would rather face his fierce incorrigible father at home than the natives in a hostile land, who had just killed his brother.

The most famous discoverer of America, Columbus, although an Italian, was entirely financed by Spain to travel west to get to the Far East, only to very fortunately bump into the Bahamas in 1492 on his way, having massively miscalculated his distances, sailing conditions and the patience of his crew.

> I have come to believe that this is a mighty continent which was hitherto unknown.
>
> *Christopher Columbus*

New World Values, Future Presidents

There were many reasons why previous ships – and indeed later ships – that arrived in 'The New World' failed to settle successfully, from not taking their wives and children to form a balanced community, to not having the right skills or required mindset that was needed to respect the beliefs of and cohabit with the ancient American Indian cultures.

However, it's thought that the Mayflower passengers were different. Many of them had acquired a greater depth of knowledge, along with an ability to see different perspectives on life, by living outside England in Leiden, Holland for eleven years.

They had also learnt new skills, and were influenced by the intellectual elite of Leiden, where the oldest University in the Netherlands was founded in 1575; a place known during the 1600s for its intellectual tolerance and nurturing of new ideas, through discussions and debates, and many fascinating new ways of thinking.

It is no accident then that many recent leaders of this new world claim to be the descendants of these original pilgrims, with their sense of high principles, values and innovative thinking. Nine presidents are said to be descended from the Mayflower pilgrims, including John Adams, John Quincy Adams, Zachary Taylor, Ulysses S. Grant, James Garfield, Franklin D. Roosevelt, George Bush, George W. Bush and Barack Obama. 16 nobel peace prize winners also trace their way back to these early settlers. Also many famous Hollywood stars can trace their origins to the Mayflower.

Whether these claims are true, is perhaps less important than understanding why there is such eagerness today for high status individuals to be seen to be attached to the high minded values and principles of this pioneering group of early settlers.

So where now – what's the future?

The bloody shattering of the 'special relationship' between the Plymouth colony and the Wampanoag tribe begs the question about who and where we are now.

Will 2020 turn out to be another major crossroads in world history, 400 years on? Will the end of the European Union, with its similar issues around freedoms, uncontrolled immigration, greed and trade, lead to further destruction of communities and trust in Europe? Have the advances in culture and technology, since the sailing of the Mayflower in 1620, made things better than they were 400 years ago? And what of us? Will we do nothing, after being ground down by a feeling of despair or foiled by the selfishness of others. Or will we learn to act more effectively as a global community?

In order to understand where we are in the world today, we've studied 20 people who were in or around Plymouth at the time of the Mayflower in 1620. We've also taken to the streets of Plymouth today to find their modern equivalents. We've asked these ordinary and extraordinary people to share their knowledge and ideas for a better world from their current perspectives, to inspire discussion and debate about what can be learnt from the past and how we can work towards global truth, peace and environmental security. Can we stop making cyclical mistakes by understanding the past? Is collective behaviour the answer? Does everyone feel they have an equal stake, for us to survive and thrive together?

The results are inspiring and insightful, connecting the history of what happened then, to the current situation of who and what we are now. Through their knowledge and wisdom, we explore what humanity needs in 2020 to create the balance necessary for 'us' to still be here in 400 years time.

> "A butterfly flaps its wings in the Amazon jungle and subsequently a storm ravages half of Europe."
>
> *Neil Gaiman, Good Omens*

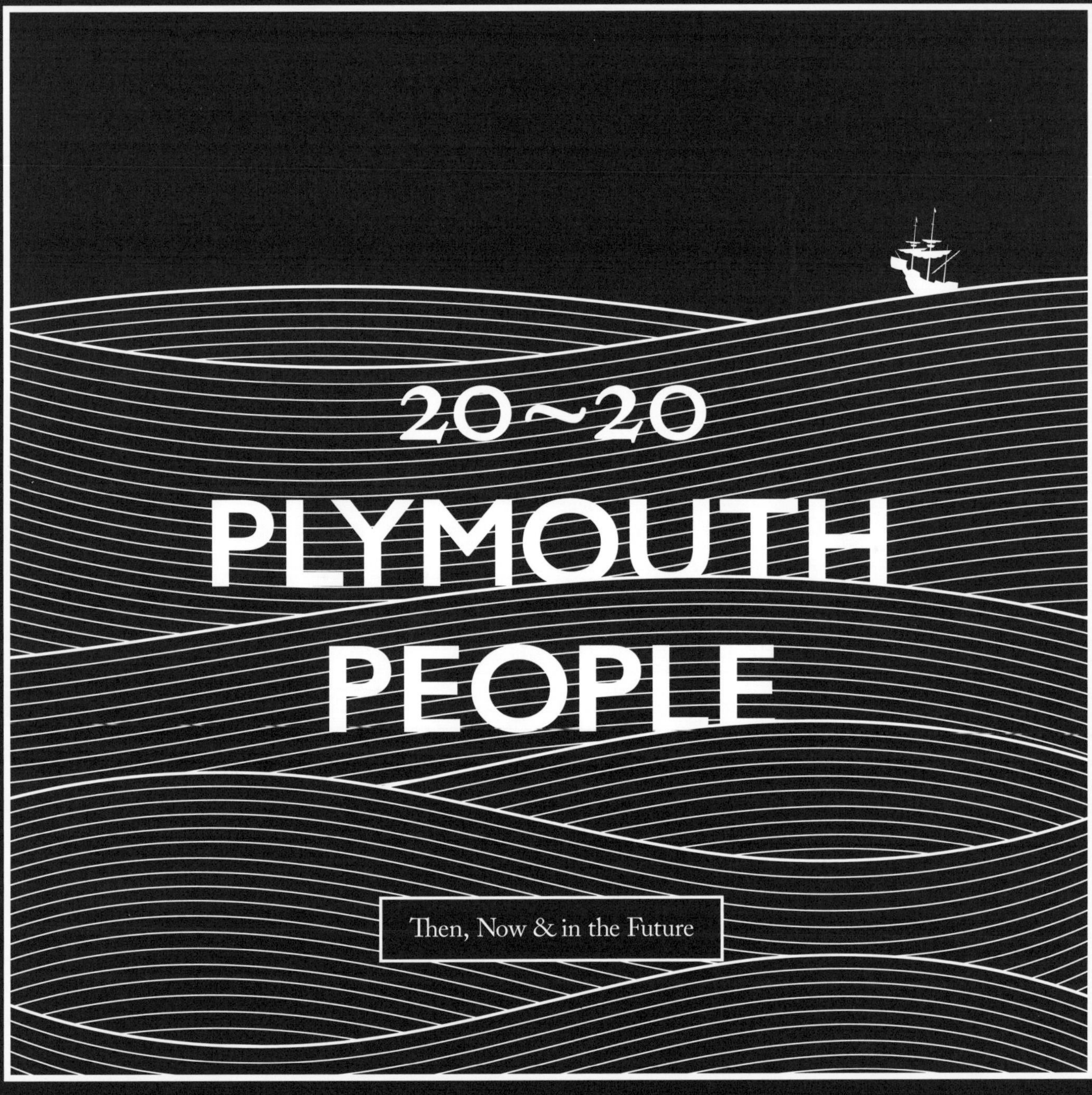
20~20
PLYMOUTH
PEOPLE
Then, Now & in the Future

20 Plymouth People in 2020

Let the following pages take you on a journey to discover twenty people who would have travelled on the Mayflower or been working in Plymouth in 1620, and their modern day counterparts. Here, you can read the stories of people living 400 years ago and imagine what their worlds would have been like. You can also discover what might lie ahead in the next 400 years through the eyes of twenty characters living in Plymouth now, who tell us about their work and what they see coming in their future.

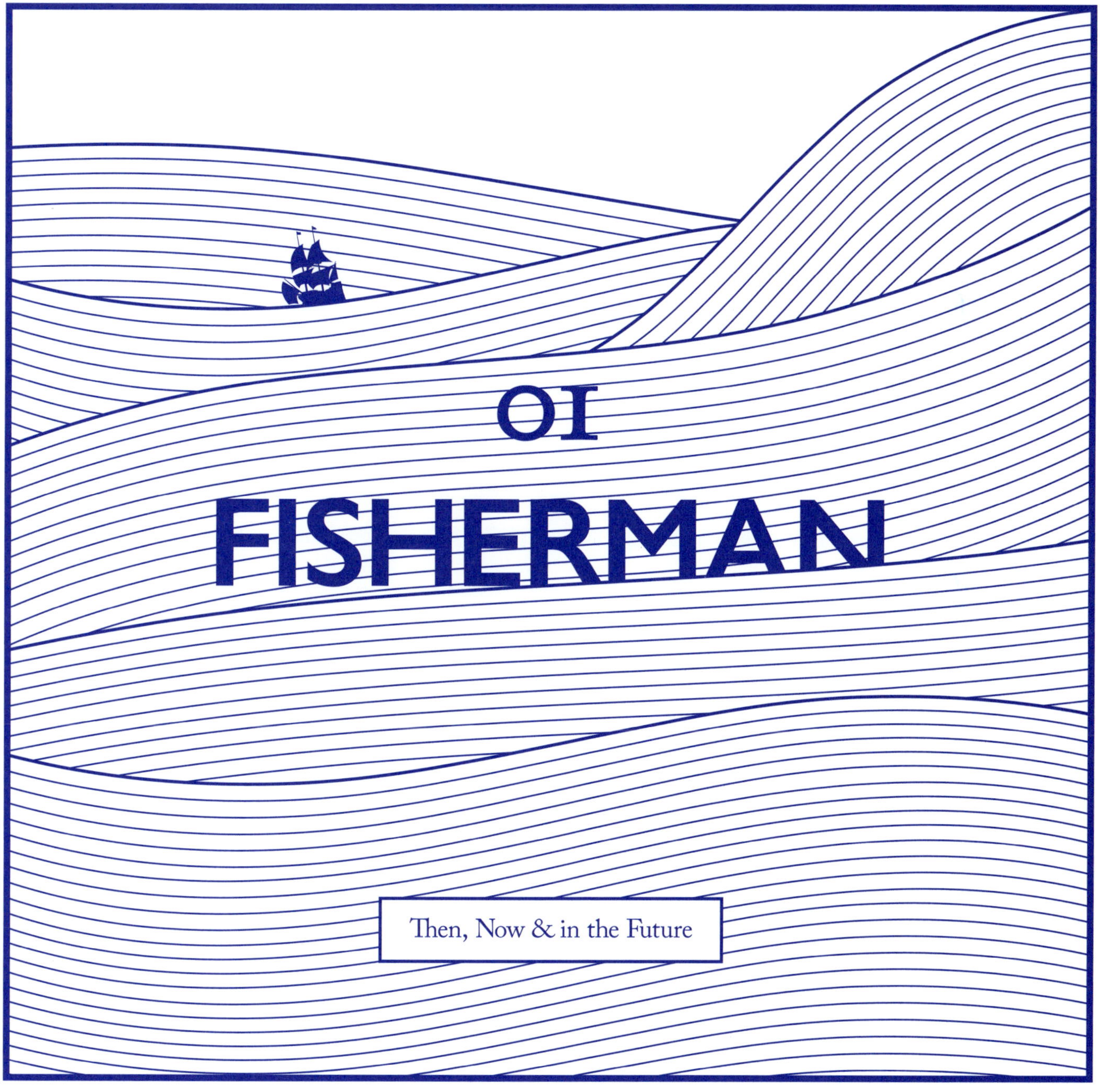
01
FISHERMAN
Then, Now & in the Future

Barbican Waterfront
Where the fishermen were

In the last 400 years, Plymouth has been transformed from a small fishing village into a large, modern oceanfront City influenced by its ocean faring ancestors who, through fishing, went on to discover treasure, scientific breakthroughs and whole new lands and cultures.

Plymouth has slowly morphed from a remote seaside settlement to a dynamic, modern tourist destination with fishing at its heart. The epicentre of Plymouth's fishing activity is Sutton Pool, where the early morning weekday fish market has become one of the biggest in the UK. Selling industrial amounts of fish, much of the catch is taken up to London to appear on the plates of the finest restaurants in the world. However, it's still possible in the early morning, to bump into a fisherman returning from a trip and buy a little hake, perhaps, fresh off the quay.

The harbour is also home to the country's largest National Marine Aquarium (NMA), run by the Ocean Conservation Trust, a charity dedicated to connecting people with the ocean. The NMA is a kids' paradise and, with its sharks, octopus, turtles and jellyfish, tells the story of the ocean, building emotional connections with all who visit. The most popular activity is 'Sleeping with Sharks', where you can have a sleepover next to the giant fish tank, with highlights that include the Twilight Tour, games and a big screen movie.

"Plymouth is going to be one of the top destinations, as nowhere in England has the history of Plymouth or a waterfront as beautiful and vibrant as the Barbican." Ben Squire

The harbour area has, in recent years, been transformed from a students' beer-drinking destination, to a place of connected waterways and ocean culture. Evidence of this can be seen most clearly at the Mayflower Steps where, from the new jetty, you can hop on a boat to the Mount Batten Water Sports and Activity Centre, the majestic Royal William Yard or even Kingsand in Cornwall.

Or, if you decide to 'Cook Your Catch', you can return from a fishing trip and relax in one of the best fish restaurants in Plymouth, The Boat House, where scallops served in a shell are caught 7 miles out to sea daily, by Ben Squire, Plymouth Boat Trips' owner/entrepreneur, and his team.

Ben came to Plymouth 19 years ago on a bus from Wales, and, thanks to a £1,500 loan form the Prince's Trust, started Fish and Trips, which is now a boat trips and restaurant hub connecting to Plymouth's waterfront.

Ben says, "The future for Plymouth excites me; there's so much happening. Mayflower 400 is going supersonic in the city. Just look around to see the momentum, from being as rough as guts with prostitutes on the Hoe a decade ago, to the greatest waterfront in England, today.

RX394
PH799
PH819

Then
Edward Winslow
Fish Merchant

Plymouth is a city that's historically been powered by the fish trade. In 1620, fishing was the lifeblood of the Plymouth economy, which had grown from a small fishing village called Sutton to become amongst the largest producers of fish in the UK in the 1600s, being chiefly dependent on the trade. Much of the infrastructure we see in the harbour today has, at one time or another, been involved in the industry over time. The Barbican was the original fishing port and the courtyard outside the fishing storehouse, now Parade Antiques on New Street, formerly called Rag Street, was where fish auctions took place. The fishermen stacked the fish on wooden beams that were hooked into the rock. Centuries later, they used a small room within the building as the first coldstore in Plymouth, which survives intact today as the office of Parade Antiques.

One of the leaders of the Leiden Separatists who signed the Mayflower Compact, Edward Winslow played an important role in the Plymouth colony as governor for three years, merchant, and diplomat, but returned to assist parliamentarians in the Civil War, before succumbing to yellow fever in 1655.

Fish were easily exchanged for gold and silver, and a ready supply of salt from the sea was used to preserve the fish, brought in with nets, for long periods. The importance of fishing to the population can be seen as far back as 1384. Competition meant that fishermen travelled from far away to fish in Plymouth waters, so Parliament decreed that fish caught in Sutton, Plymouth and the Tamar estuary must only be displayed in the towns of Plymouth and Saltash.

The commodity became a mainstay of the newly formed standing navy, staffed by the fishermen, adventurers, privateers and pirates, who had long controlled the waters around Plymouth. But fishing was difficult and dangerous before the Eddystone Lighthouse was built in 1696. It guided boats away from danger, until the construction of the Plymouth Breakwater in 1812, behind which fishing boats could shelter from the roughest storms.

Edward Winslow, a signatory to the Mayflower Compact, secured a patent for fishing grounds and trade with his friend, Massasoit, chief of the Wampanoags, as well as being free to follow the Separatist way of life.

Now
John Cabello
Antiques Dealer,
Ex Fishing
Merchant

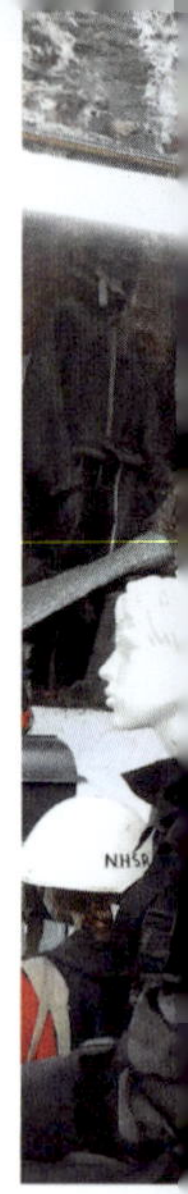

John Cabello
Antiques Dealer

From coins to costumes to curios, you are met by a pouncing tiger as you enter Parade Antiques of The Barbican – an Aladdin's cave of antiques, fascinating artefacts and bric-a-brac. It's run by John Cabello, formerly a fisheries man in Plymouth, who is now an antiques dealer, presiding over a treasure trove of unusual and interesting items sold all over the world, from a glorious 17th century warehouse overlooking the Barbican waterfront. The initial impressions of the building and its contents are like a scene out of the movie Night At The Museum. Beyond a Dalek, looking like it will exterminate you, a creepy Cyberman, and the aforementioned tiger, as your eyes adjust, you can see it's full of amazing things to buy, each with its own special story to tell. Wherever you wander, it seems to be animated by a kind of magic. Its historic items and gadgets include a Star Trek 'transporter'; when looking at it, one can almost hear those immortal lines, 'Beam me up, Scotty'!

Everything in Parade
Antiques is for sale.
Well, as long as the price is right!

Parade Antiques also has an enormous amount of fascinating historic memorabilia including coins, military uniforms, guns, swords, sculptures and associated antiques, one of which is an impressive German suit of black armour from the early 1600s, displayed in a glass showcase. It's a place which John has filled to overflowing, after decades of collecting amazing antiques. "The place kind of grew," says John, as he inspects some objects just brought in by a seller. "It began as a hobby and escalated into a career."

John is actually a scientist by training and after graduating in Fisheries Science from the University of Plymouth, he pursued a career in one of the industries in which Plymouth has grown so successful: fishing.

"At the time English shellfish, such as lobster, were

prized on the other side of the English Channel, while, in contrast, were being used as pet food in England, where they were most abundant," John explains. He got involved in exporting shellfish to the Continent, where he soon learnt how crucial it was to get shellfish to their destination, alive and as quickly as possible. "I'd drive a 40-tonne truck through narrow lanes to various remote UK fishing ports to buy shellfish direct from fishermen. When the lorry was full, I'd drive to the other side of the country and meet with the French and Spanish merchants waiting on this side of the channel tunnel."

John found the work incredibly stressful. Even though the truck was converted to hold large tanks of salt water, oxygenated by an elaborate system of pumps, he was constantly worried his cargo would die. But John was able to condense a week's work into two days, leaving him time to browse the many antiques shops on Plymouth's waterfront. Places sold anything from Georgian furniture to collectible oil paintings.

As Plymouth's fishing industry has changed, so its fishermen have diversified, like John Cabello, who has followed his heart from fishing for lobster to fishing for curios, not in nets, but on the internet.

As John filled his house to overflowing with his many purchases, and the backbreaking work of carrying heavy crates of shellfish became increasingly unattractive, he was encouraged by his wife, to take on his own shop and trade antiques instead of fish. "She was tired of dusting it all at home," he says. So, John sold the lorry and opened an antiques warehouse and has barely eaten a crustacean since. Today, only a few of the old antiques shops he used to frequent, remain and John's is by far the biggest. He's glad he made the move. "Antiques gather dust, but they do not die on you," he says.

Over the last 25 years, enabled by technology, Parade Antiques has grown and amassed an incredibly eclectic array of wares covering nearly every interest you can imagine. "Our recent growth is a consequence of the internet, which has opened our collection to a worldwide audience", he says. "Before, it was: what sells locally? Now, it's: someone somewhere will want this teapot and we can ship it to them." But, it can be an unpredictable business. "There are many influencing factors, from the irregularity of supply to the ever-changing prices at auction. Fashions also change, and the brown furniture, once the mainstay of the antiques shop, is now relegated to the storeroom, in favour of more unusual items."

"But the Dalek, Charlie Chaplin costume, suit of armour, deep-sea diving regalia, and the stuffed Tiger are rock solid investments," says John, confidently. In what other job could you buy things that you coveted as a child and, as an adult, be able to pass them off as legitimate business purchases?

The Future
Holding on for dear heritage

John Cabello
Parade Antiques
27 New Street
Plymouth PL1 2NB
+44 (0)7765 408 063
john@paradeantiques.co.uk

“Our wish to own stunning things will remain. I hope in four hundred years time we will still have a love for the past and history, so we will protect our heritage, and that places like this will continue to satisfy this distinctly human impulse of hunting and gathering stunning things. I doubt very much if artificial intelligence could ever reliably judge what is beautiful.”

John Cabello, Antiques Dealer

02 WRITER

Then, Now & in the Future

The Old Quarter, The Barbican
Home to writers and artists

The Barbican was once the strategic defence against foreign powers seeking to raid England. It's come a long way since the Mayflower pilgrims gingerly descended the harbour steps into a small ship.

Named after a fortified gate, 'A Castle Barbican', it's thought that it was once the entrance to Plymouth Castle, a late mediaeval fortress that guarded access to Cattewater, before the Royal Citadel was built.

The fishing market (now the third biggest in England and relocated to the other side of Sutton Pool), was originally the mainstay of Plymouth's economy and industry, and is still home to many fishermen, with a few streets still retaining the character of the original fishing port.

In the 1800s, the area was identified by the government as one of the worst examples of slum dwelling in Europe, with families living 10 to a room – comparable only to Warsaw – so was cleared out, following the Public Health Act of 1848, with many decaying buildings demolished. But, luckily for the Barbican, it was not considered worth bombing in the Blitz of 1941, so, unusually for the city, some of the Barbican's heritage buildings remain intact. Twenty properties are now protected by The Plymouth Barbican Trust (Association), which has worked hard since 1957 to safeguard the remaining Tudor and Jacobean buildings. The Trust was started in the 1920s by architect Arthur Southcombe Parker, and supported by Nancy Astor, and is largely the reason that the old quarter still exists. Today, you can sit on a stone seat in the Elizabethan Gardens, listening to the hypnotic sound of the fountain, immersed in the time of the Mayflower, while reading Plymouth 1620 – 2020 A Guide, by local author, Chris Robinson. It's a guide to the principal attractions for those arriving in Plymouth by boat in 1620. Or you can walk along the most concentrated area of cobbled streets in England and enjoy a modern dining experience infused with history.

The Barbican, one of the few places in Plymouth to escape the blitz and slum clearance, has one of the highest concentrations of cobbled streets in the UK, and is now a magnet for lovers of history, food and waterfront culture.

The Tudor Rose Tearooms & Gardens, situated between the bookshop and the Elizabethan Gardens, were recreated to commemorate the 350th anniversary of the sailing of the Mayflower.

For spit and sawdust magic, check out the unpretentious Dolphin Inn; a centuries old pub, on the waterfront, with original stone floors. These, plus a vibrant selection of shops, bars and restaurants, are the principal attractions of the modern day Barbican, just a short distance from the Mayflower Steps.

Plymouth
Elizabethan
House
MUSEUMS
LIBERTY
OPEN

Then William Bradford Writer, Governor

William Bradford's writing provides us with great insights into the minds of the early Mayflower settlers. In his journal, Of Plimoth Plantation, covering 1608 to 1647, he connects us directly to the Mayflower story, detailing the tribulations of the Separatists in England, their move to Holland, the epic voyage to 'New England' and the first 27 years of settling in what is now Plymouth, Massachusetts – or Patuxet, as the Wampanoag Indians called it for thousands of years.

Born in Yorkshire to a rich family, but, owing to multiple family deaths, he became an orphan for some time, before inheriting great wealth. He used his riches to procure a place on the Mayflower, having been a keen follower of the Separatist movement of Scrooby.

The voyage was terrifying, ultimately leading to the loss of his lifestyle and the death of his wife. William arguably was nonetheless one of the first to sign the Mayflower Compact, the set of rules for self-governance written by most of the adult men on the Mayflower.

One of the most poignant images of the Mayflower story is the Compact's beautifully uneven infinity style handwriting used to add gravitas to this seminal work. Through his writing and 30 years as the second Governor of the Plymouth colony, William became a key influencer of the American constitution and its spirit.

Bradford's journal is fascinating in that he discusses so much of what still troubles the governments of today, like the first failed attempt at a form of communism, tested for several years by 'honest people' but found wanting, owing to a lack of incentive to excel.

He also identifies the failings of capitalism, pointing out how the increase in land ownership and wealth causes physical separation between people, leading to poorer communication, then greater confusion and the illusion that only more material wealth can improve the situation; a view that is not so different from that of many, today.

"All great and honourable actions are accompanied with great difficulties, and both must be enterprised and overcome with answerable courage." From Of Plimoth Plantation, written by William Bradford, who overcame immense hardships to inspire the foundation of a successful colony.

Now
Chris
Robinson
Writer

Chris Robinson
Writer

It was during a school tour around The Elizabethan House, in Plymouth's Barbican, over 50 years ago, that Chris Robinson's teacher made a comment that shaped his life forever: 'Until you know and understand what is on your own doorstep, you will never properly know or understand the rest of the world'.

Since then, Chris has become a writer and artist, the leading documenter of Plymouth and its history and a world expert on the City and its stories. Today, Chris can be found at 34 New Street, his Barbican bookshop, Pen & Ink, in a Grade II listed timber Tudor building. Built as a sea captain's residence, with a spiral staircase constructed around the mast of a sailing ship, the building became multi-tenanted – an extended family of six or seven on each floor – with no internal bathroom or toilet. Deemed unsuitable for residential accommodation in the 1950s, it was used for a time as an antique print shop, before Chris snapped it up to follow his dream.

Chris was fascinated by history from a young age. Aged nine, he arrived from Australia to live in Plymouth, with his Scottish mother Brenda, and father, Des, a Plymothian through and through. Des had joined the Navy at 15 years old and his father had served with the Royal Marines during both World Wars.

An only child without TV or siblings to play with, Chris's principal pastime was drawing in pen and pencil, and painting. He didn't, however, attempt an art 'O' Level at school. "I did not want to draw different angles of a vase or an onion," he explains. "My father taught me perspective at an early age, and I wanted to produce drawings that people could step into."

Chris found exams challenging and, even though he went to Leeds University to study psychology and sociology, and then Warwick University in 1976 to write a Masters thesis on 'Youth Culture and the Rolling Stones', he continued to write and draw in his spare time.

"While the city of Plymouth is by no means perfect, it is nevertheless the most beautiful city for its size in the Country. The sunlight bouncing off the Portland stone, reflecting back onto the wide streets, makes the city centre stunning." Chris Robinson.

Returning to Plymouth in 1978, aged 24, he married and took a studio in 44 New Street in the Barbican and proceeded

to sketch Plymouth for the next four years. By chance, in early 1982, he was introduced to the editor of the local newspaper, The Evening Herald. "I have written for the paper ever since – 37 years and I have never missed a week!" he beams.

What started out as a passion to produce line drawings and stories, has developed into a major career for Chris, authoring over 30 books on Plymouth and becoming an expert historian.

"I love sharing my knowledge with other people and helping them to appreciate the stories behind what we have here in Plymouth," he says. "If every picture of our civilised world tells a story, it is only because everything manmade tells us something about mankind, and something about ourselves."

Nowhere could be more interesting to write about than Plymouth, with its fabulous history, wealth of green spaces and amazing marine park, says Chris Robinson, author of over 30 books on the city.

"I think it is important to record a lot of this information, so people in the future understand how we lived in former times. I doubt whether or not any of my three children will come back from London to carry on my work, but I hope there is someone out there with a passion to pick up on the best library of images and local information, aside from The Box."

Chris still feels his first hardback history of the city, Plymouth As Time Draws On, is his favourite, "I was so naïve in 1985; the print bill, (at £22,000), was more than my mortgage at the time. The printers, Latimer Trend, who I still use, had confidence in selling it as a hardback with a dust jacket. The first 4,000 copies sold quickly, so we printed more the following year."

Forty years on, and Chris is still learning new things about the City, as he researches subjects, like the history of local tin mining. "Between three and four thousand years ago, people were coming over to Plymouth and Dartmoor for tin - an essential element in the Bronze Age," he says.

"They saw us as the Cassiterides – the Tin Islands. Plymouth still looks a little like an archipelago when you come here by sea. South-west Dartmoor and Cornwall were the main sources of tin then and much of it was shovelled straight out of the riverbeds in those days. Mount Batten, was the main trading point."

He is excited about his new book, Plymouth 1620 – 2020 A Guide. "I wanted my latest project to be a tourist guide for people to see what Plymouth was like in 1620 and which buildings from that period are still here today."

The Future
Can we predict it?

Chris Robinson
Pen & Ink bookshop
34 New Street
Plymouth PL1 2NA
+44 (0)1752 228120
chrisrobinson.co.uk

“In 400 years time, Plymouth, based on how it has grown over the last 400 years, could have the population of London’s today. But we can’t predict the future now, any better than the people on the Mayflower could then. Who, then, would have thought we would be fishing plastic out of the sea instead of fish? But plastic is not the only issue – we also need better, fit-for-purpose education. The state system has sidelined drama, debate, sports, and art … all life skills, important for developing minds and inspiring creativity. Mental happiness is key to a healthy society and essential for another inventive and fulfilling 400 years.”

Chris Robinson, Writer.

03

COOK

Then, Now & in the Future

North Hill Roundabout
The route to food

North Hill is a Mecca for students and the professional classes. With two iconic buildings and a multitude of small businesses and food outlets, it powers the City's minds and bodies.

Plymouth's city centre offers food for all tastes and budgets. Transformed over the decades, following its obliteration in WWII, the centre is a mix of some of the finest examples of postmodern architecture in the country, divided into distinct zones: the intellectual district of North Hill, the busy shopping area of Drake Circus and the city centre, studded with an eclectic mix of eateries from around the world.

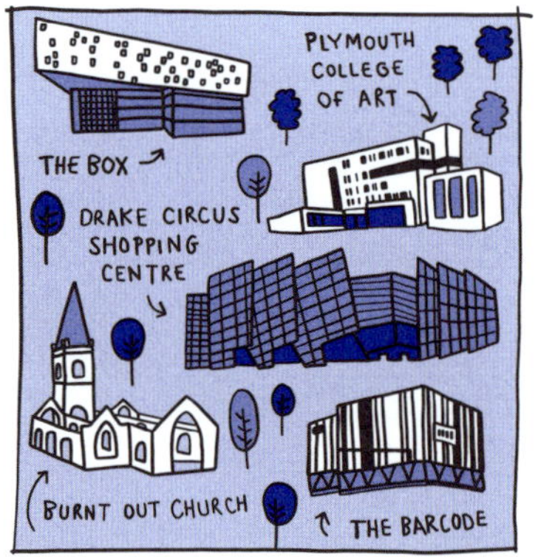

The large North Cross Roundabout, which pulses with traffic, is like a human head, with Armada Way as its spine and roads connected like nerves to the different areas: up on North Hill there's Plymouth University, with its iconic copper Roland Lewinski building and House theatre and professional enclaves of lawyers and accountants. Drakes Circus, home to over 70 shops of many different kinds, is on the east shoulder with the shiny new 21st century cultural experience, The Box. To the west lies the soon to be modernised train station; and from this centre road, arteries wind all the way down to The Barbican and The River Plym, to the east. Perhaps driven by the 30,000 student population and professional classes, who surround it, there's also food to please every taste, fanning out from this most central of roundabouts.

Brand new The Box, highlights Plymouth's rich seafaring heritage and includes 7 galleries and 7 exhibition spaces

Excellent places to eat include the Bac Bar, ideal for those who like to work in the early evening then socialise late into the night. If you want a night in, you can grab a quick tasty Thai from Mr Woks. Or try The Roundabout, a curvaceous and spacious highly fenestrated half circle of a building. Artsy Ebrington Street caters for students with its 'oh-so cool' Prime skate-café, social enterprise Bread & Roses and, of course, Hangry – a fun, affordable eatery. And for the unashamed coffee addict, there is also the popular Caffeine Club with its homely atmosphere, old style advertising boards and grandmaster murals.

If you want to plumb the depths of a subject with your lecturer, you could do worse than treat them to 'a bite' at the Reservoir Café on the Uni campus, or, perhaps more fittingly, the Classrooms club. On the other side of the roundabout, Drake Circus lures professionals into its steel framed glass mall with promises of Bill's and Yo Sushi. But if brain food – and real food – are what's on your mind, Plymouth Art College, incorporating the very cool Plymouth Arts Cinema, showing great arthouse films alongside its café and restaurant, is hard to beat.

Then Fone Family Baking

Standing outside Jacka Bakery, 38 Southside Street, it looks like just another building in a busy street full of tourist shops. Venture inside and it's easy to go back 400 years, to when the Pilgrims made their last English walk from Blackfriars Distillery towards their embarkation point. They would have passed this solitary detached building. Then, it had windows on both sides, still to be seen in the walls upstairs, as well as at the front, with an uninterrupted view of Sutton Pool.

How nice it would have been for the Pilgrims, after buying the famous hard tack biscuits for their epic journey, to have some bread here – considered a special treat in those days and mainly for the rich, except, of course, for special occasions like Holy Communion. If only they had baked biscuits with apple peelings inside, many more of them would have survived that first harsh winter, without the onset of scurvy, easily cured with vitamin C.

The bakery was originally owned by the Fone family from 1597. This prominent Plymouth family name also boasts the 1619 Mayor and merchant, Thomas Fone. Eventually, the bakery joined with the Warren family and became Fone Warren, selling Fone's 'Captain's biscuits'.

Fone's Bakery ceased production of 'ship's biscuits' about 100 years ago, owing to the biscuits being too hard and too salty for modern day tastes, despite the habit of dunking them in tea for softening.

Officially the oldest bake house in Britain, it still has the original oven, albeit with a later metal insert, as well as an Elizabethan balcony and, most enigmatically of all, an extraordinary lump of wood with a cannon ball buried in it, under the stairs. In the loft at the back, you can see the original wooden roof from the 16th century.

According to the 1600s recipes, the baker would have made flour-based lard-filled stodgy cakes with ale, weighing 20lbs, and other fare that didn't perish on long voyages. Jacka, harking back to the area's trading traditions and environmental philosophy of re-use, have tote bags so you can carry away your delicious cinnamon swirls to enjoy a taste of history. Locals describe it as quietly groovy, extremely friendly and amazingly good at baking, so go and have a treat.

Now
Jessica Sneyd & Vicki Rowan
The Real Junk Food Project

Jessica Sneyd & Vicki Rowan
The Real Junk Food Project

The Real Junk Food Project Plymouth has been the talk of the town, over the last three years. It's run by Jess and Vicki, who intercept unsold or unused food and turn it into delicious, freshly cooked meals at pop up restaurants held in community spaces around the city, where local diners can 'pay what they feel'. The project is part of a food revolution that was started in Leeds in 2013 by Adam Smith. It aims to address hunger and the serious issues of landfill and massive global food waste.

Both Jess and Vicky love what they do. "We both wanted a job which made a difference to the world and made people actually THINK about how we can better treat the planet and its resources. We wanted to demonstrate that cooking is not scary or intimidating, as so many think," says Jess. They can't remember a time when they were not cooking. Vicki says, "Apparently, when I was tiny, I would stand on a stool and stir the porridge. My mum, who was a fantastic cook and largely responsible for my abilities today, would give me bread or pastry to play with, despite the mess; I've been passionate about food and cooking ever since!"

"Vicki has taught me a lot about baking. She is amazing at making wonderful cakes out of things I'd never thought of; often vegan and always delicious. San Pellegrino has featured a lot recently in lemon cakes, and she makes a brilliant rice pudding cake from left-overs, eggs and chai spices!"
Jessica Sneyd

The pop-up dining model gives them flexibility to go anywhere in Plymouth and feed anyone. "People tell us that 'Pay as you feel' is brilliant, as they can take their children out for lunch without worrying about being able to afford it or how to prepare such food," says Jess. But the Real Junk Food project is definitely not about 'junk food'. "The project WON'T save everything from landfill – like horrible microwave burgers, foul energy drinks or stuff that has not been stored properly. We don't use anything we're not sure about." Instead, the food they make is influenced by some of the world's best cookery writers. "We're inspired by Madhur Jaffrey cook books, 'Peace and Parsnips' by Lee Watson, 'Real Food' by Nigel Slater, and the Flynn brothers, who do 'The Happy Pear' books, which are excellent for making plant-based foods look vibrant and enticing." Jess and Vicki are now writing their own cookbook and aim to encourage more people to grow their own fruit and vegetables (preferably heritage ranges) thereby decreasing pollution and carbon-release from imported goods and reducing the over reliance on supermarket chains.

In the future, everyone will have to grow more, cook more and eat fewer calories. Vicki says, "It's great news that eating habits are changing and we are seeing a rise in plant-based food consumption, as people eat less meat. I feel very passionately about this and I'd love to see a less carnivorous outlook." They are also pleased to see a lot more people conscientiously buying local, in-season

produce, from box schemes and smaller shops/farms, instead of the larger companies. Jess says, "I really admire The Growing Project, The Green Cow Dairy, Good Earth Growers and the Keveral Community of Growers. All these producers are small and aim to be sustainable and kind to the earth. They are very happy to give us their surpluses to avoid waste."

Junk Food Project diners from the Plympton Pop Up: Jo Burt, Margaret Burt, Anne Cuddefor and Linda Harris, have strong views on why the project is successful. "People aren't content with enough, anymore – they want more, more, more," they say. "Nowadays, couples both work because they want too much. But there are now people who can't even afford to buy food, despite being in work, which means they, ironically, can't go to food banks. There's also a real stigma attached to it.

"Not enough people are growing their own and certain products are being overproduced; there's too much thinking about growth and profits at the expense of sustainability. Poor people are forced to buy convenient, cheap, but inferior food. We should go back to getting our ration of butter in a greaseproof wrapper and Sunday closing – like after WWII. We live in a very fragmented society," agree Jess and Vicky. "The Junk Food Project is a unique way of bringing the community together and not being so wasteful, which needs to be the new normal. We love the fact that our project is exposing food waste, addressing climate change, feeding hungry bellies and helping to build healthier, happier communities of people, which in turn will build a healthier country."

"It's horrible to think of so much food going into landfill, when so many pensioners and rough sleepers are hungry; more people need to know about The Real Junk Food Project Plymouth."

The Future
Free Food for the Future?

Jessica Sneyd & Vicki Rowan
The Real Junk Food Project, Plymouth
The Greenhouse Lower Clicker Road
Menheniot Liskeard Pl14 3PJ
+44 (0)7510 138 595
realjunkfoodplymouth@gmail.com

“The combination of an exploding population’s drain on natural resources and climate change means large amounts of food will need to be produced in relatively small spaces. The world will have to rely heavily on: technology and AI for our farming, and bakeries, using things like insects for protein. But will food be interesting enough? Will we manage to create beautiful dining experiences with swedes, potatoes, insects and micro-herbs? Maybe, the food system will be demonetised as we all end up eating similar regional foods; that would really change the ‘eating out’ landscape!”

Vicki Rowan and Jess Sneyd, The Real Junk Food Project Plymouth

04
DISTILLER

Then, Now & in the Future

Southside Street, Barbican
The original distilling district

Walk into any bar in Britain's Ocean City and it's a fair bet you will spot a sign saying, 'Welcome to Plymouth – twinned with tonic'. The words 'Plymouth' and 'Gin' have become synonymous with authentic gin, but there's a fascinating story to tell behind gin's genesis in the heart of the city.

Gin has enjoyed a slow rise to the top of the Spirits League, putting Plymouth on the map, since the time the Mayflower sailed in 1620.

The world renowned Plymouth Gin was first distilled by John Coates in 1793 in what's now the delightfully cobbled Southside Street, which makes it the world's oldest distillery.

It has not only been home to one of the world's most popular gins, but also, since the early 1400s, the building has been a place to praise the Holy Spirit, a refuge for foreign Huguenots, a meeting place for nonconformists, and was also claimed to be the final sleepover spot for some of the pilgrims, the night before they boarded the Mayflower. The historic and iconic gin distillery is now a must-visit for tourists and locals alike, with its choice of three tours to experience, before enjoying a gin cocktail in the upstairs bar, and dinner opposite in the award-winning Tanner Brothers' Barbican Kitchen. On the other side of the street is the bonded warehouse where the ingredients and final products were stored.

Gin & Genocide:
Plymouth is a city that celebrates success and pleasure, and commemorates failure and horror, in nearly equal portions.

Plymouth Gin is on a delightful cobbled street studded with interesting arty shops, eateries and whiffs of the Mayflower. Try a Blue Badge walking tour with Jane Dymock if you want to really get beneath this street's skin. Get your chocolate fix at Chocaccino, while 45 Southside Gallery shows contemporary exhibitions and stunning artisan work by artists of Cornwall and Devon.

Victoria Sewart features interesting jewellery, some made from ocean plastics. From here, it's a short walk to Madam Vilma Sparks and David, of Gypsy Acora, thought to be the best clairvoyants in the south. Once you know your future, you can celebrate or commiserate with a multi-award-winning round of the classic seafood favourite at Harbourside Fish & Chips on the buzzy waterfront.

At the far end of Southside Street is the Mayflower Museum, which tells the epic story of the Mayflower voyage and doubles as the Tourist Information Centre. It's opposite a set of steps clearly labelled Mayflower Steps, but shhh! We have a secret for you: the real Mayflower steps are hidden away in the Admiral MacBride pub across the road; people say you can find the remnants of them in the women's lavatories if you look or drink hard enough.

PLYMOUTH GIN
1793

Then
Monks
Distillers / Apothecaries

Alcoholic beverages and medicinal preparations have been distilled in Plymouth, since the 1400s, when the monks concocted all kinds of remedies, many to ward off the plague and other major illnesses of the time. Thereafter, the world renowned Plymouth Gin was known to have been first distilled in 1793 by John Coates on the site of the former Great House of a local merchant.

But it was the Bols family, who started the world's first commercial distillery for gin, in Holland (the name comes from Dutch jenever, meaning juniper water), selling it from Amsterdam in 1575. They cleverly developed a strong relationship with the VOC (Dutch East India Company) through whom they procured the special herbs and spices required to make their gin, and then sold the gin back to them for distribution around the world.

The drink came to prominence in England from 1618, when, during the 30 years war in Europe, the English troops, fighting alongside their Dutch allies against the old Catholic foe, Spain, observed their Protestant allies drinking the fortifying stuff before confronting the horrors of battle. This is where the famous phrase 'Dutch courage' comes from and has come to mean any kind of alcoholic fortification of the spirit before some challenging task or other.

The Society of Apothecaries, was formed in 1617 by royal charter, having been split off from the Grocer's Company.

The British went on to use it in the Navy as it was often healthier, along with beer, than drinking the more bacteria prone water, stored in wooden barrels, before the invention of metal containers. And, as the 30 Years War progressed and the supply of brandy from France dried up, more readily available grain-based drinks proliferated, with gin at their helm.

It has also had its darker side exposed in the Victorian days, known as 'mother's ruin' and during Prohibition in America, the Plymouth Gin distillery exported a thousand crates a week to New York.

Opposite the distillery is a classic example of a bonded warehouse, which was once used to clandestinely stash booty from high seas piracy, before being used to store the distillery's finished products before shipment.

Now
Sean Harrison
Master Distiller

Sean Harrison
Master Distiller

The Master Distiller oversees distilling, marketing, operations and continual improvement of taste, experience and the tours, to keep Plymouth Gin the world's No.1.

It's no accident that Plymouth Gin, one of the world's most popular drinks, was developed in a global seafaring city. The gin is made up of seven botanicals, as gin distillers call them, sourced from around the world. The Plymouth Gin Distillery, located in the heart of an international port, made it perfectly situated to develop this complex drink, as the botanicals are sourced from many different countries. Moreover, 220 years ago there were only rough tracks for overland transport, so, being in a port was of the utmost importance for easy access to ingredients from around the world.

Juniper berries are the heart and soul of any great gin, the best of which come from Umbria in Italy. The other botanicals in Plymouth Gin are coriander seeds from Eastern Europe, lemon and orange peel from Spain, angelica root from Saxony, orris root from Italy and finally cardamom pods from Guatemala.

Today, Plymouth Gin is presided over by Master Distiller Sean Harrison, whose job it is to carefully select the botanicals that give it its signature taste. Each year, Sean battles against the unpredictability of Mother Nature to find the perfect taste and smell profile of essential oils that create Plymouth Gin.

Eight months of the year are taken up with sourcing the botanicals, depending on their annual harvesting cycle. Many, many samples of each botanical are sourced and individually assessed; one of each of the botanicals is carefully selected every year to maintain the taste and heritage of Plymouth Gin.

The 7 Plymouth Gin botanicals, along with Neutral Grain Spirit, distilled from wheat-grain, and Dartmoor water from the Burrator Reservoir are placed in the 113 year old Pot Still. Once the Pot Still is loaded or charged, steam heats the nine ingredients to boiling point. The liquids then evaporate, so extracting the essential oils in the botanicals and attaching them to the Neutral Grain Spirit as they are squeezed through the swan's neck of the still and then condensed back into a liquid using cold water. Voila! Plymouth Gin is created.

Sean Harrison, Master Distiller, has a nose for the finest blend of gin with botanicals that make it such a classic and enduring British drink.

The fine art of making top quality gin is in how the distiller operates the Pot Still by hand; opening the steam valve to regulate the heat, and using his nose to make the right cuts at the right time and then organoleptically assessing the day's run to ensure Plymouth Gin has been made.

Using natural ingredients can have a sting in the tail; not every juniper berry (as with all the other botanicals) has the same amount of essential oil and this leads to a subtle difference in every batch and this is why the skill of the distiller's nose is essential to ensure consistency. "That's the craft," says Sean.

Plymouth gin's historical success is attributed to the fact that at 'Navy Strength' proof level, the gin's ingredients do not dampen a ship's gunpowder, thereby proving suitable for fighting ships in early years! On top of this and the fact that the botanicals were readily available, John Coates, back in 1789, when he set up the first gin distillery, had the benefit of fresh Dartmoor water and the dream sales team of the Royal Navy in its heydays of travelling around the entire globe with the stuff, both for the officers themselves and the people they met along the way, including those who needed softening up.

The old ways are best you might think, when you taste the traditional recipe used by Sean Harrison, Master Distiller of Plymouth Gin.

Now the number one place to visit in the city, the distillery is a wonderful conglomeration of bulbous shiny metals of marvellous contours, colours, pipes snaking this way and that, and dials popping out like eyes everywhere. Huge holding tanks sit in pride of place looking like a cross between Charlie and the Chocolate Factory and a Heath Robinson contraption.

To get the full feel for Plymouth Gin and an inspirational education, the gin tours reveal the real spirit of this most historic Plymouth gem. For those wanting to go one step further and learn the art of distilling, there is a tailor-made tour to get you well on the way, and for those wanting to learn the art of distinguishing one great taste from another, there's the Connoisseur's Tour. You'll find it easy to become a connoisseur of this king of spirits and refine your organoleptic evaluation skills.

In his quest for continued perfection, Sean Harrison has recently introduced another great flavour, saying, in typical cognoscenti-style, "Mr King's 1842 Recipe is a true one-off craft gin that we will never be able to recreate. Even if we were to visit the same Italian hillside next year, the climate and harvest conditions would affect the juniper, resulting in a different taste profile."

The Future
Gin Gin! Your good health!

Sean Harrison
Plymouth Gin
60 Southside Street
The Barbican Plymouth PL1 2LQ
+44 (0)1752 665 292
info@plymouthdistillery.com

“

400 years from now, gin could be the most ubiquitous drink on the planet, but not because of its powers to intoxicate, rather due to its possible health-giving properties. The botanicals added to the gin can include just about anything natural in the local environment that refines taste. We could live in a world where the local brews reflect the best local wild health giving plants and places where people with certain ailments will travel, to enjoy a botanicals drink with a unique regional flavour.

” *Juliet Coombe in discussion with other guests on a Plymouth Gin tour.*

05 RELIGIOUS FIGURE

Then, Now & in the Future

Catherine Street and North Hill
A religious hub

The religious landscape of Plymouth has changed dramatically. From a city subject to the absolute rule of the Church of England to a town hosting a diverse range of religious beliefs to be found all over the city.

The great edifice that is the Minster of St Andrews, with its over 1,200 years of history and beautiful brightly coloured John Piper designed stained glass windows, has always played a pivotal role in Plymouth's history. Until the early 1900s, it was the parish church for Sutton, one of the three towns that were combined to form Plymouth. Outside the main entrance, a bronze resin sculpture of St Andrew, a fisher of men, perfectly straddles the entrance arch to net potential new recruits from along Royal Parade. The church is a hive of activity, catering for a wide range of groups: Minster Maids, Mothers' Union, Who let the Dads out? Noah's Ark, Cradle roll … the list goes on.

Walking in off the street, you can get an enthusiastic tour of the church, its history and much of the history of Plymouth by a volunteer keen to guide you through the fascinations of the past. After all, this is a place where the 15-year-old Katherine of Aragon first gave thanks for a safe voyage from Spain, Drake will have prayed here before his many escapades, Mutiny on the Bounty's William Bligh was baptized and King Charles II performed touching for the king's evil (a lymph node disease). But St Andrews is just one of a multitude of religious institutions across the City.

Once the longest street in Plymouth, Catherine Street bustles with religious history and activity, incorporating five different places of worship but all with the Ten Commandments at their heart.

Take a walk around the centre of Plymouth and you might never find the Jewish synagogue. "They don't want to be found," people will tell you, but this is simply not true. Plymouth was once the most prominent Jewish community in the UK, building the first English Ashkenazi synagogue in 1762 – which, far from hidden, was built overlooking the town square as it was back then, in a much more commanding position. The original square has since been filled in with other buildings. Just down from the synagogue is Living Stones Baptist Church, a thriving multicultural church set up by five families in 2006, where you can declare your faith as a 'living stone', or explore the core values of worshipping: missionary, sacrificial, inclusive and prophetic at Catherine Street Baptist Church. Beyond the end of the street you come to the Unitarian Church, formed in 1662, where you are invited to a lively and vibrant congregation. A short walk away is the spectacular Sherwell Church with its Mayflower window.

AYE, CALL IT HOLY GROUND THE SOIL WHERE THEY FIRST TROD
THEY LEFT UNSTAINED WHAT THERE THEY FOUND FREEDOM TO WORSHIP GOD.
THIS WINDOW IS GIVEN BY ALICE CORNISH CATER IN MEMORY OF HER BELOVED BROTHER
SAMUEL AND OF THE LONG ASSOCIATION OF HER FAMILY WITH THIS CHURCH

Then
Henry Wallis
Vicar of St Andrews Church

Henry Wallis, the first puritan vicar of the Minster of St Andrews, was very similar to the Mayflower Pilgrims in his beliefs, as was most of the town's population; only diplomacy separated their different causes. After the Reformation, Plymouth was fiercely Protestant, having been so closely involved in fighting the tyrannical champions of Catholic rule, the Spanish empire.

By 1572, with a town of around 5,000 people, Plymouth's finances were in poor shape, owing £120 (c. £30,000 in today's money) to Queen Elizabeth I. The Council duly asked permission from the queen to run its own finances and choose its own vicars. She agreed on the condition that the town did not get into debt again. Then, free to determine its future, the town employed highly knowledgeable 'lecturers' to lead the church, instead of a vicar, so they could rent out the vicarage, not have to pay the fees of a vicar and not fall foul of the authorities for having a vicar with puritanical views.

In 1603, that changed with the crowning of James I, who initially made an attempt to bring the state bishops and puritans closer together and so, Henry Wallis was made vicar in that year and remained so until 1633.

The church was stripped of much of its Catholic decorations, seen by Protestants as idolatrous. Likewise, the vicar's attire was a simple cassock, gown, and cap.

It's highly likely that Wallis will have have conducted the Mayflower pilgrims' last service in England before they set sail on the high seas, no doubt conducting special prayers for their safe passage to the new world.

At least 1,200 years old, yet not having been awarded the status of Minster Church until 2009, St Andrews Church has seen more of the comings and goings of Plymouth than any other building. Gutted by an incendiary bomb during the blitz, the church has been rebuilt into a stunning blend of ancient and modern.

In *Plymouth Minster – A History of St Andrews*, Jack Spence has written a fascinating in depth history of the church, encompassing a good deal of Plymouth's history, including how Bishop Nick McKinnel became its first Rector in 1994.

Now
Jerry Sibley
Plymouth
Synagogue
Custodian

Jerry Sibley
Plymouth Synagogue Custodian

At the time of the Mayflower, religion was not the kaleidoscope of religious choices it is today. You had to be loyal to King and country, receiving punishments if you did not pay your dues, and attend a Church of England establishment, of which he was the supreme head. However, as trade links grew, new ideas took hold and people came from all over the world, religious options multiplied.

Today in Plymouth, in addition to Catherine Street and its multiple denominations of Christian churches, you can go to Piety Mosque for Muslim prayers in 19 Greenback Avenue, or learn about Buddha's teachings at Kadampa Centre in Sutherland Road, or join a hidden Jewish history tour with Jerry Sibley.

Jerry is the Custodian of the oldest Ashkenazi Synagogue in the English speaking world and his curated experiences at the Catherine Street place of worship have been awarded certificates of excellence on TripAdvisor for the last three years. What's the secret? "If I am honest, although the building is fabulous, it's the old stories, local history, the people, the connection with Christianity explained and, of course, a healthy dose of humour that has brought it alive over the last 10 years," says Jerry, who is a Christian, not a Jew.

"I'm not a teacher or historian, just the tea boy with the posh title of Custodian, reading around the religion, its people, Plymouth, old books, maps and visiting rabbi's/peoples' stories. The version of events are my own thoughts on how they fit together from a Plymouth Jewish angle, viewed by a Christian." Jerry Sibley.

Jerry's tour explains how, in the first few centuries after Christ, the term 'Christian' was not in common use; Jews and Gentiles faithful to Christ would follow 'The Way'.

"I'm not a teacher or historian, just the tea boy with the posh title of Custodian, reading around the religion, its people, Plymouth, old books, maps and visiting rabbi's/people's stories," says Jerry. "The version of events are my own thoughts on how they fit together from a Plymouth Jewish angle, viewed by a Christian.

"Sherlock and Watson are my heroes and the inspiration behind my questioning everything here. I like reverse engineering, or, to be more precise, forward engineering to see how my own religion has emerged and to put all we have today into context," explains Jerry.

Jews have been recorded in log books as having lived in Plymouth since Drake's time. Services were regularly held in people's homes until 1762, when they built the wonderful synagogue you see today. "The religious tolerance here, away from London and the main cities, has been constant throughout," says Jerry, and is perhaps the main reason Plymouth stood against the rest of the southwest against the Crown, during the Civil War. In the 1800s and 1900s, the synagogue was a hub for over 250 families and was so packed and popular with the local tailors and business trades that it was standing room only for some. For over a hundred and fifty years, many Jewish merchants cut their cloth on Rag Street and were well known for their tailoring skills.

New Street, ironically recognised as the oldest street in Plymouth, and the skilled workforce thereon, became responsible for the production of the smart British Navy attire. The Jews have been a positive force in many walks of life in Plymouth, also producing their more familiar gold and silver jewellery and ornaments. "In the Lord Mayor's chambers you will see on display, 6 gold goblets given by the community," says Jerry. The synagogue has an amazing interior, with its splendid Bimah (central platform), typical of a naval wooden boat construction of the period – like the stern of one of Nelson's warships. The craftsman hired to design it were boat builders from the dockyards. So, with no architectural plans to follow, they did what they knew best, which was to create, in a naval style, the central focal point of the Synagogue that remains unchanged to this day. The Holy Ark, however, was brought over in parts from the Netherlands and assembled on site – a sort of Georgian flat-pack! It consists of a majestic baroque style, with gold and white column, carved edifice, made from wood, with flourishes and plush red curtains, embroidered with the ten commandments in gold, which have, hiding behind them, the Holy Scrolls, breastplate, covenant, pointer, and high priest's bells and pomegranates.

It's one of the more incredible aspects of the war that the synagogue survived untouched by the blitz, and was narrowly saved from the post war planners' grand design, as a building, but not as a community. Many Jews left Plymouth in the early 1960s firstly to Bournemouth, London and Glasgow, many more moved to Australia, Canada and the USA. By 1968 the community found themselves unable to employ a Rabbi. However, the Synagogue's spirit, despite its tiny residual population, lives on in its stories and fascinating tours run by Jerry. He makes tourists think, with sayings like "hold onto your heads" as you head off. A nod to Saint Catherine, who they failed to kill on the wheel rack, so, beheaded instead. As a Christian, Jerry Sibley is a great example of a man embracing the positive aspects of another religion, and promoting understanding and cohesion between faiths. Once you have been on his amazing synagogue tour, do check out the hidden Jewish cemetery by the Citadel, he rediscovered in 2016.

"The religious tolerance here, away from London and the main cities, has been constant throughout," says Jerry Sibley, Custodian of the oldest Ashkenazi Synagogue in the English speaking world.

The Future
Life support on life support?

Jerry Sibley
Orthodox Synagogue
Synagogue Chambers
Catherine St, PL1 2AD
phccaretaker@yahoo.co.uk
plymouthsynagogue.com

Joe Dent
St Andrews Church
Royal Parade
Plymouth PL1 2AD
+44 (0)1752 661414
standrewschurch.org.uk

“

The Church's challenge, in 1620, now and in 400 years, is to be both faithful and contemporary, living by the apostolic truth of Jesus Christ, but living in a way that engages with the world of its day. The Mayflower pilgrims embarked on their adventure of faith, leaving behind what they saw as the repression of the Church and State. Four hundred years from now, expect that same tension to be around. Some will embrace a multi-faith, multicultural world, some will feel threatened. But the need for spiritual adventure and authentic community will remain deep in the human heart.

” *The Rt Rev'd Nick McKinnel, Bishop of Plymouth, former Rector of St Andrews.*

06 TEACHER

Then, Now & in the Future

Plymouth Guildhall
A place to share wisdom

The grand Grade II listed Plymouth Guildhall, a vibrant city hub, hosts all sorts of events from markets, rock concerts and tea dances, to opera. Just as well it narrowly escaped post war demolition then!

The Plymouth Guildhall, built in 1874, is a Gothic Revival style gem to be found in the heart of the city centre, surrounded by hotly debated 1950s post-war architecture.

A dynamic space, with a balcony gallery at one end, it has hosted music legends Lloyd Webber, Status Quo, Queen and many important historical events, including, on November 28, 1919, the election of Lady Nancy Astor to parliament, the first woman to sit in the House of Commons.

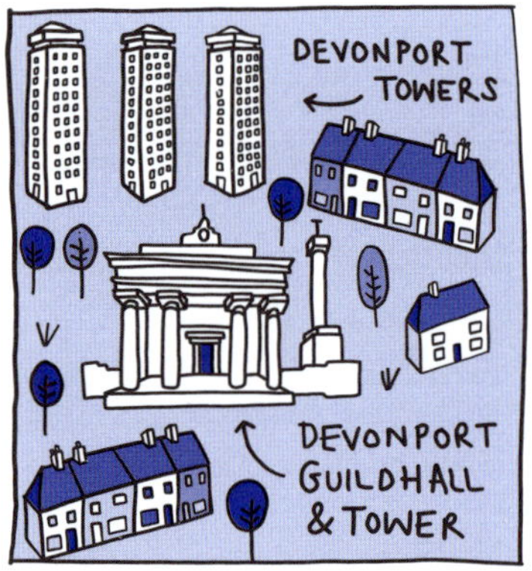

On a commemorative plaque outside the Guildhall, it says, 'Lady Astor was formidable in politics and an indomitable champion of just cause; her charm and wit was matched by her unflinching courage in adversity.'

Stone carvings of an astronomer, artist, writer, stonemason and other artisans of historic importance, sit lifelike in little alcoves along the north face of the building overlooking the main thoroughfare – fascinating snapshots of Plymothian lives before photography.

Gutted by a WWII incendiary bomb, this beautiful iconic 19th century building escaped demolition by a single vote, in grand plans that some argue, controversially, were almost as damaging to Plymouth's heritage as the blitz.

Inside, you will learn how the Guildhall was gutted, owing to the horrifying shelling of the city during the Plymouth blitz in World War II and staggeringly saved from complete demolition by a single vote in 1951. Paton Watson and Patrick Abercrombie envisaged a Beaux Arts city which would have meant its demolition. Thankfully it was voted down. Lovingly restored and reopened to the general public in 1959, as a multi-purpose edifice, it now hosts the city's most important gala dinners, university graduation ceremonies, proms, award ceremonies and fairs.

Perhaps, most striking is its high, pointed tower and the fourteen colourful modern style stained-glass windows around the hall, each depicting a key moment in the city's history.

A visit to the Guildhall puts you within easy reach of many city highlights. Annexed to the building, is the dazzlingly posh Treasury Bar Cafe & Restaurant, serving 'ginspirational' cocktails with about 150 gins to try.

At Christmas, the amazing City Christmas Market is right outside, and often there are funfairs and endless community events right on its doorstep.

From here, you are within walking distance to the library and the lively Plymouth city market, where you can buy fresh produce and a snack, before going to a performance. In summer, enjoy a picnic in one of the nearby green spaces, like The City Jigsaw Gardens.

Then William Brewster Teacher

William Brewster was a pioneer in every sense of the word. He started his Mayflower journey as a teacher in Scrooby, where the Separatists were developing their ideas and community: Puritans regarded teaching as second only to preaching the divine word. After a brief spell at Cambridge University at Peterhouse College (the oldest), studying Greek and Latin, he did a stint in the service of William Davison, Secretary to Queen Elizabeth I, which had taught him diplomatic and political skills, thanks to a trip to Holland in 1577 to negotiate peace with their Spanish Ruler, soon forging an alliance with William of Orange in defence against the tyranny of Roman Catholicism. While in Holland, Brewster saw and heard more about reformed religion.

In Scrooby, Brewster hosted Separatist meetings at Scrooby Manor, which he looked after for the Archbishop of York. Increasing restrictions by the authorities soon convinced the congregation that they should emigrate to the more sympathetic climate of Holland. But leaving England was illegal at the time. Their first foiled attempt in 1607 led to arrests, but in 1608 Brewster and others were successful and they settled in Leiden, where he was selected as the ruling elder. Brewster made a living by teaching students of Leiden University, to speak and write English.

While living there, he also printed books and leaflets, some highly critical of the Church of England. The most controversial, the Perth Assembly, was sent back to England. As a result, King James ordered his arrest and both Dutch and English authorities hunted him into hiding. When it was time for the Mayflower's departure, Brewster came out of hiding and joined them with his wife, Mary, daughter, Love and son, Wrestling, to journey to the New World in 1620. There, he became the senior elder and leader of the Plymouth colony, where, to this day, four islands – and a turned chair – are named in his honour!

In 1620, poor children didn't go to school. Boys learnt through apprenticeships or jobs such as tanning and forging. Richer children went to Petty school before Grammar School. Girls from wealthy homes were often taught music and needlework privately or at home, by governesses and tutors.

Now
Catherine
Hamilton
Opera Singer /
Teacher

Catherine Hamilton
Opera Singer / Teacher

If you walk past Catherine Hamilton's house in Plymouth, it sounds like an opera coming from her living room. "I amuse my friends by saying things like, 'I've got to learn to sing this opera in German, by next Thursday!'" she smiles. Catherine is an extraordinary Plymouth-based soprano, who has performed all over the world – from The West End to Germany and for HRH Prince William – but now shares her talents and expertise with students to help them grow as musicians.

Her exceptional, sparkling voice has put her centre stage in the West End show, Masterclass, at the suggestion of her concert pianist friend. "It was both thrilling and terrifying at the same time, to be performing live at the Shaftesbury Avenue," says Catherine. "I felt I'd really made it, sitting in my own dressing room, with bulbs round the mirror!"

She toured Germany with Das Phantom Der Oper before returning to London, and her classical roots that brought her such amazing early success, to sing opera and oratorio. She now counts making an official recording of her singing for HRH Prince William as just one of the amazing opportunities in her career, along with touring Europe and singing in the Devon and Opera Holland Park Summer season. Catherine's love of singing started when she joined her church choir at the age of seven. Two years later, at primary school, her teacher noticed her talent and persuaded the County Music Advisor to listen to her.

"For many opera singers, the ultimate ambition would be to sing in any of the great opera houses in the world. Although travelling to sing is immensely enjoyable, there is nothing quite like performing in my adopted home town of Plymouth." Catherine Hamilton

Struck by the beauty of Catherine's mesmerising voice, they suggested that she audition for the Royal Academy of Music, and at ten years old, she became the first Junior Exhibitioner in its history to be accepted as a singer – and she has never looked back.

Growing up, Catherine enjoyed every aspect of musical life. Singing in choirs meant that she sang a lot from the late Renaissance era. "Each age influences the next and 400 years ago was the beginning of the Baroque era; so much of the Oratorio music that I love singing now dates from that period."

After having her second child, she moved from London to Plymouth, as a result of her husband studying at Plymouth College of Art and Design and fell in love with the creative arts scene that the city inspires.

Nothing, she was to discover, beats singing while looking out to sea, and watching her two girls enjoy the magical freedom of which Plymouth is so proud. Today, she splits her time between performing and teaching at home and, when she has time, at the university. She really enjoys the mix of singing and taking her students to new levels in their singing, "It is great to be able to bring current performing experience to my lessons and to feel I have the relevant knowledge to convey how best to achieve this."

She advises anyone following in her footsteps, into a music career, to find an inspiring music teacher and train from a young age, to get the skills to progress with confidence. "Not having the right teacher can adversely affect your skills and ruin your voice," she says. "Tastes change over the years and each teacher will bring their own unique style. I like to focus on a strong technique, so my students are free to express themselves through the music. As singers, we are fortunate to have the words to help us communicate emotion to the audience. She also advises getting another qualification. "Being a performer", she explains, "can be a precarious profession, so it's probably good advice to have another string to your bow; in my case getting an L.R.A.M. teaching diploma." And she warns, "However good they are, all performers need to prepare themselves for staying upbeat in the face of potential rejection letters from a round of auditions!"

She loves singing in Plymouth and counts The Guildhall as one of her favourite venues. The Great Hall seems to come to life when Catherine sings Haydn with the Philharmonic choir; her sparkling soprano voice filling this stunning grade II listed building, from the 19th century, rebuilt internally in the 1950s. It's fitting, then, that another keynote performance beckons, the culmination of her personal and professional epic: she is to be the soprano soloist for a specially commissioned work by Paul Foster, to commemorate the Mayflower. Written for the Plymouth Philharmonic Choir, she'll perform it on the 5th July, 2020 at Plymouth's Guildhall. It's a great opportunity to hear her sparkling voice in a wonderful historic building.

An exceptional singer from an early age, Catherine Hamilton has soared the professional heights. She now teaches her students that music can transform and enrich everyone's life.

The Future
A virtual voice has no hope

> Much of the wonderful music that we appreciate today will continue to give pleasure to future generations. With the speed of technology, it is exciting to wonder what the advances in Virtual Reality could bring to life in the future. Listening to great musicians in spectacular settings, yet in the comfort of our own homes; this would solve the problem of booking seats or having to queue up at the bar in the interval! However, I am convinced that AI could never mimic the infinitely variable emotions of the human voice, which moves us in a way that goes to the very heart and soul of our being.

Catherine Hamilton, Opera Singer & Teacher

07

ACTOR

Then, Now & in the Future

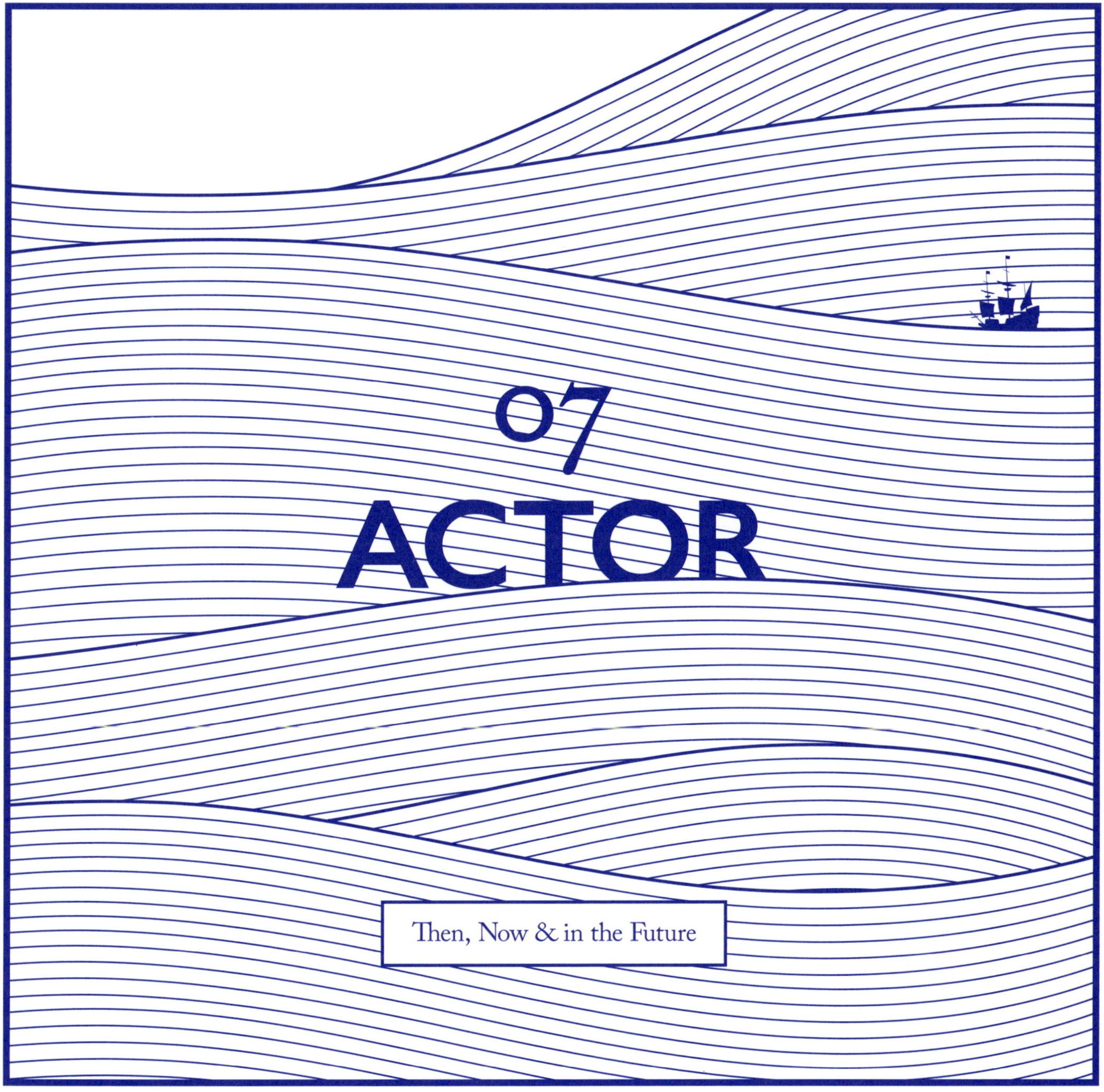

Theatre Royal Plymouth and the theatre district
Plymouth on the World Stage

If all the world's a stage, and all the men and women in Plymouth merely players: they have their exits and their entrances; and one person in their time plays many parts, so, here, in the heart of theatreland, you can be a player, too.

For world-class entertainment and superb productions, nothing beats the Theatre Royal Plymouth on Royal Parade. Since its opening in 1982, by HRH Princess Margaret, it has consistently broken new ground for the South West. Mathew Bourne's Sleeping Beauty has premiered there, as well as many popular West End shows that have started their tour there or passed through to huge acclaim, like Cameron Mackintosh's The Phantom of the Opera, and Disney and Cameron Mackintosh's magical Mary Poppins.

The Theatre Royal's secret weapon is TR2, a 'state of the art' theatre production and learning centre, tucked away in nearby Cattedown, that builds and rehearses the shows, before they are taken to the national stage. It enables most national touring productions to premier at the Theatre Royal for a short, or not so short, run. TR2 also provides a unique national level asset for aspiring children in the city, with its theatre courses and workshops. New for 2019 was the impressive 'Messenger' sculpture installed outside the Theatre Royal – the largest cast bronze statue in the UK. Messenger's pose is described as 'small, crouched and loaded with the potential to spring forward at any moment – a metaphor for Plymouth and its creative ambitions.'

The new Messenger sculpture, designed by artist Joseph Hillier, was inspired by a split-second pose by Nicola Kavanagh during a rehearsal of The Theatre Royal's production of Othello.

Since the Theatre Royals' first Charity Gala, when Leonard Rossiter, Dickie Henderson & Gene Pitney brought the house down, audiences have consistently said it's one of the most welcoming theatres in the country. The Drum Theatre, a smaller space within the main theatre, is committed to innovative playwrights, who have something to say and want to challenge our ways of thinking.

Just round from Derry's Cross is the Athenaeum Theatre, a mid-century gem recently saved from closure and now established as a charity, to promote learning in science, technology, literature and art. Founded in 1812 by architect, John Foulston, you can become a member, like Stanley Gibbons and Charles Darwin; the latter prepped here for HMS Beagle in 1831. The original building was blitzed, but the new one boasts visitors like The Beatles and Arnold Schwarzenegger. If you fancy a bite to eat before a show, try Rumpus Cosy, a social enterprise dedicated to good food and cosiness, or Bella Italia, Wildwood and local tapas Lorenzo's.

TRP
THEATRE
ROYAL
PLYMOUTH

Then William Shakespeare Actor

"Life's but a walking shadow, a poor player that struts and frets his hour upon the stage. And then is heard no more." William Shakespeare. Back in 1620, acting was a very different profession from our Netflix, Hollywood and celebrity-driven culture. Troops of actors would have all been male. Players toured the local areas and performed exciting new works like Shakespeare's, in places like Plymouth's Boringdon Hall, with its spectacular setting in the main hall, overlooked by two galleries either end, and using the main stone entrance as a focal point for performances.

Shakespeare died in 1616, just four years before the Mayflower set sail from Plymouth harbour, and having already revolutionized the English written and spoken word – those getting on the Mayflower would have been familiar with his work.

Indeed the link between Shakespeare and the Pilgrim Fathers (or The Forefathers or Oldcomers as they were known before 1820) was stronger than one might think. The original Puritan Dissenters lived in Southwark, where Shakespeare lived and The Globe theatre was built. The Dissenters were jailed in the 'Clink' – Southwark prison.

With Shakespeare's popularity at the time, it's likely those on The Mayflower introduced The Bard's works and sayings into America. But full scale export of Shakespeare happened later in the 1600s when successors took the Fourth Folios to Virginia settlements.

His rise to fame had been remarkable. In his early years he had acted on stage in cameo roles, like the ghost of Hamlet, to scathing reviews. But his lack of thespian abilities did not hinder future accomplishments as a writer and poet, to which his acclaimed 39 plays, 154 sonnets and two long narrative poems bear testament.

Many of these works of enduring brilliance, like Macbeth, Othello, Hamlet, The Tempest, and King Lear, are still performed all over the English speaking world and are still core texts of current English examinations, over 400 years later.

"Most will argue that there has been no equal since Shakespeare's time and today, can you think of anyone who will be read in 400 years time, let alone be an enduring part of the school curriculum?" Ruth Mitchell.

Now
Ruth Mitchell
Actor

Ruth Mitchell
Actor

"The main things an acting student should have are commitment and a passion to learn," says Ruth Mitchell. "They need to be able to watch and hone their craft, two skills key to delivering a great performance. They should be hungry." Ruth should know; she has spent a lifetime creating theatre.

One of her favourite roles was playing one of Shakespeare's greatest male heroes, Hamlet. "It was amazing, as it showed me how different the male actor's perspective is on stage, to that of a female actor." The experience made her choose her parts more carefully from that point onwards. In contrast to Shakespearean performances, "Now, my shows have autobiographical aspects to them, which are slightly different, as I make it quite obvious that a percentage of the show is about me or my life. If Shakespeare were alive today, he would be writing soaps and stage shows," says Ruth.

"I think he would be trying out all forms of communication, including being a blogger and influencer, with huge followings on social media."

It was The Bard who helped Ruth and initially inspired her to dream of a career on the stage. Her parents were both lovers of theatre and were members of an amateur dramatic society in Yorkshire. But a visit to the birthplace of Shakespeare in Stratford-upon-Avon made the 14 year old Ruth decide that acting was what she wanted to do with her life. She worked hard, honing her skills and carving out her theatre career in London for sixteen years, followed by four years in Stratford. Then her partner got a job at the Theatre Royal in Plymouth. They all moved and this shook up her ideas about what one can do with theatre.

Living in the South West with a young child made Ruth become more experimental with her work, as it was not feasible to find acting jobs in other areas of the country. "I had to create my own style of distinctive work here in Plymouth because at the time the theatre didn't have opportunities for local actors." She developed well-researched female lead solo stories and, between acting roles, set up a company called Ripple with fellow actor Derek Frood and created Plymouth audio trails. The trails took participants to hidden places with hidden stories, like the Jewish Cemetery right in the centre of town. "We got a lot of interest," says Ruth. "People in Plymouth knew about the door in the

"Contrary to what most people think, my theatre costumes are not created with big budgets. I find most of my costumes in charity shops and for period pieces, like WWII, I raid our family attics." Ruth Mitchell.

shadow of the citadel and wanted to see what was inside, like a secret garden. The trail is a fascinating journey through the lives of around 15 Jews from the 1700s through the 1800s." These fascinating characters are brought to life by the great acting of Ruth and David.

One of the most interesting characters that she has played recently in a play called The Secret Listener, is a woman called Olive Myler, who lived in Devon and whose life was shrouded in secrecy, eavesdropping on German radio stations during WWII. Olive never went out, had her groceries delivered and was rumoured to be working for MI6. "She had signed the Official Secrets Act, so she couldn't tell anyone what she was doing. Her neighbours didn't know what she was up to, even though it was glaringly obvious, with a fifty foot aerial in the garden". To create, write and perform the work, Ruth partnered with the local museum in Olive's village and the National Radio Society, which works out of Bletchley Park.

She also loved acting on TV's highly successful Ruth Rendell mystery, Harms Done, where she played a very suspicious character … "They turned out to be a red herring. However, it was fun to play the potential baddie and then have a big revelation at the end," says Ruth. And while Ruth has worked in every medium – TV, radio and theatre – if asked to pick her favourite way to deliver a message, she says it's always the stage: "Because it's immediate and you can change a person's understanding of something over two hours, something Brecht also believed to be true." Watching Ruth act, it's hard not to agree.

Now an Associate Lecturer teaching acting skills at Plymouth University, Ruth feels it is tragic that less drama is being taught in schools and that children are not getting that first experience, which can hook you into the art of storytelling for life. "Whether you're an actor or not, it teaches you how to get up and play a role to communicate ideas and stories. What is a more important skill for life?"

If all the world's a stage then Ruth Mitchell has played many parts in it. The Plymouth-based theatre maker has brought to life everything from secret walking trails to Ruth Rendell mysteries.

The Future
Future Drama

Ruth Mitchell
Actress
c/o Theatre Royal
Royal Parade PL1 2TR
+44 (0)7931 521 113
ruthmitchelltheatremaker.com

“Traditional theatre will change, as we will make it for different spaces. We will be more inclusive and audiences will be more diverse. Experiences will be more immersive and possibly more game like, where people have to make choices to follow the plot or change it by being involved. There will be virtual reality theatre productions and shows where we have to wear the equipment to experience the performance, as if we were actually stepping into a given time period in the story. But everything is cyclical so maybe in 400 years we will come full circle and be watching Shakespeare again in doublet and hose!”

Actress Ruth Mitchell

08
LAWYER
Then, Now & in the Future

The Law Courts & The Civic Centre
Where lawyers earn their crust

Plymouth's law courts sit on the cross hairs of the architectural paradox of Plymouth: situated in the heart of the city and civic life, their 1960s façades reflect the surrounding mid century architecture while clashing quietly with the Gothic majesty of the Guildhall and nearby Elizabethan gems.

Plymouth City centre was the only UK city to be totally rebuilt after being shattered by WWII bombing raids, its radical design aiming to signal a clean, bright, democratic and optimistic future. Uniquely, it was designed in 1943 in a single plan by Sir Patrick Abercrombie. The result was modern, futuristic and minimalistic – a look that TV's Kevin McLeod has proclaimed 'heroic' and 'beautiful'. "It's rare that you get out of something as devastating as a world war, the hand of genius. It comes from a time when we didn't have much," he said. It now boasts the largest number of listed mid-century architecture in Europe. English Heritage now likens postwar Plymouth to medieval York or Georgian Bath. But it's not a look to everyone's taste: Plymouth's own Council fought attempts to list its Civic Centre, branding it 'cheap and nasty'.

Plymouth's law courts proclaim their moral and religious stance on justice with the words: TURRIS FORTISSIMA EST NOMEN JEHOVA' – The name of the Lord is our strongest tower.

In the centre of this mid century jewel, stand the 1960s built Plymouth Combined Courts, consisting of four courts: two for crime, one family and another for over spill of cases, and the Magistrates Court. One of the main law centres on the Western Circuit, the Plymouth Courts are serviced by two barristers' chambers, at North Hill and Crescent.

Juxtapositioned around these minimalistic, functional structures are buildings of historic interest, but for very different reasons. To the east is The Greedy Goose,

one of Plymouth's top restaurants, housed in one of the oldest buildings in Plymouth, Prysten House, a Grade 1 listed merchants house built c.1498. Evocatively Elizabethan, it's a feast for both belly and an architectural eye. Tucked away nearby is the beautiful Merchant House which, built in the early 1500s, is the finest example of an Elizabethan house in Plymouth. It's first known owner was the privateer William Parker, who, thanks to his position as a respectable merchant, and pirate, was an Elizabethan phenomenon! He was a close buddy of Sir Francis Drake and, after becoming Lord Mayor of Plymouth, having helped fight off The Spanish Armada, reputedly on the Mary Rose, took an active interest in the Virginia Colony, dying just two years before 1620. Nearby, try Roma's café for a cappuccino, while you watch humanity, and a few lawyers, fight for justice in the law courts, or the The Bank for a regal lunch.

Then
Sir Walter Raleigh
Polymath

There are few more colourful characters in history than the polymath, Sir Walter Raleigh. Young Raleigh studied at the Inns of Courts in the Middle Temple of London in 1557, yet never practised law. Instead, this English landed gentleman and favourite of Queen Elizabeth I, became a writer, poet, soldier, politician, courtier, spy, explorer – though arguably his most famous contribution to UK life was the introduction of tobacco.

In the 1600s, being a lawyer was a somewhat fluid profession, with no need for a university degree to practice law. Instead gowned and be-wigged 'barristers-to-be' lodged, dined and learnt their trade at one of the four Inns of Court in London. It was very much a matter of who you knew. Without exception lawyers and judges were male, white and well-heeled landowning gentry. There were no barristers based in Plymouth at the time and no court that tried murder, piracy or witchcraft in Plymouth, the closest being the assize courts in Exeter or Launceston. A 'grand jury' of landed gentry would investigate a case and decide if a prosecution should begin, while another determined sentencing.

The 'common law' of England had taken proper root in Magna Carta in 1215 and would have provided the foundation for their deliberations. Even after 800 years, it continues to be the most important legal document ever written, asserting the right to a fair trial, and not to be imprisoned without due process of law. Lord Denning, the legendary Judge, describes it as, "the greatest constitutional document of all time – the foundation of the freedom of the individual against the arbitrary authority of a despot." Perhaps, if Raleigh had practiced law better than he studied it, he would not have conducted his own defence for plotting against James I, and lost his case. The judgement ultimately led to him losing his head in 1618, though it was the actions of his deputy and son, who went against his orders, that sounded the final death knell on his extraordinary life.

After a Royal pardon on condition he did not upset the Spanish, the Crown were forced to appease them after Raleigh's disastrous second quest for Eldorado ended in an erroneous attack on a Spanish settlement. Devon's most feted son, Raleigh, had to go.

Now
Jo Martin QC
Criminal
Barrister and
Recorder

Jo Martin QC
Criminal Barrister & Recorder

Jo Martin is a ground-breaking lawyer, who reflects not only how much the law has changed, but how much society has changed. "Her incisive eye cuts to the core of a case with ease," Legal 500, 2018, Leading Silks. Not just a talented barrister, she is Plymouth's first Queen's Counsel (QC) in 400 years and it's first ever female QC. Jo follows in some pretty formidable footsteps: the first ever QC in England was Sir Frances Bacon, who was appointed in 1597, when the role actually involved advising the Queen. Nowadays there are more barristers living and working in Plymouth than there were crew members on the Mayflower. And while much has changed, from the Bar Vocational Course that trainee lawyers must complete, to the relative openness of the profession to all backgrounds (as of 100 years ago it became open to both sexes), some things remain the same. Would-be barristers still have to join Inns of Court and eat a number of dinners there before they can qualify as a barrister. They continue to wear the medieval looking wigs and gowns which were first established in Edward III's reign (1327 – 1377), based on the correct dress for attending the royal courts. Today, the horsehair wigs are still used to set the context and seriousness of the court proceedings.

And the crimes? "People in London think that the only crimes tried in Devon are for sheep hustling or pasty stealing," says Jo. But lawyers' case loads in Plymouth include a wide spectrum of crime that reflects society's bigger challenges, including major child abuse, large scale drugs importation and frauds.

Prior to moving to Devon, she worked for both the Crown Prosecution Service and the Serious Fraud Office at the Old Bailey before becoming a Devon Chambers heavyweight in all areas of Criminal Law.

Becoming a QC was no easy task. "The application was extensive," says Jo. "It took many days to complete and then you have to get twenty references, including twelve from judges. It was quite demanding."

"With technology outpacing changes in the law, the evidence available to the police when investigating a crime, can be extensive. As lawyers, we read the papers carefully to find the unseen things and make connections; eg. looking through phone records for anomalies. One detail can win or lose a case." Jo Martin QC.

Jo works mostly in the Crown and County Courts in Armada Way. "The robing room is where all the action takes place," she says. Roughly the size of a classroom, it has a long table on which barristers put their legal robes and files for each trial. "Barristers can be very macho. Everyone chats loudly about their cases and you do hear random graphic conversations; all criminal trials are unfortunately weird and disturbing in different ways. Stereotypes around gender do still exist," says Jo, "as more women are instructed to prosecute and defend in rape cases, perhaps because they are seen as being more sensitive to the issue, whilst men are instructed on more murders, frauds, and drug-related cases, perhaps, because of a belief that the male brain is more analytical."

In the 1620s, witches were not represented in Court, leading to great miscarriages of justice, but it's an offence to accuse someone of being a witch or using magic, now. One big difference between then and now, is the range of sentences available to the judge. "It is an enormous relief not to work in an era where hanging, or cutting off limbs, is the norm," says Jo. She believes short term sentences of two years are increasingly ineffective. It was on a visit to Eastward Park's women's prison, shortly after qualifying as a Recorder, where she saw at first hand how the prison staff had insufficient funds to rehabilitate short term inmates effectively. "It's likely that short sharp two or three day periods in prison are probably just as effective as two years in getting young people to change their behavioural patterns; there is a very pressing need to address this issue at the earliest opportunity," she says. Time for the law to adapt again to society's needs.

> "The legal system is always playing catch up: whilst old offences may be a thing of the past, new laws are needed to cover 'sexting' and 'upskirting' – not something to trouble the Pilgrims". Jo Martin, Plymouth's first female QC.

"Fortunately," says Jo, "while crime in Plymouth is not as grim as in the capital, where tragic deadly knife fights and acid attacks now abound, it does have its share of significant crimes as well as regular 'town on gown' fights, where locals fall out with the student population on Mutley Plain or Union Street." And while the legal system in Plymouth is the same as the rest of the country, over the years, Jo has noticed a unique aspect of a Plymouth jury, "If we have a defendant with navy connections, the jury is often less keen to convict". There are also issues with Plymouth being a comparatively small city where everyone knows each other, so, in recent years, some high profile cases have been moved to Bristol in order to obtain a fairer jury trial.

The Future
Virtual Law Not a Reality

Jo Martin QC
Devon Chambers
8 The Crescent
Plymouth PL1 3AB
+44 (0)1752 661659
jo.martin@devonchambers.co.uk

"I hope we still have jury service in 400 years. It's key to successful democracy and a rare opportunity, along with voting, for us all to play a role in society. Algorithms are already used for sentencing, like structuring guidelines, determining the likelihood of recidivism, and could be used to calculate speeding sentences, but the law will always be about people and every case different. In 400 years, we will probably be cashless and crime will be more cyber and virtual. With no high street shops, there will be nowhere to shoplift, whilst organised piracy will be less on the open seas, and more in the virtual realm."

Jo Martin, QC Devon Chambers

09 LORD MAYOR

Then, Now & in the Future

Plymouth Hoe
Plymouth's civic focus

Plymouth Hoe is not just a pretty space. The majestic amphitheatre, where the land meets the ocean, plays a vital role in supporting cultural vibrancy and acting as a showcase for historic and cultural events like the Mayflower 400th anniversary commemorations.

"The Hoe is a place of huge importance not just historically, but as a modern day focus for city life," says The Lord Mayor of Plymouth. It's known as the place where Elizabethan Sea Captain, Sir Francis Drake famously took his time finishing a game of bowls before heading off to defeat the Spanish Armada. Today, it's a fitting backdrop for a host of key events, like Remembrance Sunday. "Even in the pouring rain, all the Armed Forces come together with thousands of onlookers to pay their respects," says The Lord Mayor. It's also the epic stage for Armed Forces Day; when the Red Arrows perform daredevil precision aerobatics in the sky; and also hosts popular events such as MTV Crashes, The Plymouth 10k run and the National Fireworks Championships.

A great vista from which to marvel at Plymouth's National Marine Park, amazing City architecture, statues galore, gorgeous coastline and sites from where world changing voyages sailed.

The Hoe is also home to Plymouth's most iconic landmark, Smeaton's Tower, the blueprint for all Lighthouses constructed after 1759 – a great spot to visit, with its incredible views across The Sound and city – as well as the glorious art deco Tinside Lido pool, open to the public for bathing during the summer months. The Hoe's undulating green lawns, overlooking the silver glitter of the sea also make it a popular place for families at the weekend. For fans of the Beatles, there's an iconic shot of the fab four, sitting on The Hoe on a sunny day. It's still possible to put your posterior on metal sculpted impressions of their posteriors, where they sat! At the eastern end of the Hoe, you'll find The Royal Citadel, the most impressive 17th century fortress in Britain and, for many years, England's most important defence against sea attacks. The Citadel has been in constant military occupation since it was built and continues to be home to some of Plymouth's modern heroes – the troops of 29 Commando Regiment.

As the Hoe embraces the 21st century, it continues to be a showcase for the city's history, and home to a new statue of Lady Astor, the American socialite, who became the UK's first sitting female MP in 1919 and an effective campaigner for social justice, improving living conditions for the poor. Lady Astor's house at 3 Elliot Terrace, overlooking the Hoe, is now the Lord Mayor's official residence and hosts visiting judiciary. Plymouth Hoe will always be the perfect natural showcase for celebrations or commemorations like Mayflower 400.

Then
Captain Robert Rawlyn Mayor of Plymouth

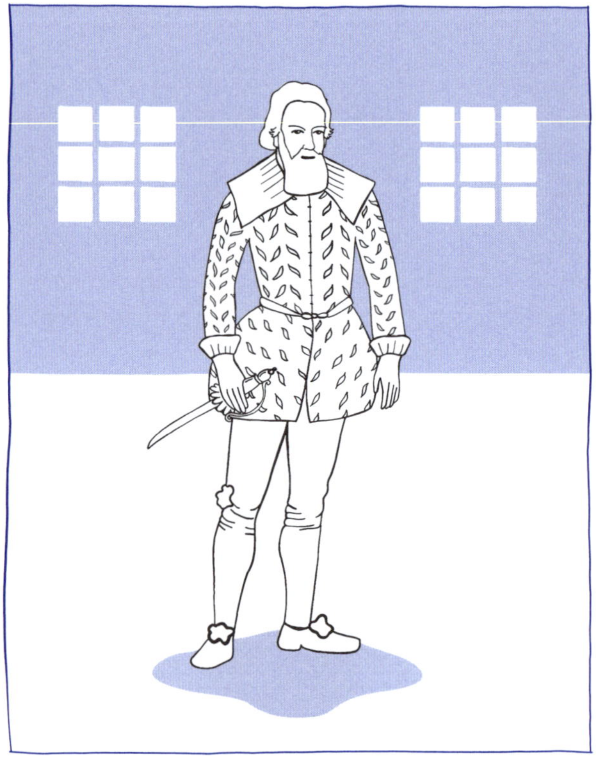

Captain Robert Rawlyn, the Mayor of Plymouth in 1620/1621 and a seventeenth century millionaire equivalent, was clearly a good egg. He paid for the building of St Andrew's south aisle and steeple, and left in his will of 1626 – '£125 (c. £16,500 today) to be lent out to poor seafaring men; £125 to be lent out to poor tradesmen and young beginners; inheritance in fee simple of two tenements in Batter Street to be given to the Hospital of the Orphans' Aid; all goods and chattels, £2,076 6s 8d, to the Hospital of the Orphans' Aid for the maintenance of the children therein, subject to a payment of £20 per year being made to his wife.' At the time of the last inquiry, in April 1910, nearly 300 years later, the gifts in both bread and flour from his will to the Hospital of the Orphans' Aid were still being administered to 34 recipients.

Plymouth's parliamentary minutes, over which the annually changing Mayors of the time would have presided, offer a fascinating snapshot of the issues around the time of 1620. For example, in 1614, the borough was instrumental in overturning the French Company of London's patent, which interfered with Plymouth's cross-Channel trade. A clock was put up in Guildhall in 1619 (the 'new' Guildhall having been founded in 1606), and a bill was passed in 1621 to free up from the New England Company's monopoly, fishing rights in American waters. In 1625, they pushed through a bill decrying the navy's failure to protect merchant shipping, while in 1626 complaints were made about Turkish pirates and Dunkirker privateers. In 1628, complaints were made about abuse of martial law by billeted soldiers and the lack of the Navy's coastal patrols to protect against the Barbary slave traders and pirates. All in a day's work for a Mayor at the time of the Mayflower voyage.

After the Golden Age of the late 1500s, the early 1600s ushered in times of great hardship and fighting over religious matters in Europe as well as the threats from North Africa and the Middle East. The Mayor of Plymouth would have been instrumental in strengthening the city and making all aware of the various threats.

Now
Councillor
Richard Ball
Lord Mayor
of Plymouth

Councillor Richard Ball
Lord Mayor of Plymouth

It's the first day of your new keenly anticipated job: Lord Mayor of Plymouth. You have prepared a simple speech for your first outing. After laying a wreath on the majestic Plymouth Hoe and saying some words in the Sensory Garden about the horrors of the holocaust and Rwandan genocide, you walk back to St Catherine's Baptist Church where a pastor begins to speak about his personal experiences of the Rwandan genocide. You are given first hand accounts of the raw horror of the machete madness in Rwanda: probably the bloodiest, most brutal episode in the history of mankind. The pastor has lost 95 members of his own family, and relates a story about a neighbouring Hutu man who killed his own wife – a Tutsi – and his ten children. One million people were killed in just 100 days. The impassioned speech creates a sort of trauma by proxy. You get up to make your speech, all eyes are on you, expecting some words of comfort and wisdom, but the words on your paper suddenly seem vapid and meaningless in light of what you have just heard, and with great sadness, you realise you are now lost for words and overtaken with emotion. Such was the baptism of fire at the Baptist Church for Plymouth's new Lord Mayor Richard Ball, a kind human soul, unprepared for perhaps the most difficult speech he would ever have to attempt.

Richard is a rare man, descended from a Plymothian mother and Polish father. "Mum was smitten by the blond, exotic sailor warrior," says Richard fondly. His father spoke not a word of English, and instead used his dancing skills and exceptional good looks to win his mother's heart. "But we are all descended from immigrants, if you go far enough back in history," he says.

The post of Lord Mayor no longer carries any executive power, in contrast to 400 years ago, when the likes of Drake could set up grand water projects. But Richard is nonetheless the chairman of an important committee responsible for many of the on-going municipal development projects. "My job is to ensure the smooth running of discussions between the two supposedly non-adversarial parties sitting opposite each other in the Council Chamber, and that various decisions are ratified according to the law and other such guidelines to development works," he says.

The Mace bearer accompanies the Lord Mayor on every single trip that involves the wearing of the mayoral chains; he is there to protect the chains rather than the mayor.

Smeaton's Tower re-erected on the Hoe as a tribute to his enduring oak tree and interlocking blocks design, the blueprint for all lighthouses built after 1759.

His job is also to make influential speeches, something Richard enjoys and puts to good use.

Richard started life in the Navy, once serving on HMS Hermes alongside Prince Charles, before specialising in weapons engineering at the MOD dockyard, then entering the commercial sector. From this experience, he has developed a deep love of Naval and Military history and so was a strong advocate for the opening of The Box, Plymouth's ground-breaking new history and arts museum. "Immensely exciting," Richard says, "an oasis in a cultural desert." Richard's Mayoral office is in the Council House, just a minute's walk from the Hoe. A masterpiece of mid twentieth century contemporary architecture, it has grooved Delabole slate cladding, and was built by Italian craftsmen, using handmade imported Venetian Murano glass tiles for the red colonnade on both sides of the building that houses centuries of the city's accumulated mayoral treasures.

The grand trappings of mayoral duties are not without problems – Richard can't go anywhere in his posh 14th century Lord Mayor's traditional robes, without one of his mace bearer friends. Only, they are not there as his friends.

Responsible for opening great events and developments, like The Box, and making public speeches, when not chairing important City Council meetings.

They are there primarily to protect the grand 18 carat gold chains, weighing 42 ounces, from being stolen. The mace with which they protect the chain, is now a highly decorated ornamental symbol of authority, a far cry from the original lethal weapon of its ancestors.

However, despite his now elevated status, Richard remains a man of the people, keen to get in amongst them and find out what makes the city tick. Richard rejects any negative descriptions of Plymouth, instead extolling the beauties of the Hoe as the city's showpiece, and the toughness of the military and naval prowess, and its ascendancy over the last 400 years. "The Hoe hosts one of the most resplendent and important Remembrance Day services in the land and, when the Royal Marines band is playing, it is the only place in the world where you can hear the music and see The Sound," Richard tells us with a smile.

The Lord Mayor, Councillor Richard Ball on the magnificent Plymouth Hoe, with his Macebearer Kevin Graham, who has been protecting the Mayoral Chains for 40 years.

The Future
More power to the people

Lord Mayor Richard Ball
3 Elliot Terrace
Plymouth Hoe PL1 2QL
+44 (0)1752 304858
lordmayor@plymouth.gov.uk

“We are planting the seeds now that will lead to enormous change over the next 400 years in the City. There will be massive investment along the shoreline of the Tamar and Plymouth’s extensive waterfronts. However, without clever use of technology, the burgeoning population, with its extravagant lifestyles and limited resources will lead to wars. There is also a danger that technology has got too far ahead of our ability to control it and understand its ramifications. We will need to deploy the brightest people to sort things out.”

Lord Mayor Richard Ball.

10

MILITARY

Then, Now & in the Future

Mount Edgcumbe
The fittest place of the survivalist

Nestled on a peninsula in the south-easternmost point of Cornwall, Mount Edgcumbe House and Country Park overlooks Plymouth, once part of the Edgcumbe estate, where the English Channel meets the mouth of the mighty River Tamar.

'It has the beauties of all other places added to peculiar beauties of its own,' said Walpole of Mount Edgcumbe. The Tudor mansion of Mount Edgcumbe was built nearly 100 years before the Mayflower sailed past its palatial front door in 1620.

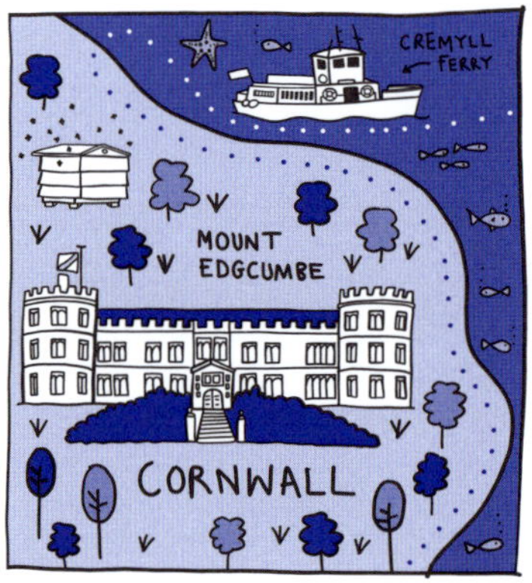

Today, the Edgcumbe estate is owned by both Cornwall Council and Plymouth City Council and has become a pleasure park attracting visitors from across the region and beyond. The gardens are a joy to explore. Plant hunters, over the centuries, have influenced what has been grown on the 865-acre estate, which is literally a living book on how the natural world has been changing over time.

The undisturbed ancient woodlands, beautiful 'Pleasure' and formal English, Italian, American and New Zealand gardens give us fascinating evolving views on medicinal plants, which, in the past, were used to cure everything from depression, in the form of pine needle tea, to growing rosemary bushes to treat exhaustion. These exotic plants, herbs and over 180 species of tree, dotted around the estate, including a 400-year-old lime tree, make it a Grade 1 listed landscape.

The Cremyll Ferry, makes it easy to get to Plymouth. The estate has been carefully developed to offer a wide range of activities for young and old. For a fine snack, visit the Stables Café, or have tea in the Orangerie. Browse over and support the pioneering spirit of the extensive range in the independent shopping village, which offers a range of activities from weaving to upcycling.

There's segway rides, frisbee golf, mountain biking as well as walks. There are regular Park Runs, weddings and events like The Proms, Vintage Car Fayre and Vintage Markets.

For those wishing to get a better understanding of what it took to survive in those early days when the pilgrims arrived at Cape Cod, with no help in sight, knowing they had to rely entirely on their skills to get everything they needed, there's Survival Wisdom. The Survival Wisdom team at Mount Edgcumbe, are training people to cope with living in hostile places, by teaching them useful ancient skills and resilience to live outside, using their hands, a few tools and craft; giving everyone a taste of the past, so we can still be here in 400 years in to the future.

Mount Edgcumbe
is enriched with over ten miles of coastline, Bronze Age barrows, battle sites, a holy well, Iron Age forts, follies, chapels and a stunning landscape, built on an ancient volcanic lava flow.

Then
The Edgcumbe Family
Soldiers of the realm

The magical Edgcumbe Estate, where the Edgcumbes personally battled and beat off the French, has an extraordinary 500-year history.

As a result of stronger military power, the Edgcumbes had reversed centuries of defensive thinking by employing 18 builders to construct their house, in 1547, to look outwards, in order to enjoy the spectacular views, rather than windowless with defensive shooting positions.

Formal armed forces did not exist in the early 1600s and the Edgcumbes would have used their own resources to defend against any attack, as royal soldiers were only deployed to protect the Crown. Nonetheless, Piers Edgcumbe joined them as a colonel during the Civil War to protect Charles II against the Parliamentarians.

A number of colourful characters have come and gone on this most wonderful and romantic of estates with its endless features, beautiful gardens, commanding position and amazing history. Regarding the defence of itself and the realm, it has had many unwelcome admirers such as the leader of the Spanish Armada and then, legend has it, Hitler, though not so much that it escaped serious damage during the blitz in 1941. While it has undoubtedly produced many heroes in its time, of note was George Edgcumbe (1721 to 1795), Baron Edgcumbe in 1761, who graduated from the Royal Naval College at Portsmouth, and went on to fight at the Battle of Quiberon Bay and the Siege of Louisbourg. In 1780, he permitted the removal of a hundred or so trees to build a battery for which he earned a viscountship the following year, followed, eight years later, by an earldom after a visit from the King. However, his marriage to the eccentric Emma Gilbert, daughter of the Archbishop of York, caused hilarity, to some extent owing to her penchant for card playing and dining with her pet pig, Cupid, but mainly for appearing as a caricature, most famously as the witch in A Witch upon a Mount's Edge with flaming hair, a crescent moon, broomsticks and a frog.

Mount Edgcumbe's guide, David Marshall will tell you that the country, over 400 years ago, was saved from invading forces on a number of occasions by those living at the estate, with its vast lands and pre-eminence in the region.

Now
Richard
Pyshorn
CEO Survival
Wisdom

Richard Pyshorn
Surviving into the future

Richard Pyshorn knows what it took for the Mayflower Pilgrims to survive one of mankind's most epic voyages. As the CEO of Survival Wisdom, a former RAF Force Protection specialist for 30 years, FRGS (Fellow of the Royal Geographical Society), and follower of Wellington's style of leadership, Richard is a very different kind of Mount Edgcumbe resident, holding regular survival courses in the grounds of the estate.

The teaching is a culmination of skills and knowledge acquired through spending thirty years in the British military, working to resolve some of humanity's most horrific and highly unpredictable wars and catastrophic natural disasters. Richard says the most important lesson he learnt from his time serving in Northern Ireland, Croatia, Serbia, the Middle East including Iraq, Afghanistan, Kuwait, Bahrain, West Africa, Belize, Germany and Cyprus was how to deal with difficult and challenging situations.

Without the right training and preparation, he says, the brain can go into cognitive paralysis, when the mind focuses on the threat – instead of on the unfolding traumatic events. Instead of going into the "Fight or Flight" mode, the untrained mind can "freeze" or become "hyperactive" when more positive action is needed. To avoid such situations, Richard would motivate and inspire his team to survive by overcoming deep fear through training, preparation and a sense of humour, thereby reversing the "freeze" or inappropriate behaviour effect, when bombs exploded nearby.

Today, thanks to Survival Wisdom and its team of ex military survival specialists, these skills are taught to people from around the world. They teach that, while the world may have changed, developing ever smarter technology and gadgets, having the Mayflower Pilgrim's core skills of resilience and adaptability, on top of an ability to respect and work with the Wampanoags, has never been more important. Richard says of the pilgrim's voyage, "Just imagine not knowing what's ahead, that you might never return and how it must have felt as the land vanished behind you. The Mayflower pilgrims only had what they took with them

"The most important principle of survival in a given emergency," explains Richard "is to own the space and create thinking time, like brewing a communal cup of tea, to take stock of what is going on and talk through the options." Richard Pyshorn.

to build homes, and knowledge and skills gained from their farming backgrounds."

Mount Edgcumbe is a place that's perfect for this type of training, says Richard. "I love the story and the vistas. When I bring people here, I deliver the context, by showing them where Darwin sailed around Devil's Point and, owing to the boat's shifting ballast, had to stay at Mount Edgcumbe at the Earl's kindness, without which he would never have reached the Galapagos Islands to develop the concept of the Origin of Species."

The aim of the action packed survival courses is to discover how to interact with the wild, using your own ingenuity; how to make simple tools like spoons and paddles; how to make crude equipment such as an axe and a knife; how to forage for plants for medicine, food, and shelter; and how to navigate using natural signs, such as the stars or geographical locations.

"And while we now have Googlemaps and Google Earth to show us what's over the horizon, however good your computer is, it can't teach you how to manage real time risks. Only proper risk training, practice-runs and in-depth research, with well-honed survival skills, will empower you to deal with uncertainty," says Richard.

When Richard worked with four amazing ladies, who achieved two world records by rowing across the Pacific Ocean from America to Australia, he showed them how to deal with the unique emergencies they might face on their voyage, such as a pirates' ambush and what to do if you lose oars or a person goes overboard in a freak wave.

The courses provide support for many different types of survival scenarios. Richard also works with Conrad Humphreys of the Channel 4 series, "Mutiny", teaching people how to stay 'safe and sound' sailing around Plymouth Sound in a replica of the Captain Bligh boat in the 'Mutiny Experience'.

Terrorist bombs and natural disasters be damned! Fight back that fear and master the unknown unknowns with Survival Wisdom.

Richard describes The Green Prescription as one of Survival Wisdom's key initiatives, which is all about connecting people back to nature, to take the pressure off the National Health Service (NHS). "It's about getting children away from their screens and back into the natural environment, where the real skill of survival is really rewarding, especially through team building exercises," says Richard.

"The difference between life and death in a survival setting is very slim, without the right mindset and basic skill set," says Richard. "Whether you have to face a tsunami or terrorist attack, why take chances? With Survival Wisdom's core skill set you can learn how to keep yourself, your family and your community alive."

The Future
The strength of the wolf is in the pack

Richard Pyshorn
Survival Wisdom
Mount Edgcumbe Country Park
Cremyll Torpoint
Cornwall PL10 1HZ
richard@survivalwisdom.com

“If we continue to be desensitised and remote from our natural environment, due to continued automation and oil combustion, we will be extinct in the next century. Surviving another 400 years requires recognising that the world is a giant operating system, and, though we are agile and adaptable, it will take awareness of changing circumstances, nurturing initiative, being generous with information and communicating plans clearly through a team of ‘green warriors’ – and above all, human spirit – for us to survive and thrive in the future. No plan survives contact with the enemy.”

Richard Pyshorn, CEO Survival Wisdom.

II

NAVAL OFFICER

Then, Now & in the Future

Devonport Naval Base
Mariners and Submarines

Her Majesty's Naval Base Devonport is the largest in Western Europe and the sole nuclear repair and refuelling facility for the Royal Navy. Nationally important to UK security, it's a heavily restricted site, but, less than five minutes drive away, you will find the Devonport Naval Heritage Museum, which tells you all you need to know!

Since it was established, forty years after the Mayflower sailed in 1620, The Royal Navy, has been pivotal to the enormous expansion of territories, ideas, trade, exploration and numerous other endeavours on behalf of the United Kingdom.

The Devonport Naval Heritage Museum, situated near to the naval base, tells the epic story of that amazing institution and so is a Plymouth must-see. On arrival, you are greeted by canons from China so ornate they make you want to display them in your living room rather than blow a ship to smithereens. In the Engine House, there's a large array of grand ornate figureheads from when wooden ships were all the rage. If you prefer metal, then you can learn about the transition from steam and wood in the Warspite Gallery.

The Grand Devonport Naval Base Dining Room (shown opposite) is part of the fascinating history of the area. The Devonport Naval Heritage Museum, run by volunteers, has an excellent collection of all kinds of naval history and models.

For those with a penchant for smart dressing and eating on board ship, go to the 18th Century Pay Office. A visit to The Fire Station will tell you the history of shipbuilding, the Sail Navy and the Police Museum.

If it's WWII monster battleships that grab you, check out the Plymouth gallery. But if you want the strong silent type then slip stealthily into Courageous's gallery, or – amazing trip alert – for a whole submarine tour, book two weeks ahead!

Once weary of naval endeavour, you'll find, close by, Devonport's exceptional 'People's Park', sitting atop a hill with the most wonderful views of the Tamar, the sea and much of Plymouth. It is a great place to relax, reconnect with nature and entertain the kids. Snack at the environmentally friendly Park Pavilion Café, or meditate in the sensory garden with wild flower meadows and a pungent flower garden.

There's also tennis, bowls, a tiny theatre, a decorative bandstand for concerts, the extraordinary HMS Doris Gun, and an old air-raid shelter.

The specialist Stiltskin's Soapbox Children's Theatre by the park will entrance your young children, offering clubs and holiday workshops in drama, art and circus skills, like Plymouth's Family Rave, Bubblicious and Story Stomps. For those who want to buy something handmade and authentic, the independent Soapbox Toy-Box sells beautifully designed unique toys with a retro twist.

Minesweeping Trawlers
From a sketch
On the spot by
W.L. Wyllie

Then
Sir Edward Cecil
Commander of English fleet

Sir Edward Cecil, newly promoted as 1st Viscount of Wimbledon, was appointed in 1625, only five years after the Mayflower sailed, by the Duke of Buckingham, to command an English expeditionary force to pillage Cadiz and surrounding areas, along with Spanish treasure ships returning from the Americas. Unfortunately for him…

In 1620, before the Royal Navy was officially established in 1660, England was on the cusp of a major sea change – for the worse; the Golden Age was over and the terrible 30 Years War had just begun, eventually to cause carnage and claim 8 million European lives of a total population of around 45 million.

This was the backdrop of Cecil and Buckingham's enormous fall from grace; for Cecil, Buckingham's fall guy, commanded the fleet of 115 ships and 15,000 mostly pressed men from Plymouth, into an ocean of death, and terrible weather.

While a very accomplished military man, Cecil knew very little about the sea and preparing for such campaigns. Dogged by ill luck and inexperience, one storm, then another, he failed to capture even some sitting target cargo ships, let alone treasure ships.

"Despite a distinguished military career and high standing at court, Sir Cecil, owing to inexperience at sea, oversaw the worst naval disaster the country has probably ever suffered. It is testament to his other achievements that the matter was brushed under the carpet."

Having not prepared the fleet with enough victuals for the campaign, Sir Edward Cecil was forced to release his sailors onto the Spanish mainland,where they found houses replete with divine Spanish wine, upon which at least 1,000 of them got literally slaughtered. For the ones that narrowly escaped, the return journey was to be no less disastrous, as they were once again dogged by terrible weather, grave sickness and now malnutrition, causing many to die of diseases as the fleet returned, horrendously bedraggled, in dribs and drabs of near wrecked ships, in what was probably the worst defeat – though one could hardly say a battle had taken place – in English naval history. Normally, a full enquiry would have followed with a grisly end for Sir Edward, but somehow the matter was completely overlooked.

Now
Commander
Steve Ward
Naval
Officer

Commander Steve Ward
Naval Officer

Commander Steve Ward is everything one expects from the Royal Navy; an impressive tactician, with distinctive leadership skills, a dry sense of humour, and always immaculately turned out. Holding his silver-topped parade stick, as he marches through the strategic hub that is Devonport Naval Base, he reminds everyone he meets, that time keeping is everything in the Forces.

In the thousand years before the English navy was formed in 1660, the 'King's Ships' were pretty effective at protecting Britain's shores on an ad hoc basis. However, with the expansion of the British Empire and its trading routes, there was a clear demand for the permanent Royal Navy to be formed.

The Royal Navy grew considerably during the Napoleonic Wars when the practice of fighting under sail developed into a great art form, later supplanted by directional cannons and shell-firing guns.

In the Naval Arms Race of a hundred years ago, the world's navies were judged on the size of their battleships and the number of destroyers, which were subject to treaty. Today, the Royal Navy is focused on maintaining its nuclear deterrent, aircraft carrier and amphibious task groups.

"The Royal Navy is recovering from political decisions made in the 1980s. The future is now bright and we are now in a great position for the next hundred years, owing to professional men and women motivated to serve in the new carriers and next generations of ships and nuclear submarines." Commander Steve Ward.

Having joined the Navy in 1985, at the height of the cold war, as a technocrat, Cdr Ward explains, "After signing up, I worked on submarines with a rear end nuclear reactor for three month periods, for over ten years, before returning to the grey ships."

There was no psychological testing for suitability for submariners at that time. "My two-years training in submarine work prepared me for being an engineer of nuclear submarines and was so good, I had nothing at all to worry about."

It was a life with which he quickly became accustomed. "On a submarine with over a hundred individuals in a constrained space, you immediately get into a routine and forget about bills and mortgages, as you can't do anything about them on a mission; once you strip these away, you discover who you are." Such close proximity on tense missions brought out unexpected qualities in his colleagues.

"The Royal Navy is all about the people; Regular, Reserve and Civilian. It's not just about the latest kit."

"We were once deployed in an area of the world where it was important to remain undetected. But one of the team fell very sick, so we had to move him. We had two camps of thought: half of the team wanted to protect and look after the guy, while the other half wanted to shoot him out of the torpedo for risking the mission.

"We didn't, obviously. But under pressure, people often do the opposite of what one expects, and I was really surprised which camp I ended up in!"

"The British Government wishes that we remain at the top table of the United Nations Security Council, so it is crucial that we always have the right capabilities to deter hostilities, but warship production is not a five minute job," says Steve.

"Successive British Governments are very conscious that through the Royal Navy, UK PLC can achieve Global Influence and project power with our Joint Strike Fighters, grey ships and black submarines in control of the waves and the skies. Aircraft carriers are a clear show of British military strength; the design of the new Queen Elizabeth class hails back to lessons learnt from the Falklands War. It is important that we always have our own air capability on our aircraft carriers, so we can deploy within twelve miles of any international coastline," says Steve.

The new breed of ASTUTE Class 'hunter-killer' submarines, known as Submarines Submersible Nuclear (SSN), can attack sea and land targets without surfacing. "The fear of having a sub in your backyard is enough to influence most situations to bring about a positive resolution," says Steve.

"When I joined the Navy, it was easy to know the enemy, but it is quite different today," says Steve, "fighting an asymmetric war against an enemy that can pop up anywhere, at any time."

Fixed wing jets and helicopters are a big draw for people wanting to join the navy. "The Royal Navy is also an organisation that inculcates strong rules of commitment, and where you can learn excellent skills for joining the civilian workforce when you ultimately go outside," says Steve. Many of Commander Steve Ward's generation joined up as a result of the Falklands War, even though initially many thought the islands were off the coast of Scotland!

The first female Royal Navy personnel went to sea in 1991, and are now in all roles, including submarines. According to Commander Ward, "The intensive training is the same for both sexes and today, having all male warships would feel strange and out of place."

The Future
Britannia's new wave?

Devonport Naval Heritage Centre
Plymouth PL1 4RW
+44 (0)1752 552 326
navynbcd-nblo@mod.gov.uk
devonportnhc.wordpress.com

"In 400 hundred years' time, if there is still a world with countries and the UK still wants to influence those countries, Britannia will wish to continue ruling the waves. Whether the whole of the Royal Navy is driven by artificial intelligence will be determined by society and what is considered acceptable at the time. Once the general public accept being flown by an unmanned aircraft to a holiday in Spain, the rest will follow fairly quickly. The British public expect us to protect them and national interests, and go wherever we are told to go on their behalf; that will continue."

Commander Steve Ward, Royal Navy.

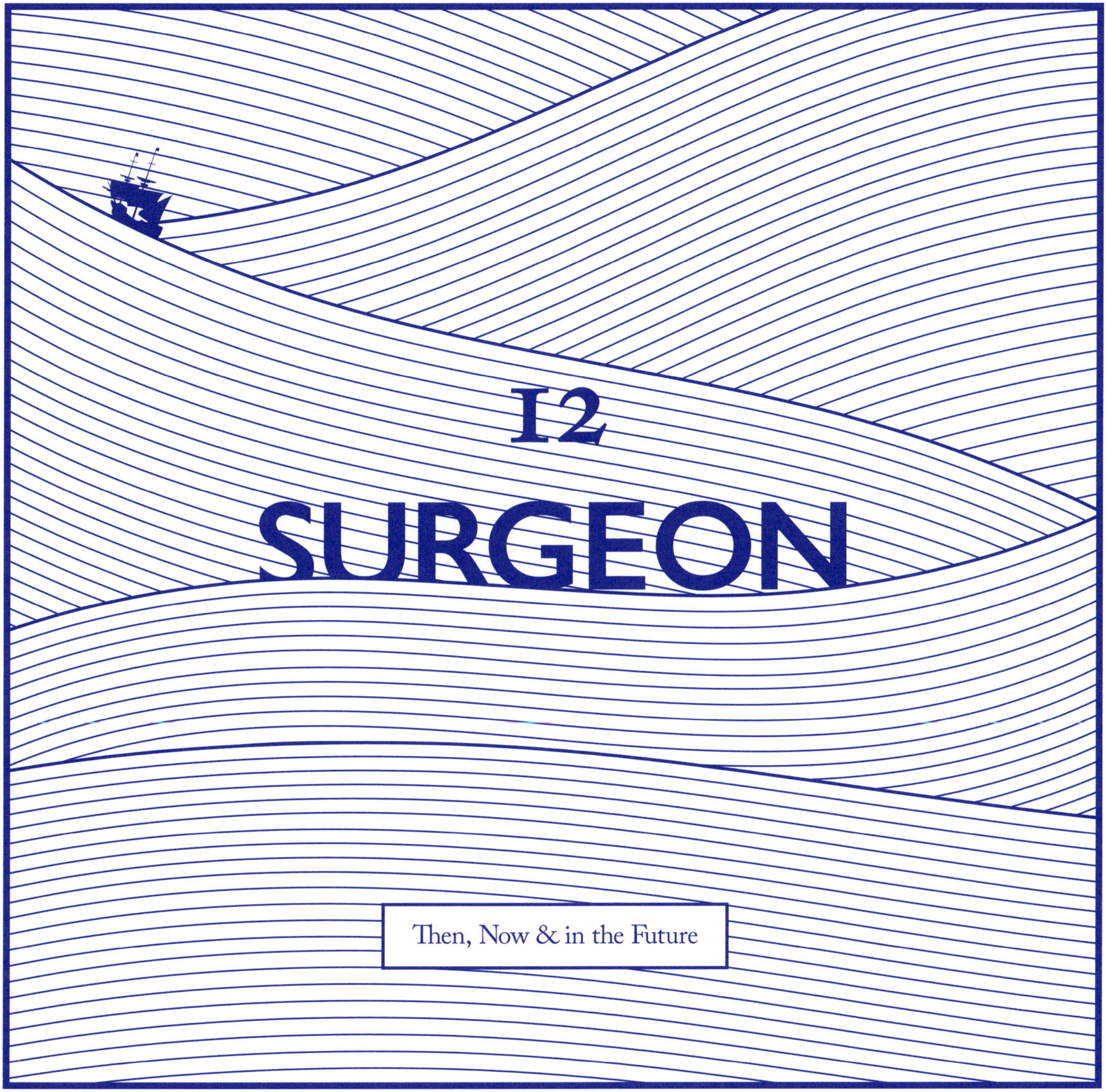
12
SURGEON
Then, Now & in the Future

Durnford Street and its environs
Home to medics

Stonehouse has been a place for all manner of things: the first naval hospital of the 18th century, the Royal Marine Barracks, St Paul's Church, the foot-ferry to Mt Edgcumbe and countless other establishments, some not quite so salubrious.

From the famous writer and doctor Sir Arthur Conan Doyle to today's Dr. Jason Smith, beautiful, historic Durnford Street has been home to many other doctors over the centuries, owing to its convenient location near the Old Naval Hospital, Stonehouse, built in 1760.

Once owned by the unfortunately monikered Bastard family from Domesday in 1086, Durnford Street went on to be named after the Durnford family, which married into the Edgcumbe family in 1472. This union linked Devon to Cornwall as they owned both the estate in Cornwall, which can be accessed across the water via the Cremyll passenger ferry, and the land stretching from Plymouth to Dartmoor.

"It is a capital mistake to theorize in advance of the facts. Insensibly one begins to twist facts to suit theories instead of theories to suit facts."
Sherlock Holmes
(Sir Arthur Conan Doyle)

Durnford Street has seen many establishments come and go, including numerous brothels that were no doubt set up to satiate the more lusty sailors and marines in the nearby Royal Marine Barracks, originally built to combat the American War of Independence (1775 – 1782).

Just off Durnford Street is Pound Street, home to the Artillery Arms, a top spot for a pint of Bass. But, if you want to do something active, there's the magical Stonehouse Lawn Tennis Club, tucked away in a beautiful corner at the end of Durnford Street, with its majestic views of the Sound, or Plymouth Cricket Club up at Mount Wise. But, just past St. Paul's Church, with its pointed spires, we see, along the pavement, a setting in stone of twenty separate plaques of pithy quotes from the great crime solver, Sherlock Holmes, the creation of Dr. Arthur Conan Doyle, as he was known in 1882. These plates are testament to his literary and medical genius while he worked here as a doctor in Plymouth, experiencing not only the dark side of his contemporary, the opium-addicted Doctor Budd, but also the misty moors of Dartmoor that inspired the 'Baskerville beast'.

Such sayings as, "There is nothing so unnatural as the commonplace," are more apt now than ever before. "Any truth is better than indefinite doubt", encapsulates the current agonies Britain endures over its connection with Europe, and the fate of its increasingly godless population. However, never before, perhaps, has the following statement been truer: "Life is infinitely stranger than anything which the mind of man could invent."

Then
Giles Heale
Barber and Surgeon

The Mayflower ship's barber surgeon, Giles Heale, could have been a woman in 1620, for it was as common for women to work in medicine, as say herbalists, as men, in England. However, the English Navy under King James I would only have allowed men to serve on board military ships.

Very little was available to surgeons in those days before anaesthetics were developed in the early 1800s, so the medical care of 400 years ago on the Mayflower would have been pretty basic and brutal. Operations would have been performed in calmer seas on a stretcher with a fresh flow of sea air on the ship's top deck. If someone really needed an operation, the options were strong opiate painkillers when available, navy strength rum or the like, and a stick on which to bite down. As anaesthetics were developed, to keep people asleep during surgery, operations could be more complex, with a greater variety being possible. Reading ships' logs, surgery remained relatively rudimentary and the Company of Barber Surgeons was exactly that: cutting things off and cutting things out, to put it simply, and skills in one discipline were considered qualification enough for the other, for a time. However, some things are still done in a very similar way today as then, such as 'bone-setting' with plaster of Paris, used from the 1800s onwards, and still used today, along with stitching up wounds with a needle and thread. John Hunter in the 1700s, often recognised as the father of modern surgery, admitted that it should be seen as a last resort in most cases. Most modern-day surgeons, for much of what they do, would not see themselves as a last resort, rather medical engineers for improving or repairing the body, with a vast array of safe surgical options from which to choose.

"A strong healing touch, an honest look in the eye, the ability to read the body language of your patient, and most of all, to feel empathy for another's suffering are all essential features of the fine human medical practitioners of today." Dr Jason Smith.

Little else is known of Giles Heale beyond being a signatory to William Mullins' will, but, given the hideous voyage of the Mayflower, the illness it caused and the effects on health of that first winter, it is hardly surprising that he returned to England the following year.

Now
Dr Jason
Smith
Doctor

Dr Jason Smith
Doctor

Dr Jason Smith is both a doctor and professor at Plymouth University, joining the Royal Navy in 1992 after studying medicine at Newcastle University. "My first job at the Royal Naval Hospital (RNH) Plymouth was in Stonehouse, where I loved working as a Senior House Officer in General Surgery in 1994. There was a real sense of family and belonging, and everyone pulled together to look after the patients. It was very civilised; I lived in the wardroom, and was woken with a cup of tea every morning, a simple but great way to start the day."

"I had no intention of joining the Royal Navy until Surgeon Commander (as he was then) Rick Jolly came to talk to the Newcastle University Medical Society and told us about his time during the Falklands Conflict and the period afterwards. He was an inspiring character, who planted the idea in my mind that a career in the Navy might be for me. I was also inspired by Dr Clifford Mann, who was my Senior Registrar in Plymouth in 1996 and went on to become a Consultant in Taunton and the President of the Royal College of Emergency Medicine. He is able to see and talk sense in a world gone mad."

Surgeon Captain Jason Smith has been a Consultant in Emergency Medicine at Derriford Hospital since 2005, having joined the Royal Navy in 1992.

Deployed by the Navy all over the world, Jason has seen the horrific results of war first hand and says, thankfully, he has not seen much of this in Plymouth – long may it last. Doctors in HM Armed Forces spend a period (typically 3 years) doing 'general duties' on ships, submarines and attached to Royal Marine units, before specialising – Jason chose emergency medicine, which has seen him deployed to places like Iraq, Afghanistan, and South Sudan as part of a UN Mission (UNMISS), where he spent four months as the emergency physician and clinical director in the medical facility. A military career of course brings unusual challenges: Jason trained with the Gurkhas in Belize and had to deal with soldiers getting human bot fly larva after a jungle military exercise, not something you do every day in Plymouth. The larvae burrow under the skin, and form what is essentially a boil – but until you remove the maggots with forceps, having starved them of oxygen using something like Vaseline, the boil won't heal.

"In general, most things in medicine are more complex than we thought only 30 years ago when I was at medical school," says Jason. "Much of what was taught has now been proven to be wrong, or at least a gross oversimplification of the truth. For example, we have learned that the way blood clots after injury is nowhere near as simple as previously taught."

"Medicine is still heavily reliant upon apprenticeships; medical school gives you the core knowledge, but it is only by practicing medicine under supervision that the nuances become apparent," he says.

Sailors don't get nutritional diseases like scurvy any more, and in fact, the diet on board Her Majesty's Ships

is excellent, but seasickness is still difficult to treat, even with modern medicines. Jason remembers as a ship's Medical Officer, "We had to send a sailor home as she was constantly seasick, ending up on an intravenous drip as she couldn't keep food down."

One of the most dangerous modern scandals is the influence of big pharmaceutical companies on the habits of doctors, such as with oversubscribing antibiotics. We must be much more careful with these precious resources or they will lose their effectiveness.

"In the future, I really hope people will not just be accessing healthcare online from their bedrooms, and that we will always be trying out new ideas like playing appropriate music to help patients in pain or distress, which we want to trial at Derriford Hospital.

"Hospitals are like businesses today, with budgets and key targets, which sometimes detracts from why we are there as doctors – to look after patients. I hope in future that money ceases to be the driving force."

Like many other aspects of modern life, Artificial Intelligence will be a part of the future but I really hope not too much, as being a doctor is a vocation and patients are not simply customers. Saving people in their hour of need is very rewarding. I think different medical practices will interlink more in the future. I actually qualified as an acupuncturist, when I was in training, to offer another treatment option to patients with musculoskeletal problems, such as neck or back pain. I don't know exactly how it works, but it seems to work well for many.

The Future
Virtual doctors? Don't test our patients

Jason Smith RN
Surgeon Captain
University Hospitals NHS Trust
Derriford Hospital PL6 8DH
+44 (0)1752 437629
jasonesmith@nhs.net

"AI technology will replace a number of doctors' activities, such as with Bayesian Networks in clinical prediction tools. In Japan they already use human-like robotic nurses, to cover the shortfall in patient care. In the UK, stroking electronic fluffy cats aid hospital patients to de-stress. We also have robotic surgery, where a surgeon can operate from a remote location; this will become more common using live-streamed instructions. However, understanding pain and two-way empathic communication separates us from robots that will never understand the complexity of body language and eye contact."

Doctor Jason Smith

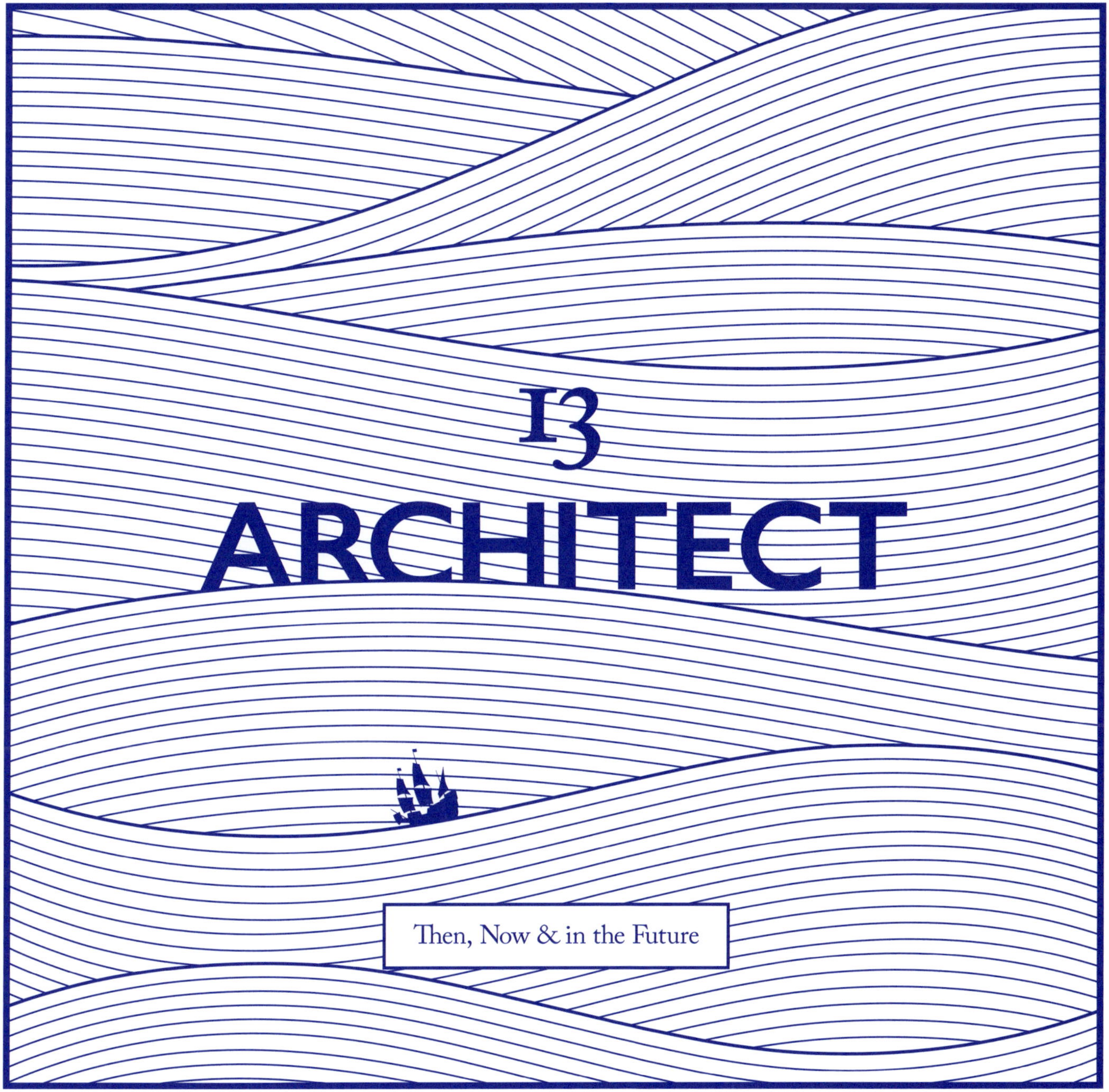
13
ARCHITECT
Then, Now & in the Future

Royal William Yard
It will never work...

"Why would you want to invest millions in a massive dead end dump like that?" Like so many stories of imagination and determination, The Royal William Yard is an enormous success story born out of very shaky beginnings.

The Royal William Yard looks across to Mount Wise and the Scott Memorial to the north west, and looks west across the River Tamar to South East Cornwall.

At the far end of the yard, you can climb up the 'Stairway to Devon', a near-floating staircase with one attachment to the sheer rock face, to take you up to Devil's Point, where you can look back over the top of the grand looking yard before venturing out into an area of significant green space that might one day grow vegetables for the Yard. For now, it is a place with entrancing views of the Sound and Plymouth's majestic seafront. Legend has it that witches were thrown into the sea off Devil's Point at Firestone Bay (maybe short for Fire and Brimstone Bay)! Devil's Point is also home to Western King Battery, a signifcant defensive line with two emplacements in front that make fine viewing platforms: the perfect spot to see an Armada of 130 galleons sailing up the English Channel, until Drake decided eventually to leave the bowling green and go to battle.

From an old derelict giant white elephant, the Royal William Yard has been converted into a hive of business activities in the grandest of settings, with awesome views.

Further east, you can look down over the wall to see Firestone Arch, a shortcut to the sea, with a short tunnel directly from the Yard, and the place where the free membership South West Stand Up Paddleboarders (SUP) launch their boards. From there, walk on to the Firestone Bay blockhouse, whose defensive role was superseded by the King's Point Batteries before it became the Artillery restaurant, which overlooks the splendid tidal pool and is next to a café.

Getting to the Yard is easy, thanks to Plymouth Boat Trips, owned by marine entrepreneur Ben Squire. There are regular ferries from Royal William Yard to the Barbican every day, and you must try his chorizo honey scallops and lime and chilli shackattacks at the entrance of the yard in the old slaughter house. Another way to travel is via the Ocean City Sights buses, which operate a hop on, hop off service in a loop around the city, visiting some great sights, or you can catch the 34/34A bus for a direct route into the city centre. However, if exhausted by a day's exploring, you can always retire to Plymouth's first luxury hotel, the nearby Duke Of Cornwall, for an exquisite cream tea in the turret, with its wonderful 360 degree birds-eye views of the surrounding area!

Then
Sir Bernard de Gomme
Military Engineer

The highly talented Dutchman and royal favourite, Sir Bernard de Gomme was commissioned to design the Royal Citadel in Plymouth in the 1660s, to defend the Crown, ironically, against the Dutch and later the French, and some say, the people of Plymouth: the Citadel, manned largely by Plymothians, was the first fortress to side with William of Orange in 1688.

This amazing fortress, in pride of position, overlooking the Sound and Sutton Pool, and incorporating Drake's Elizabethan castle of 1598, the Royal Chapel of St Katherine's of 1666 (the original was built in 1371), and a blockhouse from Henry VIII's reign, was originally designed with bastions arranged in a pentagon. It was finalised with one bastion absent, giving the aerial appearance of having fallen away down the hill towards the Barbican, so that it could have its own harbour and wharfs and to connect with the people and their trades. Much of the tailoring and victualling were done from here, before the latter was moved to the Royal William Yard, to be nearer the newly constructed docks at Devonport.

Probably the most important military engineer of the 1600s, highly accomplished in serving the Royalist Army engineers, 'Surveyor-General of Fortifications', with 63 designs of fortified towns to his name in the Low Countries, Knighted by Charles I, and Engineer-in-Chief to Charles II.

The entrance to the citadel was guarded by a ravelin, while the north side of the fort was built in a similar way to other designs of the time, having a ditch in front of a tall stone wall with an earth bank on top of it to stop artillery shots. The 12 metre high walls were made from local limestone while granite from Dartmoor was used for dressing. To make sure all the walls could be protected by artillery, three angled bastions were built, pointing into the ditch.

So far, so good, until Samuel Pepys came along and announced, "De Gomme hath built very sillily". The Citadel however has stood the test of time and is still in use by 29 Commando Regiment, who provide artillery support for the Royal Marines of 3 Commando Brigade and de Gomme was also credited with producing plans for some 63 forts in the Low Countries.

Now
Jackie
Gillespie
Architect

Jackie Gillespie
Architect

Jackie Gillespie is one of the most instrumental and inspiring architects in Plymouth's regeneration story. A partner in the award winning Gillespie Yunnie Architects and part time lecturer at Plymouth University, she has worked with property developers, Urban Splash, since 1999, on the conversion and repurposing of the Royal William Yard in Plymouth, one of the most significant sites of historic military buildings in the United Kingdom.

> Regenerating heritage buildings into contemporary social spaces that incorporate transport links, user experience, congregation, conveniences and other factors in their design.

Built by Sir John Rennie and Joseph Whidbey, it's a fascinating 19th century industrial complex that was used as a victualling yard for the Royal Navy to pick up ships' biscuits, clothing and essential items like rope. But in the nineties it had fallen into disuse, the MOD having no further purpose for it. "The Navy was the pulse of Plymouth, since the late 1600s, and the city revolved around them. The Royal William Yard had been used for victualing for over a century and employed lots of people from Plymouth. But, after closing in 1990, it was left derelict for a long time," says Jackie.

Then, along came Urban Splash, award-winning property developers from Manchester. "Urban Splash, the trendiest developers in the country at the time, could not believe their luck, being awarded a beautiful Heritage building project with amazing sea vistas," says Jackie. "The people of Plymouth simply could not see why anyone would want to live inside very old warehouses – 'familiarity breeds contempt' – so the greatest challenge of all was changing people's mindsets, to make them think it was a fun and amazing place to live or visit."

Initial regeneration discussions centred around turning it into an out-of-town shopping centre, or very large luxury hotel and spa. But Jackie's dynamic team felt that a mixed-use development of homes, offices, shops and restaurants would provide the most benefit for Plymouth. With others, Jackie led the delivery of £40m worth of regeneration construction that transformed the redundant naval dockyard into a vibrant visitor attraction, business centre of excellence and thriving sustainable artistic and artisanal community.

Her dynamic firm breathed life back into the Brewhouse, the Mills Bakery, the Cooperage and the Slaughterhouse, by redeveloping them into 220 contemporary apartments. Creatively converting different spaces throughout the yard into a mix of commercial and retail outlets, including lively restaurants and Ocean Studios, with over a hundred artists, was deeply challenging, as the buildings are all Grade 1 listed. To address the lack of natural light to the bedrooms, they used glass block wall divides, something the visionary Victorian architect, Sir John Rennie would definitely have appreciated.

Twenty years later, 220 heritage designed apartments, and 110 square metres of office space have attracted people from all over the world, who love the place and lifestyle – and the local people finally appreciate its importance as a destination. "Today, the yard is one of the most happening places in Plymouth, with luxury accommodation, unique heritage architecture with tours, live street theatre, yearly light shows, and exciting weekly events," says Jackie.

Sir John Rennie, the Yard's original architect, was also ahead of his time. He built the yard, from 1825 to 1835, on bare land, as a sort of factory for the Navy, using the grandest of designs – neoclassical Georgian.

As the son of the Plymouth breakwater designer, he was also a superb engineer, and used all sixteen acres to create the world's most impressive production site for the Navy. Rennie's bold entrance, with a statue of King William, summed up his regal aspirations for setting the tone of the place. From the moment you enter, you are left in a state of awe and wonderment over the sheer grandeur of the place. Rennie made sure everything had its place and position according to the social structure of the times and designed a highly organised, hierarchical site. As both an architect and engineer, he developed new building materials and created ingenious stone compartmented walls to stop fire spreading in the buildings like the bakery. It was not easy to do, as the Navy put all the best materials and money into building bigger and better ships at the time; although he wanted to build everything from granite, he was forced in the end to mix it up with cheap quarried local stone.

Architect, Jackie, who also loves post war brutal Plymouth architecture of the 1950s, has moved on to work on the regeneration of another Plymouth icon, the heritage Civic Centre. She feels fortunate to be one of only 15% of women working in architecture in England, and in a city with such diverse styles. "As people change, the buildings they want to live in must change, too. You can see this by observing people on the high street; a place that must adapt, owing to the way people are now buying things online. This shift from pure retail, to retail withentertainment, is just one of the many challenges of bringing the buildings in the city centre, back to life."

"People want shared experiences if they go shopping in the high street today, so the new retailers need to make everything a personalised memorable interactive experience, like making your own jewellery at ID Fashion."

The Future
Alternative energies for an alternative future

Jackie Gillespie
Gillespie Yunnie Architects
The Lower Tweed Mill
Shinners Bridge
Dartington TQ9 6JB
jackie@gyarchitects.co.uk

“I see The Royal William Yard as being a creative, artisanal, sustainable, foodie community that grows its own food on the headland. I see the high tech community using renewable transport, from sailing to electric trams, linking it environmentally to the city centre in sustainable eco-friendly ways. In four hundred years, the community could create energy using wind, sea and tidal power and develop exciting new marine industries. Plymouth is so lucky, as it is not like London with the countryside miles away from it; everything is on its doorstep, from the sea to amazing unused green spaces.”

Jackie Gillespie, Architect.

14
ARTIST
Then, Now & in the Future

Plymouth Sound
A place to hear the waves and see The Sound

The grand seascape at which you gaze from Plymouth Hoe, inspires like no other, with endless iconic features like Drake's Island, Plymouth Breakwater, Mount Batten breakwater, and Mount Edgcumbe, not to mention miles of craggy coastline dotted with villages and the great South West Coastal Path.

It's no wonder that Plymouth Sound, with its unique environment; tourist playground, fishing fleet base, fish market, marine research cluster, historic naval dockyard, commercial port and amazing wildlife, has been designated the UK's first ever National Marine Park, set to dominate the headlines in 2020 and beyond.

However, what's less well known is that The Sound and surrounding areas have around 600 shipwrecks hidden in their deep waters. It is one of life's ironies that to survive long into the future, a ship has a better chance of being preserved as a wreck on the seabed than it does above water. 'There is one ship that dates back to the 1600s, with a covered portion left in situ, to preserve it for future generations, when they will likely have deeper knowledge and better equipment to research it.

"Every time I park on Devil's Point overlooking the Sound, and walk to my studio, I cannot believe how lucky I am to be here." Ayse Phaneuf.

Why so many wrecks? Over the millennia there have been thousands of boats come and go in The Sound and the sea can be very unpredictable, which is why the engineering genius, that is the breakwater, was built in 1814 to protect the Sound, in addition to the series of lighthouses on the Eddystone rocks from 1696.

The charting of these various wrecks has been achieved in large part by the SHIPS (Shipwrecks and History in Plymouth Sound) project, through the efforts of countless divers, researchers, archaeologists, historians, finds experts, illustrators, lawyers, engineers, and naval architects.

Artist and marine archeologist Ayse Atauz Phaneuf, who has helped fund this project with her non-profit organisation (ProMare) between 2013 and 2017 says, "SHIPS project does excellent archaeology, and trains their volunteers and participants; it is great fun to hang out with these people."

Aquanauts, operating out of 88 Vauxhall Street is a one stop shop for all diving needs, including PADI training, instructor training, technical dive training and the hiring of a charter boat with all the kit you need, for very reasonable prices. You may also book guided wreck tours with them, especially on wrecks identified by Ayse's team.

As for above water fun, Plymouth Boat Trips run about 7 boat trips from the Barbican, or get active with sailing, windsurfers, paddle boards, kayaks, or power-boating from Mount Batten Watersports & Activity Centre.

Then
Rembrandt
Artist

Dutch artist, Rembrandt was probably the most significant artist practising at the time of The Mayflower. His work was seen as ground breaking because of the way he reflected the lives and concerns of people in the 1600s.

He was born in 1606, in Leiden, Holland, one street away from Pieterskerk (church), next to which the Mayflower Pilgrims moved in 1609. It was from here, under the leadership of Pastor John Robinson, they would plan their passage to a new world, eleven years later.

Rembrandt would have made childhood friends with these foreigners. Some of the pilgrims, including Robinson, ended up staying in Holland and would have frequented the young artist's studio, where he became renowned for depicting the human condition in his now very famous and dramatic oil paintings.

His life-like portraits and high contrast handling of light and dark, captured the story and conflicting emotions evoked by the religious liberation of the time, like his painting of the Blinding of Samson. His colossal masterpiece, 'The Night Watch' is studied even today.

Rembrandt spent much of his youth, life and training in Leiden, very close to the where the Mayflower Pilgrims spent 11 years, before making their voyage to the new world. He is regarded as the greatest etcher and visual artist of all time.

Rembrandt brought in a new era of thinking that influenced artists well into the next century. His work embodied the same principles as the Mayflower Pilgrims – he firmly believed that integrity and dignity are key in all civilised societies. His depiction of the kitchen maid, crouching down with buckets and a floor brush, broke new ground by capturing the lives of ordinary folk.

By contrast, his detailed renditions of the rich, in his grand master portraits, give us an insight into the nobility of the 1600s and the growing contrast of Protestant ideas and dramatic social changes, with widespread rejection of Catholic Baroque.

One of Rembrandt's self-portraits has been discovered in Buckland Abbey, and likely influenced Sir Joshua Reynolds, born in 1723, in Plympton. Another visionary artist, who recognised the importance of British art, he founded the Royal Academy of Art in London in 1768.

Now
Ayse Atauz
Phaneuf
Artist

Ayse Atauz Phaneuf
Artist

Between the broken bows of ships that Ayse explores, marine life has taken up residence, swimming around her as she draws a tool or artefact, catching her eye and then finally inspiring her to create a dazzling new type of art.

It was her work as an underwater archaeologist that inspired Plymouth-based artist Ayse Ataūz Phaneuf to create her dazzling tropical fish-scapes at her paint splattered studio in Royal William Yard.

"The strong connection of the Royal William Yard with The Sound inspires me. I can smell the sea and hear the seagulls while I work." Ayse Phaneuf.

After decades of being an underwater archaeologist, Ayse has learnt about our ancestors from the artefacts they left behind, as well as from her job, documenting, in detailed line drawings, everything from about 1700 BC.

Her eyes sparkle, as she talks about the depths of the sea and the ghostly shipwrecks she has explored, some of them many centuries old, revealing how she is influenced by past artistry. The sea is where she first learnt how different cultures connect and interact through trading raw materials and objects. She says, "Shipwrecks are like time capsules of these bonds, cradling the artisan masterpieces and utilitarian implements that once belonged to the long gone sailors, merchants, passengers, explorers, adventurers and those who traveled in these boats."

Inspired by the beautiful shoals of vibrant patterned purple, lavender, orchid and azure blue fish, darting in and out of the manmade marine parks she explored for her underwater archeology, Ayse decided to create a project that allows you to move the fish around and create your own marine patterned colours. Colours can represent sacred wisdom and enlightenment.

"In art, since ancient times, tropical fish have been depicted as powerful and energetic life forces, representing wealth, in people's minds, and boundless opportunity," she says.

To make her fish mural, she experimented first with clay, then papier-mâché until finally deciding that plaster, mixed with glue, worked best for this exciting interactive art piece.

Encouraged, by her university professor mother in Turkey and city planner father, Ayse developed an early love of art. "I learnt to do everything by hand as a child," she says, "and that's why I have always been interested in art."

Ayse's studies of the ocean floor have revealed fascinating insights into early man. "People were crossing the seas tens of thousands of years before they planted anything," Ayse says. The oldest artefacts found in the ocean date back to the second millennium BC. Designs and technologies associated with these ancient ships, grew organically, according to the kind of trees that grew in the area, and what knowledge they gleaned from other environments beyond their horizons.

Ayse loves the centuries old creative thinking processes that were involved in ship construction, and how ship designs have developed over time.

Her fascination with mapping the nautical archaeology of the world's shipwrecks can be seen in all she does. Measuring and drawing the spacing of the nail holes in the timbers of ancient ships, to study the construction methods, taught her that detail is everything, when creating a work of art.

After decades of studying wrecks, she is now drawing the objects that would have been used on the Mayflower voyage and to build new homes in America. Drawing artefacts requires a detailed eye and a deep interest in how people conducted their lives. "Often, we're very excited to discover artefacts that were built, created, and used by our ancestors. We value, admire, study and learn from them about how knowledge and artistry have progressed. We often find these objects aesthetically pleasing."

"But I wonder what the people of the future will think of us, depleting the earth's resources to produce huge quantities of objects that fill this planet, and what knowledge our remains will provide to future generations. I doubt that the majority of what we leave behind will be admired and appreciated in a similar manner."

She describes the symbolic meanings of fish, as she demonstrates her rock painting collection, which harks back to a primitive era, when rocks were used for making the earliest tools, weapons and later, sculptures. Each rock painting is different and, unlike her black and white archaeological drawings, are colourful illustrations of coral flowers, sea creatures and lizards.

"The earliest underwater artefacts found here in Plymouth are lead anchor stocks from the Roman era (about the 1st century AD). They constitute irrefutable evidence that the Romans sailed to Plymouth (as opposed to the previous belief that the Romans reached southern Britain via land)."
Ayse Atauz Phaneuf

Shipwrecks, like time machines, take us back to identifiable points in time. Ayse has brought to life a hidden oceanic world, from which we can learn. She reads wrecks like Sherlock Holmes reads crime scenes, seeing things the rest of us don't notice and making connections between seemingly random discoveries, 'there is nothing more deceptive than an obvious artefact'.

The Future
The art of the possible

Ayse Atauz Phaneuf
Artist
Royal William Yard
Plymouth PL1 3RP
+44 (0) 7729 426 283
massivebonsai.com

“Artists express people’s frustrations and lack of control using provocative work, highlighting complexity and impossibility, or escapist approaches that create calming environments. Future art will be less commercial but more interactive, immersive, and personal. Once, anyone could create art – think handprints in caves – until it became for those exceptionally talented, trained, financially endowed, and connected, to support production of masterpieces. The future is exciting as everyone can once again express themselves artistically and reach wider audiences, owing to technology.”

Ayse Atauz Phaneuf, Artist

15

FASHION DESIGNER

Then, Now & in the Future

Royal William Yard
Tailor Made – Victuals, Rituals, Rags and Riches

Royal William Yard is a stunning Grade One listed ex Naval Victualling Yard that stands magnificently on the Devil's Point Peninsular with wonderful views across the Tamar estuary to Mount Edgcumbe in Cornwall. Over a quarter mile up Cremyll Street, catch the Cremyll Ferry for pedestrians, with free parking, to Mount Edgcumbe in Cornwall, saving an hour's round trip by road.

Regenerated in recent years by award-winning Manchester based hip urban redevelopers Urban Splash, The Yard is now, according to Lonely Planet, one of the must-visits on the tourist map, as a thriving hub of restaurants, bars, artist's studios, offices and accommodation. Designed by Rennie and constructed between 1825 and 1831, the Royal William Yard is steeped in history and considered to be one of the most important groups of historic military buildings in Britain and the largest collection of Grade I Listed military buildings in Europe.

Its building names: "Slaughterhouse", "Brewhouse", "Cooperage" belie the original uses of the stunning greystone buildings, which miraculously escaped the attention of the Luftwaffe as a military installation, and have recently been sensitively repurposed as accommodation and restaurants.

It now boasts an array of both local and more widely known eating and drinking experiences, including Bistro Pierre, Wildwood, Wagamamas, Las Iguanas, Hook & Line, Seco Lounge, Le Vignoble and Prezzo as well as Residence 1 and an Everyman Cinema.

The Yard hosts a wealth of events and places to explore, like the award-winning Good Food Market, regular music sessions, Wimbledon on the green, Weekend of Wonders, yoga on the lawn, stand-up paddle boarding, running groups, outdoor cinema and theatre, to name just a few of the activities on offer.

There is an on-site marina offering berthing and a regular ferry service, and you can go out to the battery on a hired rib in August to get a close up view of the national fireworks championship, enjoying the nautical traffic jam camaraderie on your return.

And, watch out! Rumour has it there's a ghost in the clocktower. It's no wonder The Yard has been the backdrop of many films and adverts, and has hosted The Antiques Roadshow, Children in Need and royal visits.

No area of Plymouth has seen such a wonderful transformation as the Royal William Yard, which has retained its majestic grandeur, while offering first rate accommodation and eateries.

If you visit one place in Plymouth – or even The South West – you'd be hard pressed to beat the Royal William Yard.

Then
Isaac Allerton
Tailor

Isaac Allerton was the second name on the Mayflower manifest and one of nine men on board to be connected with clothes making. Allerton was a tailor amongst other things, a trade he perfected whilst living in Leiden, Holland. The pilgrims spent ten years there, before sailing to Plymouth and were only permitted to work in laborious jobs.

The pilgrims learnt skills in clothes making from the Dutch, who used an array of dyes, such as the blacks and browns from oak and alder tree bark, red from rubia (madder plant) roots, one of which is called fittingly rubia peregrina (peregrino means pilgrim in Spanish), yellow from the weld plant that has been used from Neolithic times, and blue from woad.

The materials used, such as cotton, wool, linen and silk, interwoven and beautified in twills, plushes, calico, corduroy and worsted, were made into even more exotic sounding fabrics: bombast, bombazine, fustian, pintado, padusoy and frisado. And to give pieces a great finish they used braiding and embroidery, skills for which the English had been famous for many centuries, and that would adorn nearly all clothing according to degrees of wealth. There has been a renaissance in the wearing of these colourful and sturdy designs by the pilgrims of the General Society of Mayflower Descendants, in Plymouth, Massachusetts, which currently numbers around 150,000 members around the world.

Contrary to popular belief, the apparel of the pilgrims was not dowdy, drab and only black. Expensive black cloth suits were only worn when they attended church and other important occasions. Detailed inventories and wills of named pilgrims show daily outfits were of all the colours of the rainbow.

The Mayflower was full of makers in addition to Isaac Allerton. James Chilton was also a tailor, William Bradford was a fustian-maker, Edward Tilley was a cloth-maker, John Tilley was a silk worker, Francis Cooke and William White were wool combers or carders, and Degory Priest had been a hatter in London. In addition to those clothing-related trades, we know that William Mullins was a boot and shoe merchant, and Thomas Rogers was a camlet merchant.

Now Denitsa Avramova Fashion Designer

Denitsa Avramova
Dress For Life

Standing in her stylish boutique, in a renovated naval bakery in Royal William Yard, one can almost imagine Deni Avramova in a baby cot, full of colourful fabrics, as she talks about her childhood in Bulgaria and the influence of her mother.

Deni was born into the fashion industry, "I was brought up by a fashion designer and went to fashion shows with my mother, from the moment I could walk. I watched her being interviewed on TV, enthusiastically talking about trends, and I fell in love with the idea of being an actor in the theatre." As a result, in 2006, Deni travelled to Totnes in Devon on an exchange programme to study theatre for three months at Dartington College and ended up extending her course by a year. "And now, I am still here," she smiles.

But it was seeing Bulgaria's fashion industry explode, from the communist era of making uniforms, into what is now a melting pot of exciting and fresh fashion ideas, that helped Deni realise that her stage could be bigger than the theatre. Slowly, with other Bulgarian designers, she started to develop her own outfits that exude passion and eternal style and inspire the expression of personal identity.

Looking around her second Plymouth store in Units 9 and 10, Mills Bakery, with its red carpet, mirrors and photography studio, it feels like a Hollywood movie set, where her customers are the stars of the show.

The rack of clothes includes all sizes and are designed to make you look sexy and fun, whatever your age. "I want to find your inner identity and bring it out in what you wear," Deni explains, as she twirls around in her not-so-simple white shirt, and throws on a hat.

Picking up beads, feathers and some leather strips, Deni starts to mix things up, showing her skilful use of colour and unique basic designs that are anything but simple in combination. "I like people to carry their personality in the clothing they wear. I quickly learnt that 'crazy and different' makes people feel intimidated and that trust is the key. There are so many motivations behind why people purchase certain things. It's fascinating."

"Instead of buying blindly without considering global consequences, people should think through what they are wearing, where it was created, why it is sold at the given price, who might have been exploited in its production and how safe the clothes are, if the dye is not fixed." Denitsa Avramova.

With a twinkle in her eyes, she shows how one outfit can show a myriad of different funky styles, just by what accessories can be added, from belts to chunky necklaces. "For Identity Fashion, being strong and versatile in our range of designs is key as it makes

them stand out on their own and brings a new dimension to an ensemble, allowing you to transform your style to suit your mood and the occasion," she says.

A move to Plymouth from Totnes in 2012 was the game changer for Deni. Her friend Debbie took her to the Royal William Yard when it was still being regenerated, and partly derelict, and there were only three other businesses open, but Deni was captivated. "For me, The Yard was love at first sight, so we approached Urban Splash with ideas. They loved us, our fluid draping, asymmetrical shapes and our relaxed unique designs, and they gave us some amazing opportunities."

Denitsa Avramova is a Bulgarian fashion designer and boutique owner who is shaping women's lives through her stylish designs sold in her boutique in Royal William Yard.

The Identity Fashion brand has grown in stature and popularity since then, in part because it has a strong sense of global awareness at its core. The sacred symbol of eternity within its logo, signifies the cycle of birth and rebirth, that in Bulgaria embraces the eternal rhythm of life. Deni has taken this symbol and block printed it on a sexy directional dress and has started to create matching earrings that celebrate her historically rich and vibrant culture; just one of her many innovative ideas.

She reflects on where fashion is today, "The public needs to be educated on how things are made and the importance of quality in the materials that are used to create garments that should be both sustainable and gorgeous, however many times you wash and wear them. I do not want people to wear my clothes today and throw them away tomorrow." She started to consider this when she began selling handmade gorgeous ceramic Bulgarian pottery that had been made in her home country, and was shocked when people stopped and asked her if they were 'fair trade' goods. "Do they ask such questions of those selling their clothes in the high street shops?" She asks, agitatedly. "I wonder if people really care about slave labour or is their apparent application of double standards an indicator of how detached they have become from the real world? Where clothes are involved, Deni says, "we are what we eat", so why not "we are what we wear?"

The Future
A City in the Making

Denitsa Avramova
Identity Fashion
Royal William Yard
Plymouth PL1 3GE
+44 (0)1752 267951
identityfashion.online

“Looking to the future, Plymouth needs more quirky people who are visionary and want to express their personality, with sustainability firmly lodged in their hearts. We should help our local communities go to a higher level with whatever skills they have, and make something good for all, in a fun way. Every creative business should be supported, to restore Plymouth’s former glory as a city of makers. Fashion needs to be part of that eternal circle and especially to support special children with creative gifts.”

Denitsa Avramova, Fashion Designer & Co-owner of ID Fashion.

16

MERCHANT ADVENTURER

Then, Now & in the Future

Home Park & The Life Centre
The Pilgrims of Football

Adrenaline, Testosterone, Serotonin, Dopamine, or whatever other natural high you have in mind, Home Park and Central Park have everything you could possibly need to keep you happy and healthy in well organised high spec outdoor and indoor environments.

Sitting atop one of Plymouth's undulating hills is a special area dedicated to the health and wellbeing of everyone.

Spurred on by Eggbuckland local Tom Daley's and Tonia Couch's Olympic successes, Plymouth City Council has developed The Life Centre – a giant yellow brick building of leisure and lifestyle that includes an Olympic-sized pool, diving boards, climbing walls, a gym boasting 150 stations and a myriad of brilliant sports facilities.

Designed to tackle some of the health and wellbeing issues of the City (you could die ten years earlier if you are from deprived Stonehouse, rather than Mannamead), it's become a huge centre for the region, hosting national level competitions and local activities.

Next door is the beloved home of local professional football team, Plymouth Argyle. Nicknamed The Pilgrims, the boys in green will keep you on the edge of your seat in the Green Taverners bar, where, over a pint, myths become legends, while marvelling at Plymouth's ancient heraldic shield.

Football has almost become a religion, so, time to watch The Pilgrims, pull together and follow their inspirational forefathers' quest to be the best they can.

Argyle's Community Trust uses the club's resources and outreach to inspire, engage and help people of all ages in the community. It runs the Mayflower 400 commemorations, and National Childcare Scheme, to help 15 to 17-year-olds achieve their potential and work as a team. And next to these two beacons of sporting endeavour is the great beacon of Plymouth's health and wellbeing mission: Central Park. The largest outdoor public space in Plymouth, it was built in 1928 to improve the town's health. From its well tended grassy shores, you can enjoy panoramic views over the city centre, Plymouth Sound and Cornwall. Broad boulevards meander through to a woodland, undulating open fields and wildflower meadows. Explore and you'll find historic hedgerows, bat and bird boxes on trees, and allotments made for those who want to get their hands dirty and grow their own. There's also a stupendous range of sporting activities available for all ages: a skate park, a bowling green, an orienteering course, cycle routes, baseball and lacrosse clubs, and a nine hole 'pitch and putt' course. The Seven Continents Adventure Playground, has a dino swing, climbing frames, pyramid net, drums, sound wheel and wheelchair roundabout, while periodic Parklife events include graffiti art, foot golf and mad science.

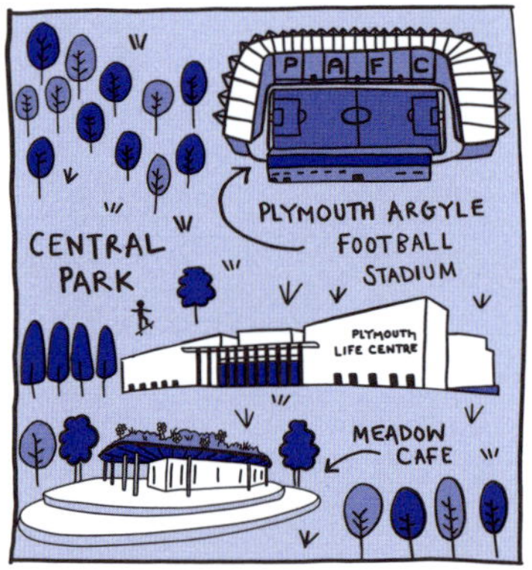

BBC RADIO DEVON
TARGET TRAVE
TAXI
PROPERLY TASTY
A TASTE OF CORNWALL

Then
Thomas Weston
Merchant Adventurer

In 1620, claiming lands in North America was dependent upon establishing viable settlements – a challenge which continued to prove very difficult for the colony of Jamestown – and impossible for previously attempted settlements of the late 16th century.

So, as soon as it was known that the Mayflower pilgrims intended to settle in America, merchant adventurers were keen to deal with them: they knew that if a settlement could be achieved and sustained, a wealth of fishing and other goods would surely follow.

Enter Thomas Weston, a merchant adventurer of London, of neither high repute nor great wealth, who was eager to take a punt on the new world and exploit what he could – clearly dreaming of the fame and glorious gains achieved by previous privateers like Drake. But, despite financing the Mayflower, Weston soon fell out with the Pilgrims on account of trying to change the terms of their agreement in his favour, to pay off debts elsewhere. Nor did he deal lawfully with the English Crown; once selling a cannon to Turkish pirates instead of returning it. And so he was declared an outlaw in 1622. In that same year, Weston sent more ships to America, one called The Sparrow, with some 'rude fellows' on board, to secretly establish another colony, Wessagusset. The mission failed when, while the governor was away, the colony executed a sick old man in place of a thief, who stole from the local tribe, which was incensed at the injustice, in their eyes, of the execution of an innocent elder. Further relations broke down when a local tribesman then stole from the colonists. According to Phinehas Pratt, who started with the Wessagusset colony and then joined the Plymouth colony, the latter initially enjoyed a good relationship with the indigenous tribes with whom they traded happily. Weston represented the kind of people that saw others, including the Plymouth Colony, as being exploitable, which appears to have contributed greatly to the eventual tragic collapse of relations with the Native Peoples. Weston died of the plague, around 1648.

"He was eager to reap quick profits from the New World, and not very scrupulous about the means," was how William Bradford described Thomas Weston, soon after he had ignominiously abandoned the colony to wreak more havoc elsewhere.

Now
James Brent
Venture
Capitalist

James Brent
Venture Capitalist

Investing and taking an active part in businesses that show promise, integrity and are ethically run for the benefit of the whole community.

Today, finance is crucial in every walk of corporate and public life. But for James Brent, financier and entrepreneur, it was his seven year journey as Chairman of Plymouth Argyle, that brought home to him how business can be a force for good in communities like Plymouth.

Plymouth Argyle, based at Home Park, has one of the largest catchment areas in football with a fan base, the self-proclaimed Green Army, stretching across the whole of Devon and Cornwall.

It was James' leadership that brought Plymouth's football fortunes out of the darkness and doldrums of 2011 and into the First Division where further investment and the regeneration of their stadium at Home Park became possible.

Not a football fan, getting involved in Argyle was not something he wanted to add to his portfolio, originally. James explains, "My involvement with the Argyle Pilgrims was rather fated. I understood the economics of football, but not the sport itself. At first I refused to give advice, saying I preferred to help with anything, even the tortuous airport reopening project, rather than football, as it's so much more political than anything else in the city." However, one thing followed another and soon he had no choice once he realised the seriousness of one of the largest cities in Europe facing a future without a professional football team.

"For me, it was ownership by accident, but a lovely accident as I ended up falling in love with the country's greatest sport." James was attracted to the powerful tribalism that surrounds the sport and, most of all, the passion of the Pilgrim community, which turns up for every game at Home Park. "The commitment and cheering of 15,000 fans make it something very special. Senior 'greens' – older supporters in their 70s and 80s – are the most wonderful group of people you will ever meet and seeing kids' eyes light up around the world, as their favourite footballer scores, is quite a special thing to see," James says, smiling. The secret to his success with this battle weary club was to encourage his brightest staff to come up with a solution to make it survive and thrive.

When signing a footballer or manager, they look for values that reflect the club's new ethos. "Integrity is the most important aspect of the job," says James. "We look for people skills, total commitment to the team, intelligence, and a willingness to learn and teach; we will only recruit the person that espouses all these essential core values."

James and the team also believe that football should be emotionally impactful and engage young people: "It can literally be a game changer for those with limited opportunities and challenging family backgrounds," he says. "But to engage young people, you have to get them through the door, get them to learn, and better still, to participate. That is the power of the football brand."

That's where the fabulous Argyle Community Trust comes in. It turns over £2 million a year and helps over 6,000 primary school kids go through its programmes. Significantly, it also successfully reaches 'hard to engage' people – whether it's young adults with challenging backgrounds or older members who need to stay fit.

James says proudly, "We were the first team to introduce walking football for the over 50s. Football is great for mental and physical health and it's great to see participants as competitive as they ever were."

In fact, statistically, the charity helps more people in Plymouth than the City Council. Over twice the number of people are involved in public healthcare via the trust than the city council. "They do this out of passion, seeing that community engagement is key," ," says James.

James has learnt a lot about football since he became chairman. "To be a great footballer is not just a talent, it takes hard work and lots of training. The man to watch now is Ruben Lameiras, who was in the same group as Harry Kane at Spurs. It is great to see so many talented players rising up through the ranks."

Argyle has been a pioneer in many ways. The legendary Jack Leslie (left), born of Jamaican descent in 1901, was the first mixed race footballer to play for Plymouth Argyle in 1921. In thirteen years, he scored 134 goals for Plymouth. He was set to become the first non-white player to represent England, thirty years before anyone else of bi-racial background was even considered at international level. He was denied the chance when the selectors were made aware that he was 'a man of colour'.

James Brent juggles a lot more balls besides football and does this from his stunning office overlooking the harbour from where the Mayflower set sail.

Remarkably, it took another thirty years for this discrimination to be smashed. His great partnership with Sammy Black saw them scoring 319 goals between them, for the mighty Greens.

The Future
The future is bright for ethical investors

James Brent
Akkeron Group
The Jetty Sutton Wharf
Sutton Harbour PL4 0DW
+44 (0) 1752 876 556
akkerongroup.com

"With eye-watering national debts and countries stripped of their assets, we can only look forward to a better future if people are prudent and hold on to their integrity, as if it were the new gold. A few good people will take the world to the next level by slaying the propaganda dragons and investing in full proof philanthropic schemes, while all others will wither and perish."

James Brent, Entrepreneur

17

BOAT BUILDER

Then, Now & in the Future

North West Plymouth
High tech marine hub

Between the old airport and Plym Valley, out on a limb but very much in on the action, you will find a place where some of the greatest scientific challenges of the day are addressed, from cutting edge medicine to exploring ancient wrecks and the depths of the deepest oceans.

It would be easy to underestimate North West Plymouth as a vaguely faceless mix of urban housing, inevitable drive-in fast food joints and light industrial units, but dig deeper and you'll find this northern city hub is a hotbed of civil unrest (the polite kind), highly advanced science and technological endeavour. Over the last decade, the north of the city has been developed to include Plymouth Science Park, Derriford Hospital and the superb modern universities of Plymouth and St Mark & St John, as well as a cluster of modern new eco-house communities. It used to include Plymouth Airport (here comes the civil unrest bit) which was sadly closed in 2008 due to 'lack of footfall' and, property developers Sutton Harbour's keen desire to monetise their real estate. As Devon and Cornwall's largest city, this closure didn't go down well, and activists operating under the name Viable, and then Fly Plymouth, swung into action, launching crowdfunding campaigns and legal action to try to reinstate their much loved and needed airport. It's all been quite polite – with the Council stuck in the middle – but no resolution has been found to date.

Near the Plym Valley, M Subs is creating the new Mayflower, the ultra high tech modern answer to the old pioneering spirit.

Plymouth Science Park, previously called the Tamar Science Park, is the biggest in the South West and is a joint venture between the University of Plymouth and Plymouth City Council. It's been home to the Hyperbaric Medical Centre, a Diving Diseases research centre, The Peninsular College of Medicine and Dentistry, as well as a number of cutting edge companies like WITT Energy and arctic explorer, Antony Ginman's expeditions. A number of other notable businesses thrive here in this state-of-the-art end of town, like TwoFour, the biggest independent TV production company outside London, and M Subs, a marine technology company, of which more later. But times are a changin'. The, now Grade 2* listed, iconic Ship building, designed in 1992 by Sir Nicholas Grimshaw, as a flagship office for local media, The Western Morning News and Plymouth Herald, narrowly avoided demolition when it couldn't attract a buyer, and has been converted into an indoor fun complex, Adrenalin, an adventure playground full of trampolines of all sizes, as well as a 'Clip n Climb', with its climbs of all shapes and colours – ensuring children can get active, regularly.

Then
Sir John Hawkins
Boatbuilders / Mariners

The Mayflower was skippered by Christopher Jones, an experienced sailor who perhaps took on more than he could chew as it turned out. 400 years ago boat-builders and sailors were often one and the same, needing carpentry skills so they could build or repair damages on the move and from previous voyages. Tasks would include replacing masts, sewing up any holes in the sails, using hand spun linen and tar, extensive scraping, re-caulking and tarring. The sailors would have slept on board in hammocks, and worked long hours to keep the boat ship-shape and seaworthy.

Boys as young as 14 were recruited and trained for 9 years to become either a first mate or a ship's master. The Mayflower was a 180-ton ship, built using around 2,000 oak trees, as the most abundant strong wood source in England, and pegged with treenails. This historic boat was around 26 feet wide, 11 feet deep, and 85 feet long (deck length including a 12 feet 'out of bounds' gunroom) – so, very cramped for 102 passengers and at least 30 crew. It would have smelt fetid from the residual stench of wine, fish and other cargo from previous voyages.

A typical boat was built with overlapping planks of wood over a set of frames, and oil or tar, which was used to waterproof the boat and prevent the wood from drying out. Great skill was required for planing the timbers of the hull such that their curvature would provide the ideal compromise between speed and stability. Around this time, in their efforts to control the sea routes, warring countries built ships ever larger and more heavily armed, around 100 cannons in the case of first rate ships, with huge crews, but to gain the upper hand against arch enemies like the Spanish, Sir John Hawkins, one of Plymouth's most famous seafaring sons, bucked the trend by building better versions of the galleon that were quicker, lighter and more manoeuvrable than the big ships, so, represented a significant step forward in naval power power and agility.

One of the great seafarers of the Golden Age, Hawkins was a shipbuilder, naval commander, adventurer, administrator and merchant of significant success, sharing the spoils with Drake, Raleigh, Queen and country, who came to an ignominious end with Drake, with both of them succumbing to sickness.

Now
Brett Phaneuf
Submarine
builder

Brett Phaneuf
Submarine builder

A polymath, science and engineering genius, who recognises that however clever or brilliant the marine craft that you create, the sea always wins.

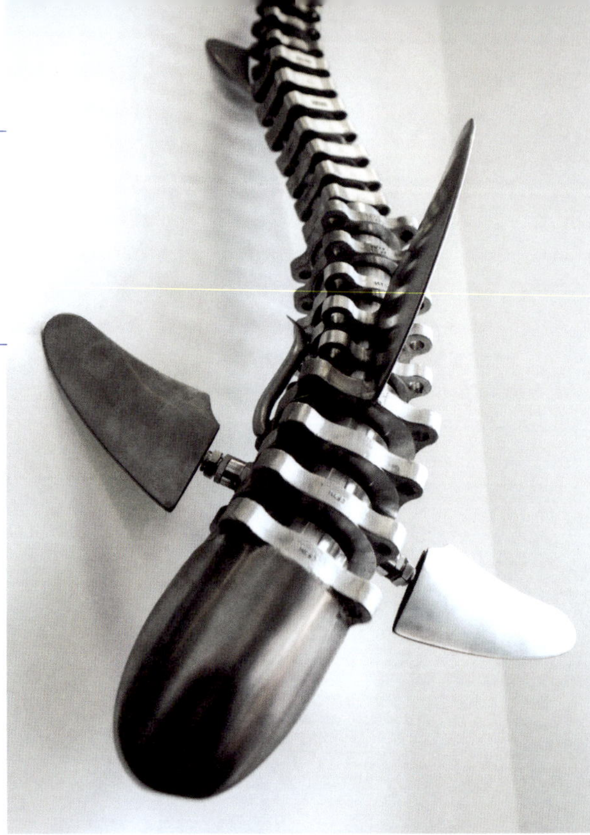

The M Subs building location in Estover is hidden away in an industrial estate of all kinds of businesses. Not easy to find, these large, uniform, bunker-like building units are where a team of sixty people create state-of-the-art world class marine engineering inventions. It's led by Brett Phaneuf, a physics graduate who loved deep sea diving, before joining the American military and studying for an anthropology and classical studies degree, which led him to underwater archaeology.

From this, his passion for oceanography grew, along with his love of exploration and marine science. "I was inspired by Doctor Bob Ballard, a marine geologist and oceanographer who worked in underwater archaeology using an underwater robotic craft, the Argo, to find the most famous shipwrecks, including the Titanic in September 1985," he says.

Brett founded ProMare, a charitable research foundation company, which quickly grew, with the increasing requirement for oceanographic and marine exploration vehicles. It was so successful that a business arm formed in Connecticut (USA) and Plymouth in 2006, Submergence Group LLC & M Subs Ltd, respectively, to build submersibles for the American Defense Department for deep-sea research. Brett has always had a visionary side to his work and so, to commemorate the 400th anniversary of the Mayflower crossing to America, Brett decided to crowdfund a modern high-tech sea-craft, the Mayflower Autonomous Ship, a vessel capable of conducting scientific research, with the endurance and reliability to operate remotely in all corners of the globe. It's being built by his team to embrace ground breaking technologies in design, propulsion, control and artificial intelligence, all in the spirit of the original Pilgrims' trip that changed the world. Brett explains, "We thought it would be great to launch 'The Mayflower Autonomous Ship (MAS)', powered by renewable energy and created by M Subs, ProMare and Plymouth University, as part of the Mayflower 400 commemorations in September 2020, taking the same 3,220 mile route as the original ship, using fuel-cells, wind and solar technologies."

After extensive trials in Plymouth Sound, it will be filmed crossing the Atlantic along the original Mayflower's route, and thereafter, conducting marine research and operations in remote corners of the globe. Thanks to Brett's expertise in learning from the underwater archaeology of sunken ships and subs, he plans to use his engineering skills to go deeper, stay down longer and discover more about how the ocean works. "I am, in truth, more interested in how to get there and extract as much data as possible. I like to work out where we are going next, how to integrate new technology, and how to explore at a faster rate and in a safer way."

"I see the term AI (artificial intelligence) as a bit of a popular buzz-word, with few people understanding what it really means. For me, it is merely vast data collection and the development and application of new mathematical algorithms, that facilitate constant machine learning; essentially to recognize patterns and work out what they mean and how to optimize a system." Autonomy can mean different things in technology. With The Mayflower Autonomous ship, or Brett's underwater vehicles, it means determining its own course and way of doing things when confronted with a novel situation. "My machines," Brett explains, "learn how to fine tune themselves and optimise the job, which is very useful in a submarine when under attack, or to avoid a collision with ships on the surface. An M Subs machine is an extremely cutting edge and valuable piece of marine equipment and is rarer than a Ferrari. It is a hyper-exotic underwater spaceship-like vessel of the sea, costing between $5 million and $40 million."

M Subs have shown us how far technology has come in 400 years by creating a commemorative artificially intelligent sea craft capable of navigating its own way, as part of a discovery expedition, across the stormy seas of the Atlantic, following the Mayflower route.

Creating a submarine is a high risk build: "The ocean always tries to crush your sub to death, however good its design," he says, "Even as you plumb the depths of the deepest oceans for scientific and animal studies." In recent times, a number of subs have been lost, where they have failed to remain watertight. "When making a submarine, you must repeatedly test it and even then, there is still some risk; I tell people, 'If you can't afford to lose it, you can't afford to use it in the ocean'," he says. However, there is a way to significantly reduce the risk – a technique MSubs have perfected. "Subs are extremely safe as they are tested over and over again, in a very regimented way. It's a much bigger risk to drive back to Plymouth from the M Subs base than driving around in Plymouth Sound with one of my submarines," says Brett, with the twinkle of a world class engineer in his eye.

The Future
Treating the sub normal

Brett A Phaneuf
M Subs
42 Sisna Park Road
Estover PL6 7FH
+44 (0)1752 696069
msubs.com

“The world needs to realise that most people do not understand how advanced technology works; to them, it might as well be magic. More technology just gives us more exciting choices but, in reality, less time. However, in the face of increasing automation of human tasks, we need to think about how to give those affected by it, who will increasingly have more leisure time than 400 years ago, a sense of purpose and existence and this will be one of mankind’s greatest challenges in the future.”

” *Brett Phaneuf, Submarine Builder.*

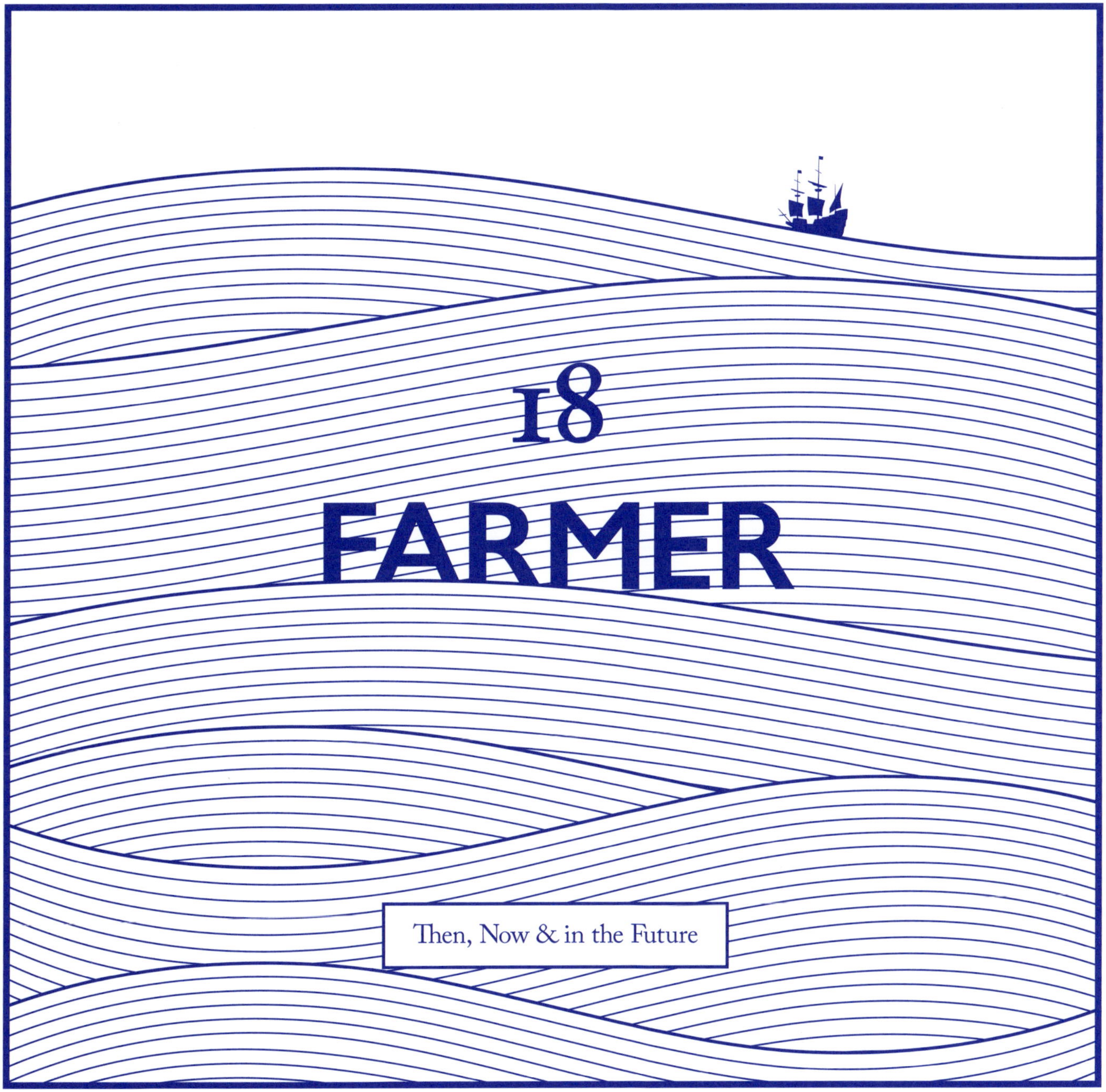
18
FARMER
Then, Now & in the Future

Derriford Community Park
Farming into the future

Few enterprises have undergone such a sea change over the last millennium as farming, with its humble beginnings as little more than scattered rural households surrounded by woodlands, to fully mechanised maximum production industrial systems on enormous scales, a trend bucked by Plymouth's Poole Farm in the heart of Derriford Community Park.

Leisurely walks through bluebell woods, watching fallow deer break cover into a hazy meadow, stepping over babbling streams, climbing steep grassy escarpments, peering over hedges thick with a symphony of songbirds and pausing often to breathe the rich air of a spring glade, replete with diverse wild flowers; all are now within easy reach of the entire population of Plymouth with its good transport links.

The 140 hectares of the city's newest park, Derriford Community Park is loosely bounded by the great Derriford Hospital to the north, the meandering river Plym to the east, the winding Devon Expressway to the south and Tavistock Road to the west. It's becoming a sanctuary for those seeking solace in nature. With the aim of reconnecting people with nature and getting them outdoors, the park is rich in wildlife and will have a new visitor and education centre at its heart, alongside Plymouth's first community farm, the oldest and closest one to the centre of Plymouth, Poole Farm. The park will connect the urban housing areas of Crownhill, Eggbuckland, Estover, Leigham and the new Seaton neighbourhood, to the beautiful Forder and Bircham Valleys through a series of high quality paths.

Plymouth is a city dedicated to nurturing green spaces for the health of its people, with Poole Farm at the centre of one of its most ambitious projects.

The initiative is at the vanguard of Plymouth City Council's excellent and visionary greening strategy. Its development has been supported by an army of local volunteers who've been working hard to improve the condition of the land, for the benefit of biodiversity, wildlife and the community. Inclusive activities include creating edible hedgerows, planting a new orchard and volunteering days; and there's a plan to re-wild a couple of badgers, making them the first urban ones since they became extinct in Britain.

Unique and beautiful, Derriford Community Park now opens up three great nature reserves: The Forder Valley, see the herons; Bircham Valley, spot woodpeckers and woodcock - both have meadows in them with species like crested dog's-tail, ox-eye daisies, purple vetch, common knapweed and common spotted orchids; and Efford Marsh, sit on oak benches beside sculptural artworks. Or join the team, building and protecting this City asset.

Then
Love Brewster
Farmer

400 years ago, Poole Farm existed, much as it does today, supporting a small number of livestock and crops, which might even have supplied the Mayflower with some of its provisions for their protracted 66 day voyage.

Advances in farming of the time would have included horse drawn ploughs that were able to penetrate deeper into the soils, and a three field rotation system with one in three years fallow. It was a time when there were still extensive woodlands, forests and common land for pigs to forage, in autumn, for delicious truffles, acorns and beechnuts. Hedgerows were being built to delineate newly purchased and reorganised lands, made possible by a new law allowing for the purchase of common land, which raised a public outcry but was too profitable to stop, and sufficiently 'democratic' to avoid an uprising! Love Brewster, William Brewster's son, was an English farmer, born in Leiden, Holland in 1611, whose fleeting contact with his motherland barely saw his feet touching the ground as he passed Plymouth, on his way to New England and then only as a nine year old. He never got to farm in England but grew up to become a freeman in Plymouth colony, where he owned land and voted.

Most of England was still forested in the 1600s, but the feudal system was a hundred years gone, so farmers were able to buy common land and trade parcels of land with one another to create a more manageable holding.

Like the rest of the original pilgrims on the Mayflower, he owed much to his friends, the Wampanoags, for teaching his people how to grow the Three Sisters as they called them; these were maize, squash and beans. Maize was the most bountiful of the crops and the Wampanoags showed the pilgrims how to plant and fertilise the seeds with marine compost. Love Brewster will have been one of the very thankful pilgrims to have been alive in November 1621 to celebrate the first New England Thanksgiving with the Wampanoags, having experienced the sickening journey across the Atlantic and an even more terrible winter that claimed the lives of half the original Mayflower voyagers. However, he died young at 40, leaving his wife, Sarah and their four children and, eventually, 23 grandchildren.

Now
Ashley Tod
Farm
Manager

Ashley Todd
Farmer

Everyone knows that today's farmers have diversified. In Devon alone you can tour a chilli farm, visit places that grow edible flowers, taste pretty good plonks from British vineyards, and enjoy the produce of farms that create cheese, fudge and clotted cream.

However, nothing could be more innovative and educational than Plymouth's Poole Farm, a local nature partnership that involves people in volunteering, learning and enterprise, and providing a gateway to the Derriford Community Park project. Plymouth's nearest and oldest farm is a green island in an urban maze, hosting everything from pioneering rewilding initiatives through to community activities for all.

At Poole Farm, all the oak trees felled, to make way for the new road, are used to further other farm projects, creating tables, seating, bee hives, signage and a pop up café. Another key initiative is planting yellow rattle, a plant that stifles the fertility of the soil, to stop commercial grasses from growing, while giving wild flowers and diverse species a chance to flourish. There's also a huge range of family friendly activities from Wildlife Wanders to den building, traditional rope making, a chance to see Dartmoor sheep, renovate chicken sheds and study animal care.

> "The farming legacy we leave behind relies on the younger generation being custodians of the land and not ignorant consumers of its produce."

For farm manager, Ashley Tod, Poole Community Farm is a way of tackling the great disconnect between younger generations, their natural environment, the food they eat and other anti social behaviours that are a growing problem in society, as a result. "If the kids volunteer and help build up aspects of the farm, they won't want to damage it; they'll own and understand it," he says.

Both of Ashley's parents work in the youth sector, fostering kids from extremely difficult backgrounds, and it was this childhood experience that taught him the importance of being selfless and working in a team. Ashley then went on to study Environmental Science at university, owing to his love of plants and animals, making him the natural candidate to deliver Poole Community Farm's vision. Key to the farm's success is the team of volunteers who manage bee colonies, teach schools about the provenance of food, forage for things like wild garlic and educate groups about how mankind domesticated wild forest foods through cultivation, in the past. So, the team needs a diverse range of skills and to be flexible.

Farm tours include learning about bees and pig husbandry. One of the most popular tours includes an ancient oak, as old as the Mayflower, which can be found in Lower Bircham Valley. "I call it the halo tree," says Ashley. "We get a great show of blue bells round it each year. As an extra, fun activity, the school kids get to blow chalk-dust on clay figurines set up next to the tree, to make them look like 'the old man of the woods', making the trip more memorable." Another highlight of a farm visit is watching stags fighting in autumn's rutting season, "A fantastic sight when they become fearless, majestically parading around, as if they own the place."

Innovation has been the secret to human survival and balance, since the Mayflower sailed, and this farm is also pioneering new ways in agriculture. As well as trialing new ways of raising cattle, the farm will soon undertake a science led, re-introduction of a pair of Eurasian beavers – the first urban beaver population since they became extinct in Britain in the 16th Century. "As 'ecosystem engineers', beavers kickstart cycles of nature," says Ashley, "benefiting biodiversity enormously, by creating channels and ponds for a myriad of species."

But at heart, Poole Community Farm is still about growing things in an entrepreneurial and educational way. Ashley says, "I see crops as an essential part of farming; we grow squashes, pumpkins and many varieties of fruits, loads of apples from cookers to juicers, along with plums, in the biggest orchard in Plymouth. We want to expand this into a land based horticultural education location and be a hub for the city."

"We plan to sell a wide range of produce from eggs to honey, through a plastic-free farm café and even sell bee colonies. It is about using the farm as a hub for the local community, working with education providers like Plymouth University and Cornwall's Duchy College, to teach sustainable farming." The farm will also teach an expanding remit to a cross-section of the community, building on NVQ 3 Animal Care, and apprenticeships.

Poole Community Farm aims to go some way towards 'future proofing' the local community against food shortages created by a breakdown in the food supply chain, thanks to challenges like Brexit. "Some say that with 'just in time' marketing that we are only ever two days away from anarchy. Growing crops in back gardens, schools, or allotments will enable a lot of people to have the skills to nourish themselves and their families, and rely less on the 'just in time economy'."

Paradoxically, Ashley is also a technology fan: "But only if it helps keep communities healthy and in touch with their natural environment and attracts people to this great Plymouth farming and wildlife programme."

Derriford Community Park's main objective is to tackle the great disconnect of humans from their natural environment.

The Future
Making nature real again

Ashley Tod
Farmer
Poole Farm Plymbridge Road
Leigham PL6 8NF
+44 (0)7500 075719
plymouth.gov.uk/derrifordcommunitypark

"I think farms will not be the rural idyllic settings we know today. In four hundred years our dietary needs will be met with novel uses of technology: growing food in closed systems – nuclear bunkers, an underground tunnel, on a rooftop or in a central city warehouse – using advanced systems such as aquaponics. In time, we will be able to take a sample of cut fillet and synthesise that part of the animal in a laboratory to create the steaks of tomorrow. This will give animals their fundamental freedoms back, living a natural life in small herds. My hope is that mega farms with poor welfare standards will cease to exist."

Ashley Tod, Farm Manager.

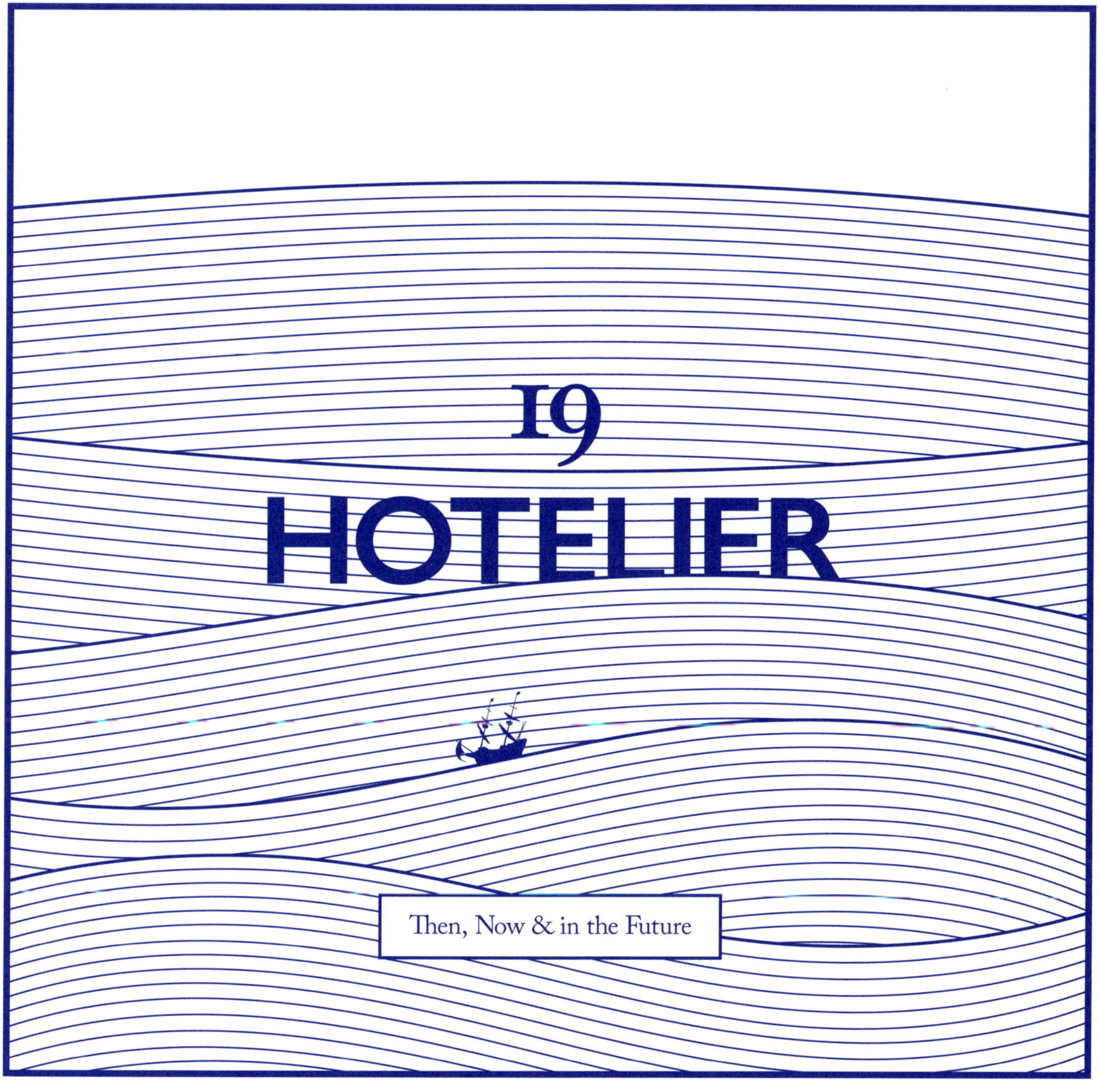
19
HOTELIER
Then, Now & in the Future

Boringdon and around
An enchanted hotel on the hill

On the edge of Dartmoor and overlooking Plympton Valley, stands the imposing Boringdon Hall. A place of history and now luxury, its stone towers and magnificent banqueting hall whisper tales of the past.

Travel uphill through the fairly unprepossessing housing estates of Plympton, and you will eventually come to the surprisingly majestic, Boringdon Hall. The Saxons named the place Boringdon – meaning enchanted place on the hill – and it's easy to see why. Especially now. This Devonshire Manor House has been converted into a magnificent five star hotel, including a multi award winning spa. But it's the hall's imposing nature and truly extraordinary history – that you can almost taste when you're there – that truly bewitches.

The house became crown property of Henry VIII in 1539 and later became a favourite of his courtier, the Earl of Southampton who sold it in 1549 to the father of Lady Jane Grey (famously queen of England for nine days in 1553). The house then became the property of the Parker Family in 1587, who extensively renovated it, although there are still parts of the house that date back to the mid 14th century.

On the edge of civilisation and yet next to the wildest of national parks, if you want to get away from it all, Boringdon delivers.

When work was complete, John Parker threw huge banquets in its fine rooms for the rich and famous, starting with the Drake's Cadiz campaign celebration. The Parkers moved out to live at Saltram House some time after 1712, so Boringdon was used as a humble farmhouseuntil 1920. Destroyed by fire in 1989, it was purchased by the Nettleton family in 2011, who turned it into a five star and 3 AA rosette hotel. The hotel's Gaia Spa has now been voted best Hotel Spa of the year in Western Europe and Scandinavia at the World Spa & Wellness Awards 2019.

The charm of the place is further enhanced by its spellbinding surroundings. Across the lovely wildflower meadow, produce for Head Chef Scott Paton, is to be found growing in neat lines under protected tunnels, cultivated by Anne, the gardener in residence, while the Boringdon bees buzz about the flowers and hedgerows under the care of Beekeeper Jean French, who will tell you all about honey's health-enhancing properties. The front garden, with two huge outspread Cedar trees partially hiding the Hall's grand façade, hosts wonderful events like the gin-tasting festival. And in the distance your eye is caught by moorlands of endless rough grass, short fir trees around small lakes and river edges. Walks traverse across valleys and to the tops of the majestic tors, like Sheepstor, overlooking the beautiful Burrator reservoir. A truly enchanted place.

Then John Parker Host

At a time when his peers were sailing round the world, exploring new lands, discovering new fishing grounds, making war on the Spanish empire and finding all kinds of natural treasures, John Parker was making a name for himself as one of the top hosts in the country. He'd inherited Boringdon Hall through marrying into the Mayhew family and set upon renovating it, to reflect his new position on the social ladder, and to provide a fitting backdrop for the social set he found himself hosting. This heavy set, bold and very old house, with its Domesday history and Saxon-like architecture, incorporated massive lintels and granite posts, and a cavernous fireplace with a monster mantel. John lovingly restored all this and extended it into a very grand affair. The main house was pushed out into the Elizabethan 'E' shape, in honour of the queen they all so diligently served. But in many ways his restoration was sympathetic to the original architecture of the old grange. He kept the huge number of beautiful windows that let in a great deal of light and the oversize doorways into the main atrium, with raised galleries at each end, which were perfect for theatre productions.

Running the equivalent of the top country hotel for his globetrotting, pioneering, new world prospecting friends and then royalty, meant a restoration of the best of the old and a sympathetic new extension, to John Parker, Boringdon Hall's owner until 1610.

The result was a fitting space for entertaining some of the greatest people of his era.

His banquet to celebrate the roaring success of the English fleet against the Spanish Armada at Cadiz must have been quite some party, which saw a guest list that boasted super heavyweight seafaring heroes like his brother William Parker, Sir Francis Drake, Sir Walter Raleigh, Sir Richard Grenville and Sir John Hawkins, amongst others. Such was the grandeur of the place and its reputation that the Queen herself visited in the following year. John Parker, no doubt, threw many more legendary banquets until his death in 1610, when the property was passed down through many more generations of Parkers, over 300 years, right to the last century, when the family moved to Saltram House.

Now
Diane Nettleton
Boringdon Hall
Hotelier

Diane Nettleton
Boringdon Hall Hotelier

Entering the estate of Boringdon Hall & Gaia Spa is like crossing an exquisite painting from the bottom corner. Drive in and an exceptionally old and grand looking manor house reveals itself across a flat and beautiful garden, bedecked with colourful flowers and metal sculpted furniture on the lawn that has been arranged to look out across the valley, with a breathtaking view across Plympton.

But it hasn't always been this way. The inspirational Nettleton Family saved Boringdon Hall from receivership in 2011. Experienced hoteliers from Newquay in Cornwall, they were seduced by the sheer beauty of the imposing stone towers, curious arrow slits, giant doorways, oak-panelling and magnificent Great Hall, decorated with James I's coat of arms over a majestic stone fireplace. Undaunted, they took on the mammoth task of revitalising the old beauty, to turn it into Plymouth's first five star hotel.

James Nettleton was the inspirational driving force behind the general restoration of the place, while Gayle Nettleton created the wonderful fabrics and beautiful interior designs. The Great Hall is now a lovely journey through history, passing oil paintings, heavy antique furniture with lion face carvings on the arms at the entrance, and sumptuous fabrics hanging from the large windows, adorned with historic coats of arms.

It was Diane Nettleton, inspired by her travels around the world and years in hoteling, along with personal experience of Mother Nature, who had the idea of creating Plymouth's first premier spa at Boringdon. It was a bold vision: to create an award-winning spa with an exclusive range of eponymously named spa products. The Gaia Spa and artisan Gaia spa products were born. "They are fittingly named after the ancient goddess of nature," explains Diane. Recognising that emotions are the main cause of imbalance in people, she now works daily, with her delightful team, to create special curated spaces that not only have one's natural wellbeing at the core of every treatment, but also the philosophical thinking behind each one of them.

Diane wants everyone to enjoy the Gaia Spa, to melt away their

The Gaia Spa
Reconnect with nature in the gardens of Boringdon Hall to gain inspiration from Diane Nettleton's handmade spa products.

stress and make time to look deeper into themselves, to unpack what lies beneath, so they can dispatch their mental clutter. "With so much changing in the world, the one constant is nature and by slowing things down for a few hours everyone can truly relax and discover the wonders of using crystals, healing stones, poultices, acupuncture, jade, wax or water," says Diane. At the Spa you can enjoy 'four hands', facials, reflexology, manicure, pedicure, painting, tinting, highlighting, waxing and then waxing lyrical with your special other half in the joint 'Zeus and Hera' day package that finishes up in a private room with chocolate and champagne. "Aromatic smells of lemon, rosemary, frankincense, ylang ylang and palmarosa reconnect you to the rules of the universe and bring sensory equilibrium to mind and body," explains Diane, sagely.

The beautiful facilities also help to balance and calm clients, with the serene environmental designs, soft fabrics and drapes, especially in the chill-out room, that gives one time to rest and reawaken, totally calm. Colour choices are all part of the healing powers that replenish the senses, so one returns to the busy world both relaxed and inspired. "We use the grounding colours, green and brown, to reconnect us with the earth," says Diane. She has even gone one step further with the Spa by treating cancer patients – with promising results. "Using natural oils in the treatments helps one find harmony and emotional balance; even after trauma," says Diane, "people say they feel better from using these ancient wellness traditions."

But the Spa is just one aspect of how the new Boringdon Hall team make guests feel special. Along with her two business partners, Diane ensures that guests can enjoy a range of exciting food and accommodation experiences at Boringdon. There are Murder Mystery dinners where the hotel's head chef, Scott Paton, creates a menu of exciting dinners from each century, or guests can enjoy the grandeur of the Sir Francis Drake Room with its lavish four-poster bed in the main house, or the indulgent Royal Suite; one quickly discovers that there are many hidden treasures. There's the evocative Àclèaf Restaurant and there's even a secret bar, hidden behind a theatrical bookshelf (clue: touch Tales of The Unexpected – and all will be revealed). Magical is an understatement, as everyone is made to feel like an A-list star in Plymouth's oldest secluded gem, Boringdon Hall & Gaia Spa, truly 'the enchanted place on the hill'.

The Nettleton family took one of Plymouth's most historical jewels and breathed new life into it. But it was the hotel's Gaia Spa, the brainchild of Diane Nettleton, that's added a new dimension to this enchanting place.

The Future
Going back for the future

Diane Nettleton
Boringdon Hall
Boringdon Hill
Colebrook PL7 4DP
+44 (0)1752 344455
boringdonhall.co.uk

"We will have to go back for the future, to recapture the good old ways of working. Today, people are looking for wellness solutions to salve their fraught lives. They want handmade natural products, blending the finest plant ingredients with essential oils. Community connections and the human touch will be more important as we tire of technology and return to the nourishment and inspiration of nature. We already recycle, having gone through all stages of extravagance; people now recognise that the rhythms of nature and interacting directly with people are more fulfilling than interacting through a device."

Diane Nettleton, Hotelier.

20

MOTHER

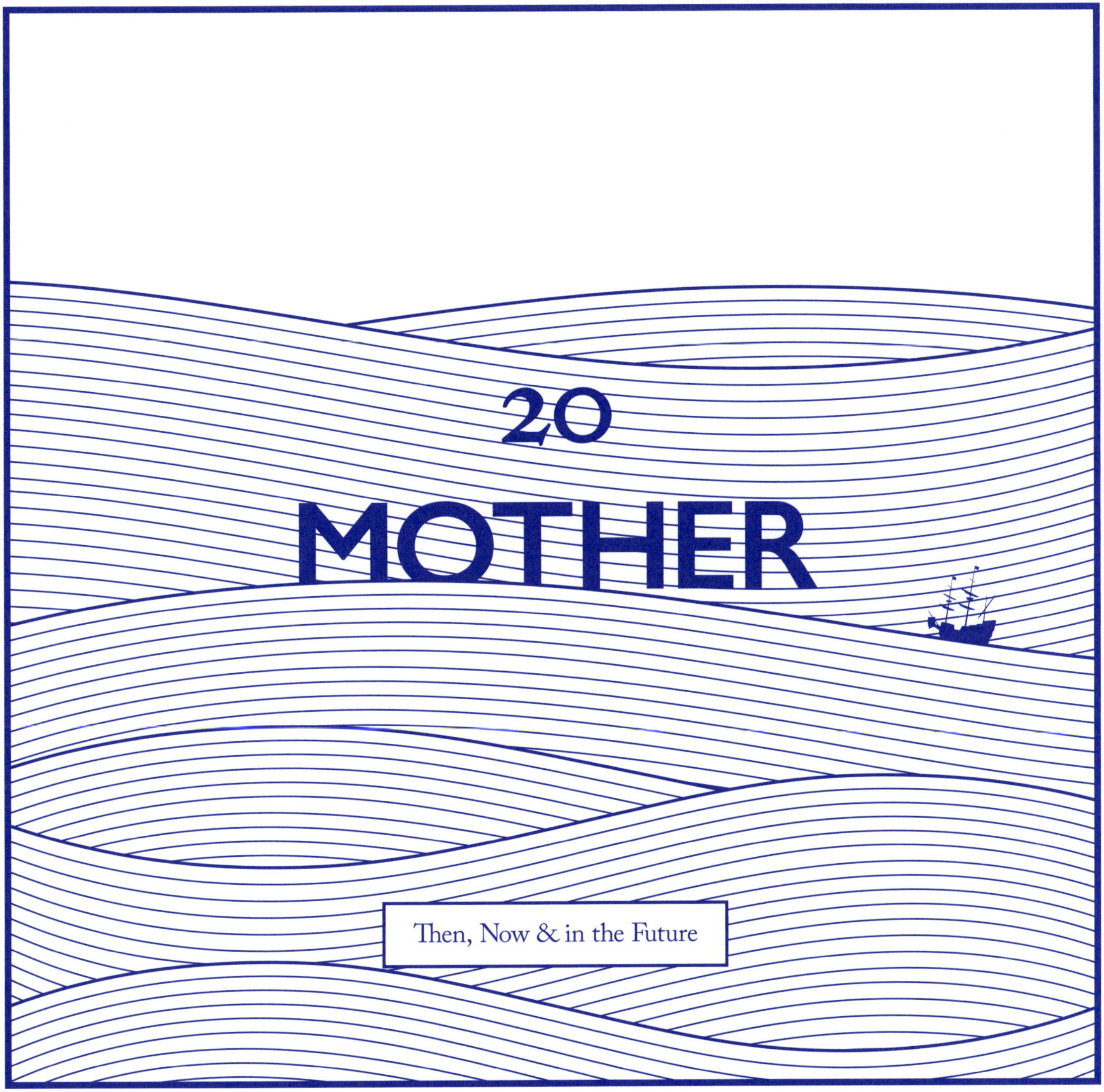

Then, Now & in the Future

Bovisand to Mount Batten
A place for families to explore

From Bovisand to Mount Batten is a stunningly beautiful stretch of coastline with incredible views of the city, out to the ocean, across The Sound, and over to Cornwall. It's studded with serious military defences: forts and batteries, reminding us of Plymouth's major historical significance in the defence of the realm.

Midway along The South West Coast Path which stretches some 630 miles, from Minehead, Somerset to Poole Harbour, Dorset, lies a stretch of coastline of both breathtaking beauty and great military significance.

Mount Batten, just across the Cattewater from the Barbican, sits on a peninsula, with its 280 metre breakwater giving the aerial appearance of a conductor with a wand, stroking the seas away from itself, while protecting Sutton Pool. It was named after Sir William Batten, who was alive at the time of the Mayflower, and was an MP and Surveyor of the Navy. Its round tower stands proud, like a king on a draughts board, overlooking The Sound. The views are stunning, all the way down the coast to Bovisand Bay, which overlooks the even bigger Plymouth Breakwater.

Bovisand Lodge Holiday Park is a paradise for parents and children alike, with luxury accommodation, sea air, a sandy beach, gorgeous vistas, the goat trail, fluttering white doves, chickens, a swimming pool, a playground and walks on the wild side.

With its fort, rescue cage and lighthouse, it protects the Sound from the worst the English Channel can throw at it and, formerly, other European and Arab nations. Two rentable apartments are named after Rennie & Whidbey, builders of this 1814, four million ton marvel. If you want to explore this coast, there's lots to do. For those who love rock hopping, exploring caves, wriggling through tight openings and jumping off cliff edges into the sea, this stretch is a coasteering paradise at higher tides. It's also a popular spot to feed your skin a little vitamin D on the glorious beaches of Jennycliff and Bovisand, while the children search for crabs and fish in the plethora of rock pools at low tide. Blast some golf balls into the distance, for a moment appearing lost in the seas of Plymouth, before dropping onto a perfectly manicured green, at Staddon Heights Golf Club, where you get the best views around of the Sound.

For those without vertigo, climb or abseil down a nearby 80 metre climbing wall. Overlooking the roundabout compass of the former RAF base, it was used for the flying boats rescue service and is where Lawrence of Arabia spent a short time incognito.

But, really, the best way to indulge mind and body in most healthy fashion is to walk the coastal path, observing as you go, some incredible viewing points and a number of old military installations.

Then
Susanna White
Mayflower Mother

The life of Susanna White, in her third trimester of pregnancy when she left Plymouth on the Mayflower in 1620, illustrates how different women's lives were 400 years ago.

Despite living in overcrowded damp and filthy conditions, unable to wash, while undertaking the rigours and challenges of a transatlantic voyage in the height of winter, she successfully gave birth to the first Mayflower child in America in November 1620, anchored off Cape Cod. He was aptly named Peregrine, meaning Pilgrim.

Living in the 21st Century, it's hard to appreciate just how creative and courageous those 19 women who boarded the Mayflower, three pregnant, were: going to a largely unknown destination where they would have to create everything from absolute scratch. Women in 1600 did not consider having careers as they do today, seeing their pilgrim husbands as head of the household, who were expected to build the house and bring home their entire income.

Mrs White gave birth, in a secluded part of the ship in candlelight, in rough conditions, to the first American pilgrim 'citizen'. Oceanus, son of Elizabeth and Stephen Hopkins, was the only child born on the Mayflower voyage.

Rather, women were considered the homemakers and their tasks on the ship and on arrival would have included teaching religion, reading from the bible to their children, gathering nuts and berries to eat, and kindling wood to build fires, once the men had built houses, and defended them against hostile tribes and other European colonisers. Cooking depended on what they found while foraging or fishing. Using plants, they handmade soap for washing, while gathering different ingredients from the forests for medicinal purposes. They took the silk worms and spun clothes and made cooking utensils like spoons, by whittling logs of wood, also creating wooden toys for their children to play with. Dolls were made out of rags, and new games from pinecones and stones, to entertain them, while they hand washed their clothes in the rivers.

But, despite their resourcefulness and resilience, 78% of the women died of pneumonias and colds, the first winter. Susanna White lost her husband, then wedded Edward Winslow, the first marriage in the colony.

Now
Candice
Hart
Mother and
Businesswoman

Candice Hart
Mother / Businesswoman

Candice Hart personifies the modern working mum. University educated, she juggles raising her young family, with running her family's successful holiday business, Bovisand Holiday Park, while at the same time supporting her husband's business, and rounding up the animals in her spare time! "Being a modern working mum is a constant challenge with motherhood, childcare and financial constraints," she says. "Today most families need both parents to work to pay the mortgage and that often means juggling more than one job." After working at Bovisand during the day, Candice also helps to administer her partner's groundworks company in the evenings.

Additionally, they bought a historic house five years ago, which needed complete renovation and modernising into five apartments. The two-acre garden takes a lot of maintaining. So, there's little time for leisure. Luckily, both Candice and her partner, Christopher, are passionate about their work and have great support from their families with raising and teaching the children what they need to know. Like many modern mums, she worries about spending enough time with her daughter, having another child and becoming a 'geriatric mother', as the doctors call older mums. "The work/life balance is a major juggling act, trying to prioritise being a hands-on mum, while being a professional career woman. I want my daughter to do whatever she wishes with her life."

After leaving school, Candice completed a degree in Maths with Finance, in Scotland and then an MSc in Hydrography in Plymouth, "I returned to work for the family business. Both courses have helped with analytical and administration aspects of running a business. I think education and life experience are so important. "I am very fortunate to be a trustee with a charity helping to fund youngsters from disadvantaged families to go to University. They are often the first in their family to go to University, and seeing how their confidence and aspirations grow over the three years is very humbling."

But now, she and her brother run the family business, a gold award winning holiday lodge park on the stunning Bovisand Bay. "There really isn't a typical working day in hospitality," says Candice, with a cleaning bucket in one hand and holding her daughter's hand in the other. "Every day is different. There is the usual stream of emails, phone calls and customers, accommodations and facilities

"Being a modern working mum today often fills you with guilt, whether it be from failing your family for not being around enough, or for not doing your job as well as you would like to or know you can. You are constantly under time pressure..."

Who could have a more idyllic work-life balance than Candice Hart, a highly successful working mother who starts the day hand feeding doves with her daughter Laura, before revving up to run beautiful Bovisand Lodge Holiday Park by the sea?

to clean and turn over, laundry to do, guests to 'meet and greet' and owners' queries and issues to solve."Most days, I'm thrown a curveball, like the goats escaping! One time, the goats made it all the way up through the fields to the Mussel Inn pub before we found them, rounded them up and brought them back again. But, that's just what keeps it interesting and entertaining!

Candice lives just over the hill from where the holiday park is located, so there are no set hours. "When you are self employed you have no set holidays either, but you are in charge of your own destiny. You get out of it what you put in, so our lives are very rich."

The family have run the park for three generations. "People's expectations have changed so much. When my grandfather started the Holiday Park, the caravans were half the size they are now and without a mains water supply or electricity! People were happy just being in a beautiful place."We also had chalets with outside toilets, but all were removed 25 years ago to make way for the indoor swimming pool and games areas, to attract more families. "We installed a couple of lodges a few years ago as people wanted 'generational staycations' with extra space and two bathrooms. "Today, we have luxury holiday caravans with double glazing, a central heating system and flat screen televisions, which is another arm of our business that we really love, as it builds a fascinating community of people around us. The pace of life also used to be much slower. Her parents took bookings via telephone and letter, using a brochure and booking form. The season was from mid March to September's end. "Now with high speed technology we have bookings all year round," she says. "People like to call and email late into the evening, expecting a prompt response."To alleviate this late night pressure, they moved to an online booking system, but paradoxically now work even longer hours, she says. "It was actually refreshing to experience France on holiday last year, where you can still enjoy a proper Sunday, when everywhere is closed."

However, Candice and her family know that the key is understanding the changing needs of her customers. "We all love the place and know we need to continue to adapt it into the future. Tourism is continually changing; you have to stay competitive; we've created four websites in 15 years! When my grandfather started this holiday park in 1958, there were only a few holiday parks around, but today, everyone's trying online rent-a-room, so we need to think outside the box. That's the challenge we love and that keeps us creative."

The Future
The Mother of all jobs

Candice Hart
Mother/Business Woman
Bovisand Lodge Holiday Park
Bovisand Rd PL9 0AA
+44 (0)1752 403554
bovisand.com

“

A mum's life 40 years ago was very different, let alone 400 years ago. Today, women are educated, empowered, have equal opportunities and freedom to make their own life choices, including not having children or getting married. In the next 400 years, there will be more flexibility for employees and technology will develop new opportunities, allowing you to work anywhere, in exotic locations for clients in other parts of the world. Our family holiday last year, saw my partner in France, calling a client in Spain, organising a meeting in Plymouth for the next week. The downside is you are never switched off!

” *Candice Hart, Mother & Business Woman.*

400 HIDDEN GEMS

Our Insider's Guide to Plymouth

400 Gems Our Insider's Guide to Plymouth

For a city built on tin, fishing, trade, the navy and discovery, in pursuit of all kinds of treasure – natural, precious and ideological – and with the Mayflower launch, 400 years ago, a great way to celebrate each year is with a precious nugget. Whether it be a fascinating piece of art, a hidden ancient ruin, a cautionary tale, a surprising thing of beauty, a hill with a view, a quirky food experience or a larger than life character, we bring you collections of great value for those wanting to enrich mind and body in Plymouth, the great turner of tides and launcher of life-changers.

THE BARBICAN, THE OLD QUARTER

01 The Tourist Information Centre (TIC), at the Hoe end of the Barbican, is a great place to discover the many exciting places to visit around Plymouth, and is run by a wonderful team, who will tell you all you need to know to get started.
01752 306330 visitplymouth.co.uk

02 Like a giant penguin grenade, a WWII mine that once defended Plymouth's shores from wanton destruction that has dogged it for centuries, sits on the quayside opposite the TIC, collecting money for the Shipwrecked Mariners' Society, founded in 1839, owing to the tragic loss of a fleet of fishing boats on the North Devon coast in 1838.
01243 789329 shipwreckedmariners.org.uk

04 Opposite the TIC, the imposing Leviathan sculpture, by Brian Fell, called 'the prawn' by locals – obviously indulging Aussie humour by, 'putting another prawn on the Barbie' – is what you get when you cross a John Dory, an angler fish, and a lobster, with a mermaid, maybe.

05 John Sparke the Younger, commemorated in a plaque on New Street, was the first property planner in Plymouth, who sanctioned, in 1584, the building of many houses on New Street, including the Elizabethan House, for wealthy merchants. He was also the first Englishman to describe tobacco and potatoes from America. He became a rich merchant gentleman, and was mayor in 1583 and 1591.

03 Plymouth Fisheries

Plymouth Fisheries, once housed in the Edinburgh Woollen Mill building, is now the other side of Sutton Pool (Harbour), where you can see giant portholes on the sides of the new buildings. Plymouth processes over 10 million tons of fish a year, worth over £15 million.

01752 204738 plymouthfisheries.co.uk

06 The Elizabethan House at 32 New Street, built in the late 1500s, as a merchant house, slowly degenerated into a slum where nearly 60 people 'lived', many in tenements erected in the gardens, and was condemned in 1919, before Nancy Astor and the Old Plymouth Society saved it. Now a museum, run by The Box, it retains its character; largely built of oak beams, with white lime washed plaster walls, a ship's mast forming the column of its spiral staircase, and a kitchen built into the rocky escarpment. The only artefact found in the restoration was a mummified rat to ward off evil.

01752 304774

plymhearts.org/elizabethan-house

10 For centuries, the sound of squeaking pulleys and warning shouts could be heard everywhere in the Barbican, when goods were constantly loaded and unloaded into the large bonded warehouses, including that belonging to the world famous Plymouth Gin Distillery, established in 1793. Dispersed all over the Barbican, warehouses are still clearly identifiable today, some with the remnants of winches, beams and hooks, such as that next to the Custom House.

11 The city owes an enormous debt of gratitude to The Plymouth Barbican Trust (Association), formed in 1957, to preserve much of the Barbican's housing heritage against a programme of modernisation, after the devastation of the Plymouth Blitz. Without their efforts, Plymouth wouldn't be half the attraction it is today.

14 It's not a load of old Cobblers; Plymouth has the largest number of cobbled streets in Britain and don't be cobbling together half-baked plans that might change this fact, as locals fiercely protect them.

07 Lady Astor was the driving force behind the Mayflower 300 commemorations, and her 'cross Atlantic' conversations led to the setting up of Plymouth University.

15 To meet the needs of empire, the much larger Custom House on The Parade was built in 1820; a time when customs officers were deployed along the purpose-built South West Coastal path, to catch smugglers bringing in contraband, such as brandy and port from France, which exceeded that going to London legally. You can now purchase delicious fare there, at Bonne Santé, while thinking about the smug smugglers as you pay VAT.

01752 310263 bonnesanteplymouth.co.uk

08 In New Street, find a small brass plaque that says, 'on this spot in 1765 nothing happened'. Actually, a huge gunpowder explosion occurred there that year, to which, clearly, no-one owned up – not me, guv!

12 Just up from Southside Street in White Lane, where classy ladies used to come down to watch the sailors and heroes of the day in Victorian times, you will find a curious looking bulge built into a corner formed by two buildings. This is called a 'modesty buttress' on account of it being built to stop pub drinkers from using it as a urinal and thereby causing offence to said ladies.

09 A couple of doors up from The Barbican Botanics Gin Room, through a small entrance and tunnel, and up some stone stairs, flanked by the Rolls of Honour for the Plymouth Barbican Association and the Mayflower Pilgrims, you will find the tranquil and beautiful Elizabethan Gardens, faithfully recreated in 1970 to commemorate the 350th anniversary of the Mayflower voyage.

13 Fishing has always been central to the character of the Barbican, with a major quay expansion built in the late 1800s, when fishing boats added steam to their sails; some original bollards remain where Southside St meets New St.

16 Another golden oldie from the golden age is the Old Custom House, on the south side of The Parade. Built in 1586, Drake himself, after raiding Spanish galleons, would have come to give the Queen and State their shares of the booty. Now, you can find treasures of the literary kind there, at The Book Cupboard.

01752 226311

secondhandbooksplymouth.co.uk

MAYFLOWER WALK

17 The 1.2 mile circular walk begins at the Mayflower Steps Memorial at the Barbican, which comprises of an arch flanked by USA and UK flags. The real steps, however, require a number of drinks at the neighbouring Admiral MacBride with a quick snoop in the ladies' toilets, apparently. Men will have to rely on their partners!

18 Right of the steps, there is a plaque dedicated to the Mayflower Pilgrims, by the General Society of Mayflower Descendants, 1620 – 2020, which celebrates the first thanksgiving in 1621, and 50 years of peace between them and the Wampanoag Tribe.

19 Left of the steps, there is a plaque commemorating the Sea Venture, which, bound for Jamestown, was wrecked on and inadvertently founded Bermuda in 1609. Stephen Hopkins, one of the passengers, was pardoned from a death sentence for mutiny, before sailing again to the Jamestown colony, returning to England in 1614, when his wife died, and finally sailing with the Mayflower in 1620 to Massachusetts.

20 Plymouth Boat trips, by the Mayflower Steps, will run a Mayflower boat tour with a special menu for 2020, using all local ingredients like bees' honey from Mount Edgcumbe, Plymouth Gin and locally fished scallops.
01752 253153 plymouthboattrips.co.uk

21 Some of the Mayflower's 350 ropes, would likely have been replaced with new ones made at the docks near where the Edinburgh Woollen Mill is now.

22 The Speedwell, bought by the Leiden Separatists in Holland, was finally abandoned by them at Plymouth, probably Sutton Pool (Sutton), on account of repeated leaks, but, after the Mayflower had set off, was declared seaworthy again; foul play was suspected!

23 Some of the Mayflower's food stocks and beer for the voyage would have been bought from the Barbican market, bakehouse and warehouses, now converted into popular waterfront cafés and bars.

24 Some say the potable drinking water to be found at Finewell Street was contaminated with cholera in 1620, so the Pilgrims stopped at Newlyn in Cornwall after leaving Plymouth, to stock up with fresh water.

25 St Andrew's Church

The pilgrims, to get to St Andrew's Church for last prayers before sailing away, would likely have walked along Catherine Street, named after St Catherine, the martyr who was beheaded in Alexandria, Egypt, after shattering the wheel rack, on which they tried to execute her; the street has since been populated by mainly religious establishments. The clergy of St Andrews would have been sympathetic to the Separatists' cause and, if it were not for the fact that the pilgrims wanted complete freedom of worship, they would have been much more content in a town like Plymouth than the north. Plymouth was more discrete with its Puritanical views, but was later to show its true colours during the English Civil War.
01752 661414 standrewschurch.org.uk

26 It is quite possible that the Pilgrims who had become master craftsmen, in clothing and attire, would have visited the former Guildhall founded in 1606, to attend a meeting of like-minded drapers.
01752 307764

27 Legend has it that some pilgrims spent a night at the Blackfriars Distillery, now home to Plymouth Gin, a meeting house at the time, and maybe where they got their 'strong water', some of which they gave Massasoit Ousamequin as a peace offering, who promptly drank it and broke into a sweat.

28 Thomas Fones, Mayor of 1619/20, waved goodbye to the pilgrims and probably owned Fones bakery, now Jacka, on Southside Street, which will have supplied the Mayflower with the famous 'Captain's biscuits' and now bakes the best bread and cakes in town.

29 There were 102 Mayflower pilgrims. One of them, an Anglican, not a Separatist, John Billington, was a Londoner hired by Thomas Weston, the merchant adventurer who was the main financier for the Mayflower. Billington, although travelling with his family, was described by Bradford, "He and some of his had been often punished for miscarriages before, being one of the most profane families amongst the Massachusetts colony". He ended up shooting dead a neighbour, while living in the Massachusetts colony, for which he was the first to be executed in 1630, having also been the first to commit an offence in September 1621.

30 Close to the Mayflower Steps, The Island House is reckoned to have been built in the late 1500s, but could be much older, according to Municipal records, which record a house so named in 1495. Some Pilgrims allegedly spent their last night here before leaving on the Mayflower. There is a large roll of honour on the wall, upon which you will find all of their names and some of their livelihoods. The most curious sounding of the professions is chirugron, meaning surgeon. Nowadays, the ground floor shop pleasures the public with Pilgrim's ice cream, a tasty break on any walk.
01752 265105
facebook.com/pilgrimsicecream

31 Read the story, marvel at the props and imagine the voyage with the scale model, while exploring the Mayflower Museum, spread over three fascinating floors above the Tourist Information Centre.
01752 306330 visitplymouth.co.uk

32 If you want to delve deeper into the extraordinary adventures of the Mayflower Pilgrims, discovering what the more colourful characters got up to; the European context; stories of their time in Northern England; the challenges of escaping to Holland; their tough years in Holland; the challenges raising finance; and the first 50 years on Plymouth plantation, book your customised walk, by calling or emailing: Charlie Keeler, the book's editor, who is passionate about the Mayflower story, Plymouth, and the history of the period.
07971808143 charliekeeler@gmail.com

CROWDFUNDED CONTENT

PLYMOUTH BOAT TRIPS & THE BOATHOUSE RESTAURANT

33 To catch and eat the best and freshest possible fish in the country, you really can't beat Plymouth Boat Trips' half day Fish 'n' Trips fishing bonanza. The fishing team provides the perfect blend of professionalism and relaxed fun for all ages and abilities, helping you catch real fish with a real fishing line, which you can have cooked, on your return, at the Boathouse Restaurant, as part of an exquisite mouthwatering feast, to finish off a truly fantastic day. "It's all about luck really," they will tell you, when asked how much skill is needed to hook a mackerel. Seasoned fishermen, and extremely friendly and helpful, they can gauge just how much to get involved and know a thing or two about where to find the fish for you.

34 Relive the naughty nineties on a boat trip, with incandescent hits and glowing colours waving along the waves, to hypnotic music.

35 Swing and sway back into the 60s and 70s Revival Party Night for 3 hours of glamour aboard the world's greatest disco boat, dancing away to those snappy hits.

36 For those about to rock back into the 80s, Plymouth Boats salutes you with the best hits, in a 3 hour groove and funk ride, surrounded by fluorescent lights.

37 Adults can have their own dance macabre at the Halloween Boat Party to enjoy a spectre spectacular night on the water and dressing up, in a glorious gore fest.

> "Plymouth is going to go supersonic!"

Ben Squire,
Owner of Plymouth Boats

39 Hard to imagine Plymouth without pirates, so treat the kids to a special Pirate Adventure Cruise for me little arty's, with dressing up, games, music and, you guessed it, a treasure hunt.

40 Dress the kids up in their scariest rags for the 'horrifying' Halloween Cruise: an hour and a half of disco dancing, music, games and the Trick or Treat Treasure Chest.

38

Plymouth Boat Trips

For a special tailored experience, take a Plymouth Boats Themed Cruise, the best of which might be the five hour sunset trip, up an outstandingly beautiful ten-mile stretch of the Tamar River, to the large picturesque pre Roman village of Calstock, visited by Queen Victoria in 1846. It has a beautiful scenic railway, old nineteenth century lime kilns, and the remains of an ancient Roman fort that could house around 500 soldiers. You will get a chance to sample the delicious brews and grub at the Tamar Inn for an hour before returning.

41 The way of St James, for those on a pilgrimage via the five Camino trails of northern Spain, is designated by scallop-shell-embossed/painted milestones, a large one of which can be seen on the roadway above The Boathouse, which marks the embarkation point for pilgrims, who, by law, had to travel abroad from Plymouth or Dover, in ancient times. Now, you can take up your scallop shell at the Scallop Shack in The Boathouse restaurant, after eating one of their delicious fresh catches from the 'Sidney Rose', cooked to perfection, before heading out on your own pilgrimage to the magnificent Santiago de Compostela, to which all trails lead.

43 Do the Calstock cruise again, but this time see that rustic bliss and lush green gorgeousness through eyes and ears filled with the sounds of the joyous Plymouth Jazz Club.

44 Carry on Cruising with 'Sid the Squid', on a Harbour Cruise, is the best way to enjoy the Ocean City, from the water, where you learn about the iconic red and white striped Smeaton's Tower, atop the amazing Plymouth Hoe, the Lido, grand houses of the Astors and Conan Doyle, the imposing Royal Citadel, the Mount Batten peninsular with tower, the Barbican, Cornwall's Mount Edgcumbe estate, Drake's Island, and a whole lot more. All this conducted on a live microphone from the wheel house, which Sid considers the best office in the world, from which to work. Here, he will answer questions and let the kids have a go at the wheel between telling everyone on board about the different historic sights of Plymouth's breathtaking coastline and surrounding areas.

45 At the end of any cruise, you can always eat out at The Boathouse and enjoy the delicious great value food, served by unsurpassable, highly trained staff. Show your boat ticket and get 10% off your bill.

46 Have your own do, with private hirings that can cater for all kinds of events like wedding receptions, parties, wakes in the wake, birthdays, anniversaries, you name it.

47 One way around Plymouth Sound is to catch the Cremyll Ferry, to Mount Edgcumbe and take a 90 minute coastal walk to Cawsand, where you can get the Cawsand ferry, aka The Red Pig, back to the Barbican.

42 Daiquiris, Wallbangers and Pina Coladas galore, and more, can be downed at the end-of-season 'All Night Happy Hour' Party Cruise along to local DJs, spinning hits.

48 Daily cruises will take you to see warships, dockyards, the Sound and breathtaking Cornish and Devonshire coastlines, with great commentary and yummy Devon Cream teas.

01752 253153 plymouthboattrips.co.uk

THE WAY OF THE WATERFRONT

49 Book an excellent value room at the Admiral MacBride, to be reminded each morning when you open the curtains, of the amazing history that is marked by the Mayflower Steps Memorial, upon which you look.
01752 262054 admiralmacbride.com

50 Next to the Admiral MacBride there are many plaques to commemorate those brave fishermen of Plymouth who lost their lives at sea. Fishing has been the essence of the city from the 1500s, especially the Barbican and Sutton Pool (Harbour).

51 You will also find a plaque commemorating the departure of the Charlotte and Friendship for Australia, the first of nine ships used for transporting convicts down under in 1788, including such as Edward Perkins, who, for the heinous crime of stealing a cockerel worth a shilling, was parted from his family for seven years.

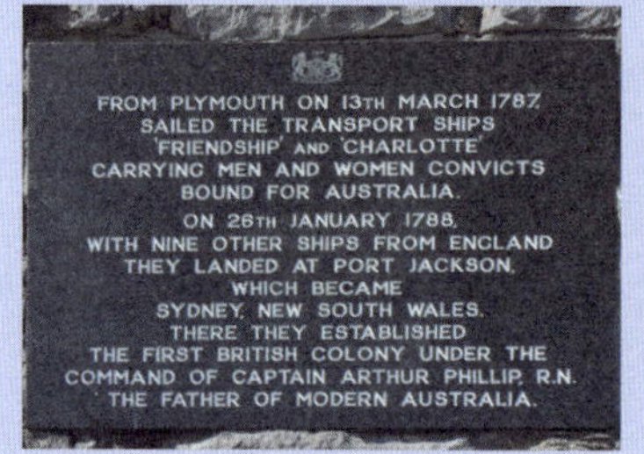

52 And a plaque that commemorates the Cornish copper and tin miners who emigrated round the world with their engineering genius that helped other countries to dig deep for all kinds of precious metals and materials.

53 A little further west, there is a plaque that celebrates giving Nelson a free run of the city; something that meant something, back in the 1800s, when you weren't from here.

54 The large golden scallop shell, near the end of the wall, commemorates the Way of St James or more alluringly in Spanish, the Camino trail, which leads to Santiago de Compostela in Northern Spain. The main Camino trails are well marked, with albergues (hostels) all the way along their routes for peregrinos (pilgrims) to sleep. Read Holly Kellam's 'The Butterfly Road' to follow a real Camino experience.
hollykellam.com

55 Further up the road is the shrine of the rescued statue of Stella Maris, Star of the Sea, complete with eight pointed pole star and protector of mariners, recovered from a wrecked cargo of marble.

56 Then, there is the Royal Australian Air Force plaque that remembers the people of Plymouth with admiration and affection. The feeling is mutual as the squadron supported sea patrols and sank six enemy submarines.

> Virgin of all virgins! To your shelter take us; Gentlest of the gentle! Chaste and gentle make us.

Stella Maris Prayer

57 "May our hearts be open to friendship and our arms reach across the sea to unite our two nations." The final words below the commemorative stone, with its red volcanic rock from St Helena (Napoleon's final resting place), embedded in granite from Dartmoor prison (used to imprison French troops).

58 Overlooking the entrance to Sutton Pool (Harbour), is the last remaining building of the emigration depot that processed over 400,000 people on their way to other commonwealth countries between 1840 and 1893, and is where the name 'passport' came into being, with papers being required for inspection before boarding a ship. The area was once the victualling yard for the Royal Navy before the Royal William Yard was built, at the height of the empire. Goods could easily be carried from the Barbican into the yard and military men from the Royal Citadel could board ships in quick time.

59 Duttons Cafe should perhaps reinvent itself as Pellew's Café or the Captain's Café, to celebrate the positive contribution of Captain Edward Pellew's heroic efforts in 1796 to save nearly 500 souls from a turbulent death aboard the wrecked Dutton ship. The ship was wrecked in a violent storm that had already snapped off its masts and claimed a sentry box half way up the hill to the Royal Citadel. The quick-thinking Pellew, later to become Admiral and awarded many other honours from performing other selfless feats, as a truly upstanding citizen, cast around for help before climbing aboard the ship via ropes and taking control from drunken sailors, to save all but around twenty souls, and being the last to leave the ship, as it sank.
01752 255245

60 At the point, just above Dutton's café, you come to two cannons with ridges worn across their barrels. The ridges are a result of being used as bollards for tying up boats, when they were set into the harbour's edge at Devonport; the navy equivalent of turning swords into ploughshares, perhaps.

61 Between the Royal Citadel and the waterfront is the imposing Marine Biological Association building, a hotbed of scholarship and scientific enterprise, home to one of largest reference libraries in the world and facilitator of 7 Nobel Prizes. Built in 1884, and awarded a Royal Charter in 2013, it's now the world leader in plankton studies, collecting data from the North Atlantic and the North Sea (more recently other regions) on plankton's biogeography and ecology since 1931, through the Continuous Plankton Recorder (CPR) Survey, Providing indispensable evidence and reference for big issues of the day such as pollution, climate change, the increase of harmful algal blooms, and excessive fishing. It boasts the analysis of over quarter of a million samples, over 5 million miles of about 700 taxa.

62 Set on a sheer cliff face below the Hoe, the Terrace Café Bar Restaurant on 74 Madeira Road is the best 'room with a view' for eating, drinking, and chilling in Plymouth.

01752 603533 terraceplymouth.co.uk

63 Below the Citadel, the Royal Plymouth Corinthian Yacht Club, established in 1688, sits within Fishers Nose Artillery Tower, part of defensive structures built in Henry VIII's time. Sadly, you've just missed a unique chance to buy it, the only private waterfront property.
01752 664327

64 In the summer, you can see the sights seated, yet from on high, in Plymouth's Open Top Bus Tour that takes you to a number of key hop on/hop off points along the waterfront and around the City, Barbican, and Royal William Yard.
01752 662271 oceancitysights.co.uk

HOE! HOE! HOE! WHAT A VIEW!

65 The small octagonal Liner Lookout Café stands in pride of place on the Hoe, just west of Smeaton's tower, and is a really sweet place to sit and marvel at the views across the Sound, with a drink and snack.
07855 949295

66 The Hoe ('high ground' in Anglo Saxon) Promenade along the top of the hill, apart from being the most incredible viewing platform for Plymouth Sound and the city, and lined with memorials and statues, hosts all kinds of amazing events, in addition to Remembrance Day.

67 The Plymouth Dome, east of Smeaton's tower on Hoe Road, was a museum from 1989 to 2006 before becoming a restaurant, and had a plaque unveiled in 1988 by the Queen celebrating the 400th anniversary of defeating the Spanish Armada.

68 The very Grand Hotel on the Hoe, built in 1879, boasted, in its day, hosting the 80 year old Prime Minister William Gladstone, and his speech to an estimated crowd of 100,000 people in his West Country Whitsun tour in 1889, where he was the subject of a great ovation.

69 At the west end of the Hoe, you will find the Viking Stone, the Rhune, commemorating a thousand years of peace since the Vikings last raided Plymouth and the Tamar, given by all five Scandinavian countries, in good faith and friendship.

70 The glorious Plymouth Belvedere ('beautiful to see' in Italian), was built in 1891, way before its namesake American car cruised about such seaside venues. The bonkers B52s played their classic, 'Planet Claire', including a Plymouth Satellite, on its top tier, in the 1980s.

71 Holding centre stage, Smeaton's Tower, owned by The Box, has 93 steps to climb for a small fee and, for £1, the illuminating book, 'The Lighthouse Keeper's Lot'. The first lighthouse to be built on the treacherous Eddystone rocks, 14 miles out to sea from the Hoe, was the ill-fated Winstanley lighthouse in 1696. The DaVinci style designer, Winstanley, boasted, much like the architect of the Titanic, that his creation could withstand any weather, which ended in his vanishing, along with his lighthouse, during the worst storm in 200 years. Rudyard's lighthouse faired better, lasting from 1705 to 1755, when a fire brought it to an end along with Henry Fall, 94 years old, who tragically swallowed 200g of lead trying to put it out. Then, in 1759, Smeaton's strong oak tree design with interlocking blocks was built, and became the blueprint for all future lighthouses. It was reassembled later, on the Hoe, as a tribute.

72 Nearby, on the grassy verge by the promenade, the Beatles' bottoms have been temporarily immortalised in metal sculptures, where they all sat on the Hoe looking out at its astonishing views. You can still sit where they briefly sat still.

73 Just up from the Ark Royal's anchor, to the north of the Hoe, is a lovely circular garden with a plaque commemorating the centenary of the formation of the Women's Royal Naval Service and Women's service in the Royal Navy from 1917 to 2017.

74 Sculptor, Hayley Gibbs, who was selected to cast a bronze statue of Nancy Astor, used extensive archive footage, both photographic and televisual, to capture her pioneering political spirit. Alexis Bowater who spear-headed the fundraising for the statue, outside Nancy Astor's former home, at its unveiling on November 28th, said, "100 years ago Plymouth made history when it voted in the first woman to take her seat in Parliament and now it's doing it again by raising the first statue of the first female MP in the House of Commons."

> "One reason why I don't drink is because I wish to know when I am having a good time."
>
> Nancy Astor

78 Lockyer Street's terraced houses flank the Hoe as it descends the hill to Armada Way, and demonstrates perfectly the pre and post WWII blitz damage, showing Victorian houses being interspersed with modern housing. On the night of 20 March 1941, during a 4-hour bombing raid, around 30,000 incendiary bombs and 1,100 high explosives were dropped on Plymouth. The King and Queen very narrowly escaped them. But the following night some 36,000 incendiaries and 1,300 high explosives wrecked the City, killing 336 civilians in just 2 days. Each night, there was an exodus of about 60,000 citizens to the surrounding fields, barns and towns nearby. From 20th to 23rd April, another blitz bombing effort almost entirely decimated the city. The bombing finally ceased after the night of 30 April 1944.

79 Valenti's Café Bar sits at the east end of the Hoe, in pride of place, to serve you snacks and cream teas inside and out, with bird's eye views of the Citadel, statues and the Sound.
01752 226122

75 Go for a great range of real ales, drinks and delicious pub grub at the classic but quirky English 'The Pub On The Hoe' with great views of the Hoe and friendly staff.

01752 202405 thepubonthehoe.co.uk

76 Traitor's Gate, on the west wall of the Citadel, is where those found guilty of mutiny or other crimes in the Royal Marines, were filed out for execution. For as little as contesting living conditions and wages, Plymouth's last, most shameful of executions took place in 1797.

77 By booking with Jerry Sibley, the custodian of the synagogue, the old Jewish cemetery can be found, just off the eastern extreme of the Hoe, in a secluded walled garden. Take a truly memorable audio tour of the grave characters with fascinating stories, recorded by actors, Derek Frood and Ruth Mitchell of the Ripple Theatre.
07753 267616 mitchellrippletheatreco.com

80 The peaceful Sensory Garden, complete with Galapagos tortoise sculpture and healing fountain, commemorates the victims of genocide, including Anne Frank of the Holocaust and those of Rwanda.

ICONIC PLYMOUTH STATUES & MEMORIALS

81 Sir Francis Drake's bronze statue, since 1884, has stood majestically tall, observing the horizon, a plotting compass in hand for circumnavigating the globe and other hand on hip over long sword about his waist, marking his fighting prowess. The original statue is in Tavistock, his birthplace, and the cast, at his peaceful retreat, Buckland Abbey. Certainly, Plymouth's most iconic character, the statue is a fitting memorial, despite some questionable actions, to a man who had one of the most colourful lives in history, as one of the greatest seafarers, a privateer of immense success and wealth, a legendary warrior, Mayor of Plymouth in 1581, and a favourite of Queen Elizabeth I.

82 It took a large crowd of Plymothians to elect Nancy Astor into power and it took crowdfunding to remember her unprecedented achievements for the nation and for Plymouth, with a statue next to her home on the Hoe, unveiled by former PM, Theresa May, and seemingly gate-crashed by Boris Johnson, the current PM on 28 November 2019.

83 'Towards another world' went Christian Victor, Prince of Schleswig-Holstein, and other officers of the Devonshire, Somerset and Gloucestershire Regiments during the second Boer War of 1899 – 1902, as commemorated in the memorial near the Royal Citadel's main gate.

84 The black commando dagger, sitting on five stone cannonballs, is a fitting sculpture of this silent but deadly weapon of choice, stealthily used by 29 Commando Regiment, to be seen at the memorial, outside the Royal Citadel's main gate, to those who fell in recent wars.

" In peace, let us pray and think, and act as aggressively and courageously as we did in war, so that we may achieve freedom, fair play, decency and integrity internationally, nationally and personally. "

Air Vice Marshal
Don Bennett

86 'He blew with his winds and they were scattered.' The Armada Memorial, with wonderful bronze sculptures, towers over all but the naval memorial, and is adorned with four plates of the chief protagonists in the famous invasion-busting Battle of Gravelines, in 1588.

87 Ever the romantic, Charles Norrington, Mayor of Plymouth from 1863-1865, erected the Norrington Memorial; a fountain depicting the biblical Rebecca of the well, in memory of his wife. Unveiled in 1881, it was intended to provide water for the children playing on the Hoe.

88 The Plymouth City War Memorials offers comforting words for the bereaved, 'They are in peace for God proved them and found them worthy for himself'.

85 The Naval War Memorial has pride of place in the centre of the Hoe, and commemorates the ultimate sacrifices made for king and country of 23,000 Naval personnel from the UK and Commonwealth who have been lost at sea, in the two world wars; over 7,000 from the first and just under 16,000 in the second. There are similar ones, to be found at the other great naval bases of the South of the UK in Chatham and Portsmouth.

89 Buried beneath the Allied Air Forces monument lies the ashes of AVM Don Bennett CB, CBE, DSO, who wrote, when chairman of the UN Association, "I have seen two great Wars in my lifetime and after each I have seen the political leaders of almost every country in the world fritter away the opportunities which their warriors have created for them. After each war, I have seen the return of pessimism and of distrust, and the vitiation of human relations by intrigue, fear, greed and dishonesty. Moral standards in matters great and small have sunk appallingly to impossible levels. In short, man in peace has proved unworthy of the dead of two World Wars. This need not be. We are the same men and women who fought beside those who died. We are of the same stuff which achieved greatness in time of war. Therefore in peace, let us pray and think – and act as aggressively and courageously as we did in war, so that we may achieve freedom, fair play, decency and integrity internationally, nationally and personally – which the sacrifices of two World Wars so nobly earned."

92 The Great War Memorial in Devonport People's Park is a giant 33 foot gothic granite cross with a white marble statue of Victory personified, to remember the sacrifice made by around 2,000 Devonport people.

93 "Had we lived, I should have had a tale to tell of the hardihood, endurance and courage of my companions, which would have stirred the heart of every Englishman," is inscribed round Robert Falcon Scott's memorial in Mount Wise; it being his final diary entry on his tragic bid to be the first to reach the South Pole.

94 'Saltash Passage, Plymouth will never forget you,' says the memorial to the American V and VII Corps, where they embarked on the momentous Normandy Landings in 1944.

90 At 7 metres tall, 9 metres wide and 10 tons, the Messenger statue crouches outside the Theatre Royal in Plymouth. Fashioned in cast bronze, in a pose from Othello, some say it is designed to inspire actors and actresses, who breathe life into scripts.

96 The Allied Air Forces Monument on the Hoe commemorates 17 countries that served in the air and on the ground for air supremacy during WWII. Interestingly, the final paragraph of the dedication honours 107,000 RAF, 84,000 United States AF and 42,200 Soviet AF, who paid the ultimate sacrifice.

91 Depicting a frozen moment of familial bliss, the Hope sculpture by Frances May Favata, commemorates 76 civilians who died in a single blast in an underground shelter on the night of April 22nd 1941, beneath what is now the Portland Square Building campus of Plymouth University. The sculpture depicts a child, representing Hope, being raised to the skies.

95 A new beautifully sculpted, dark bronze memorial figure, clothed in heavy coat and cap, calmly searching the sea's horizon with binoculars about the neck, now adorns the Hoe, to honour the considerable services to the United Kingdom of the Merchant Navy and Fishing Fleet, who regularly brave forbidding seas to bring in precious cargos.

CROWDFUNDED CONTENT

VIEW FROM THE TOP – CROWNE PLAZA

99 Order a Roast Rump of Moorland Lamb À La Dijonnaise and think how, 400 years ago, it could have been acquired by simply walking out of the front door, when most of the Hoe was a field grazed by sheep.

97 At 32 years old, Marco Pierre White was the youngest chef ever to get three Michelin stars in 1994. He also trained chefs like Gordon Ramsay and hosted a number of TV cooking shows as the bad-boy of the cooking world and first celebrity chef.

98 The fabulous 'L' shaped restaurant, with near 360-degree views around the city, will have you living history whilst eating steak from the famous Campbell's Farm, the same place from which the Queen gets one's steaks.

100 Plymouth's Pièce De Resistance, Marco Pierre White Steakhouse Bar and Grill is situated in the penthouse of the Crowne Plaza Hotel and has one of the world's most epic and breathtaking views, where you get to look out over the Hoe to the Atlantic Ocean, Plymouth Sound, Drake's Island, the grand breakwater, Mount Edgcumbe estate, Stonehouse, and the chimney stack of Nancy Astor's House.
The country's greatest amphitheatre, the Hoe, unfolds below you, and through the panoramic giant glass restaurant windows, you can piece together the history and hidden secrets of this fascinating city of exploration and exploits.

101 From this height, 400 years ago you would have seen the small town of Plymouth surrounded by walls and four grand gates, two with drawbridges, to your west/north west, which is now nothing more than an elusive memorial plaque denoting where the West gate once was before it was torn down in 1783.

102 If you sit facing east in the restaurant, you will see the Barbican, from which you could have seen the Mayflower embarking on her voyage in 1620, moving slowly out to the south before sailing towards the ocean's horizon heading west.

103 Drake's Fort and St Catherine's Church would have dominated your view of the east Hoe in 1620, only to be subsumed, some 45 years later, into the Royal Citadel, built by the vengeful Charles II, still incensed by his father's execution. After officially taking control of the former parliamentarian Navy that protected Plymouth from the Royalist siege, he renamed it the Royal Navy from 1660, and built the Royal Citadel at the same time, famously pointing some of the cannons towards the city as a warning. In macabre and somewhat morbid style, he also had Cromwell's body, along with Cromwell's two closest allies, exhumed and publicly hanged, then beheaded, with their heads being displayed on 20 foot spikes at Westminster Hall for a mind-blowing 24 years.

104 Where else can you get a bird's eye view of the November 5th celebrations or national fireworks championships, marvelling at Catherine wheels that celebrate the failed attempt to execute St Catherine on the breaking wheel while looking towards St Catherine's Chapel, within The Royal Citadel.
ihg.com/crowneplaza

105 Looking beyond Devil's Point, marvel at how Cornwall's Mount Edgcumbe estate once included most of what you see around you and right up to Dartmoor.

106 In keeping with the modern trend towards iconic historic figures, St Nicholas' Island, formerly St Michael's Island, became Drake's Island from 100 years ago, and has plans for a living museum, heritage centre, and possibly a water-sports centre.

107 Be stirred but not shaken with a Vodka Martini, whilst having a grandstand view of the Red Arrows, as they fly in formation past Smeaton's Tower.

108 Delight in a Negroni or a Clover Club cocktail, both containing Plymouth Gin, while you regard the chimney of its makers within the ambiguously named Blackfriars Distillery. Experts claim that the Blackfriars were never present in Plymouth and that it was more likely the Greyfriars or Whitefriars (aka Carmelites), though the latter were said to have taken up residence the other side of Sutton Poole in a religious building comparable to the size of the Minster of St Andrews as it was then.

109 As the stars come out, take your time over Marco's delicious signature dish, 'Fillet of Beef À La Forestière with woodland mushrooms', and, while spotting theatrical celebrities, sip away at the highly delectable 'Mayflower commemoration Plymouth Gin cocktail with Elderflower Cordial, lemon juice, topped with Prosecco and garnished with a lemon twist'.

> "Staff treat us like family with a warm welcome. Breakfast still spectacular and bed so comfy."
>
> Kevin R, TripAdvisor

110 As you finish with a devilishly good sticky toffee pudding, think how Devil's Point might have acquired its name from Drake's antics with witches. Legend has it that witchcraft actually defeated the Spanish Armada and that the incantations to raise a storm were performed at this point with Drake, who sold his soul here to the devil and continues to walk the earth, waiting for his drum to be sounded again. When the Mayflower sailed, witch-hunting was at its peak with hundreds of 'witches' in Europe being executed, with the Holy Roman Empire as it was then, at the epicentre, where the Reformation then Counter Reformation began 100 years earlier.

111 In the early 1600s, you may have got your side of sourdough from the windmill, a stone's throw away, used for grinding the town's corn to make flour, at the top of the hill outside where Nancy Astor lived.

112 Drinking a 'Blood and Sand' cocktail, while looking through the southern windows, see if you can spot the Eddystone Rocks, 14 miles out, which, until 1696, wrecked many unsuspecting passing ships, until Winstanley built the first lighthouse.

01752 639937 info@mpwsteakhouseplymouth.com

PLYMOUTH'S NOTABLE HISTORIC RESIDENTS & VISITORS

113 William Elford Leach was a marine biologist and zoologist, who singlehandedly overhauled the British classification system of post-linnaean zoology.

114 Stanley Gibbons set up his famous stamp dealership in his Dad's chemist, around 1855, at 15 Treville Street, then 8 Lockyer Street, before going on to bigger things in London, and boring 4 of his 5 wives to death; or was it the other way round, him also being a chemist? They all died from internal organ damage of one kind or another.

115 Tobias Furneaux, born at Plymouth Dock, was the first skipper to circumnavigate the globe in both directions, after captaining HMS Adventure alongside Captain James Cook's Resolution in his second great voyage of discovery that had them crossing Antarctica in the mid 1770s. He also brought back the first South Sea islander to see Britain.

116 Captain James Cook is remembered for his 3 voyages from Plymouth to the Pacific, from 1768 to 1779, in a memorial on a remote island of Hawaii where he was killed by Natives in 1779.

117 Captain William Bligh, raised in Plymouth, famously skippered the Bounty in 1789, when Fletcher Christian led a mutiny in the Pacific that set him adrift with 18 of his crew in an open sloop, to navigate an incredible 3,600 miles to Timor. He was rejected again by his charges in the Rum Rebellion of 1808 in Australia.

118 Elizabeth Tillie sailed on the Mayflower, aged thirteen, with her parents, aunt and uncle, all of whom died in the first winter, leaving her orphaned in a strange land. She married John Howland, an apprentice to Governor John Carver who died in April 1621. They raised ten children, all of whom married, giving them 88 grandchildren. Imagine Christmas in their household! Their descendants include: presidents, Franklin Roosevelt and both Bush's; actors, Alec and Stephen Baldwin, Humphrey Bogart, Christopher Lloyd and Dr Benjamin Spock; the founder of the Mormon church, Joseph Smith; and the poet, Ralph Waldo Emerson.

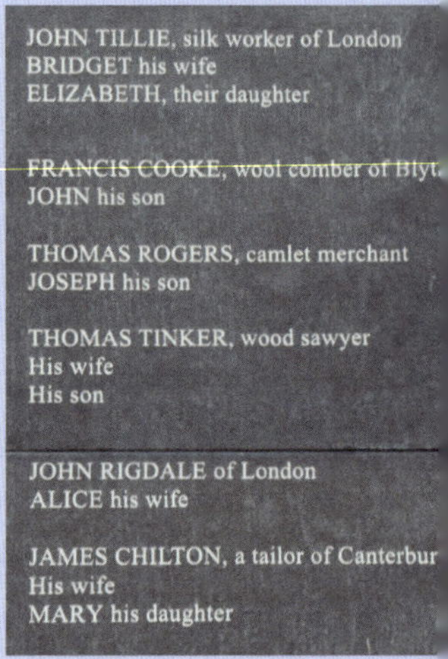

119 Sir Arthur Conan Doyle lodged, in 1882, with his university buddy, Dr Budd, a few doors down from Nancy Astor, but not for long, as he discovered his business colleague had become insufferable, having become addicted to opium while treating an injury. Such was his disappointment that he moved away shortly afterwards.

120 Nancy Astor lived at 3 Elliot Terrace, which she generously donated, along with her expensive necklace, to Plymouth Council, who now use the building for special functions and judicial hosting. She was the first female MP to take her seat in parliament in 1919, campaigning hard for many 'human rights' issues, including the plight of those who had to suffer abuse from alcoholics. She championed, through a hostile house of 500 MPs, the 'Intoxicating Liquor (Sale to persons under 18) Act, 1923'; the first act to be passed by a woman, resulting from her maiden speech and sheer determination. This led to 'black tot day', the last Royal Naval issue of beer rations to its sailors.

121 In 1571, John Hawkins, son of a merchant, became MP for Plymouth and was Treasurer of the Royal Navy in 1578. Besides the exciting tales of piracy, discovery and trading, it is thought the fire ships that scattered the Armada at Gravelines were his idea. Hawkins also spied on the Spanish as a trusted advisor and did much for charity, but will be remembered as a ruthless slave trader, that proudly included an image of a bound slave in his coat of arms.

122 Vice Admiral Robert Fitzroy, who captained the Beagle to the Galapagos Islands, from 1831 to 1836, has been commemorated by the Fitzroy Building at the University of Plymouth, for his services in founding the Meterological Office.

123 Ever heard o' Hearder? Jonathan Nash Hearder was a Plymothian electrical engineer and educator, who found alternative ways to help the blind to see and also invented the induction coil in 1853, used in x-ray machines, old lights and radio transmitters.

124 Charles Darwin's study, aged 22, of fossils and his later explorations of the Galapagos Islands, with their wonderful array of creatures, led to his opus magnum, the Origin of Species that gave rise to the Theory of Evolution. Some think that, while advancing our understanding of how species have developed, it has also encouraged racism through its corollary, 'survival of the fittest'.

127 Nearly a thousand years ago, as detailed in the Domesday Book, Judhael of Totnes, 'of venerable memory', having helped William the Conqueror defeat King Harold, owned lands in Devon stretching to both coasts, including 98 estates, 107 manors and a castle in Barnstaple. His duties included upholding law and order, assisting tax collection for the Crown and helping raise an army for the King, if required. In his latter years, he 'shed the weight of his flesh' to live out his days at the monastery of St. Martin.

> "There is nothing more deceptive than an obvious fact."
>
> Sir Arthur Conan Doyle

125 Rebecca Rolfe, aka Pocahontas, arrived at Plymouth in 1616 having converted to Christianity and married John Rolfe, but, heading back to America, she tragically died in 1617 on the way.

126 William Cookworthy, who lived where Southside St meets Notte St, was a Quaker minister and chemistry genius, who came up with an alternative to the highly popular and expensive china from China. He patented his own hard porcelain in 1768, made at his Plymouth China Factory, using Cornish china clay from St Austell.

128 Judge people by their fruits. Fred Stott OBE was a true man of the people and enormous contributor to Plymouth. Stott Close in Efford is named after him and a Guildhall plaque dedicated to him. He was a: productive post-war councillor, shipwright, Welfare Officer, Lord Mayor 1960/61, staunch Methodist preacher, pastor over a pint, Dartmoor Prison preacher, believed 'if you educate women then you educate families', open government champion, Library & Museum Committee Chairman, JOTP, Freeman of the City, who everyone stopped in the street for a chat. A veritable hamper of fruits.

HISTORIC SITES AROUND PLYMOUTH

129 Is the B-Bar in Castle Street named after the Barbican or a former failed attempt to clean up the street in the 1850s, by renaming it Bethel Street? Go, eat, ask and decide.
01752 242021 b-bar.co.uk

130 John Foulston built the stunning Egyptian-styled Oddfellows Hall in Ker Street, Devonport, in 1823, which is a quite unique looking building that evokes an extraordinary spirit, typical of this enigmatic City.

131 Mount Batten, as part of the lands of the Danmonii, who inhabited Cornwall and Devon in pre Saxon times, traded tin from about 4,000 years ago until around 50 AD.

132 All the world's a stage and the stages come and go, get burned down, rebuilt and finally demolished, in the case of the first one built in Plymouth in 1762, called The Dock Theatre in Cumberland Gardens, Devonport. At the height of its popularity, during the Napoleonic Wars, Sarah Siddons played Lady Macbeth; we all know what happens to theatres that host that particular play! Close your eyes, imagine the scene and you might see it in your mind's eye, but don't utter the words.

133 The 'Hands across the Sea' plaque outside St Andrews commemorates the Plymouth, Michigan delegation to Mayflower 350. 'Let this tree forever be the symbol of friendship between the two cities, July 15th 1970.'

134 Another case of 'resurgam', Derry's Cross, the centre of Plymouth in Victorian times, was almost completely destroyed during the blitz, except for the bank and the free standing Victorian clock tower built in 1862. Although now swamped by much bigger modern buildings, they were seen, after the war, as symbols of defiance.

135 The Merchant's House, nestled quietly in one of Plymouth's oldest streets, St Andrew Street, is the city's finest surviving example of a 16th and 17th century residence. The seven rooms ooze history, each one with its own central theme displaying Plymouth's past history of trade, transportation and WWII. Feel the nostalgia of olden times before the world became so busy and complicated with technology, and see how your half and the other lived, in the past. The Victorian school shows how education has changed over the centuries, particularly in the last century, with the introduction of mass education.

136 Mount Pleasant Redoubt in Blockhouse Park, Devonport, is one of the highest parks in Plymouth, enjoying expansive views across to Devonport, the ocean, Dartmoor and the cityscape. Redoubts were to where Armed Forces personnel could retreat when under attack, or regroup after attacking the enemy, so were thrown up quickly as a result; this one in 3 months. It was built during the American War of Independence (1775 – 1783), just over 150 years after the Mayflower arrived in Massachusetts, to resist the combined fleets of Spain and France, who had allied with the Americans and sailed into the Sound, threatening an invasion. There is a full scale redoubt reconstruction with blockhouse in Plymouth, Massachusetts.

137 The 115th Infantry Regiment and the 29th Infantry Division of the US Army departed from Barn Pool, Mt Edgcumbe for Omaha Beach for the famous WWII D-Day landings in Normandy where they suffered mass slaughter before successfully turning the tide of the war.

139 Guy Burgess, one of the Cambridge Five spies, who famously gave away important secrets to Communist Russia, was born and raised in a well-to-do family living at 2 Albemarle Villas in Devonport, which would have, being the largest naval base in Western Europe, been a target for Soviet missiles during the Cold War.

140 Around the time of the Mayflower, a wealthy Plympton landowner by the name of Childe, who perished out hunting during a snowstorm, despite taking refuge in his freshly disembowelled horse to keep warm, had offered his considerable land holdings in his will to whoever could build a tomb and bury him. See Childe's tomb on Dartmoor and imagine the rush.

141 The very grand HMS Drake, Exmouth Block, in Devonport, is the only remaining barracks of five that were built in 1907. It is a reflection of the importance of the Royal Navy at the time and the power of the Drake brand.

138 'I'm the king of the castle' contested King Stephen when Plympton Castle's owner, Baldwin de Redvers, rebelled against him in 1136; only, in this case, he had it besieged and burnt to the ground. Not one to take it lying down, Redvers rebuilt the castle in the 1140s after recovering his property and being made Earl of Devon by the Holy Roman Empress Matilda. A later castle owner, Fawkes de Breaute incurred the wrath of Henry III in 1224, who sent the county Sheriff with 10 knights and 60 sergeants to besiege the castle by force, de Breaute's surrendered after 15 days. The castle keep can still be seen today.

142 Finewell street, near the city centre, is so called because it was once the City's main source of drinking water, whereas Buckwell Street's water was only fit for washing and feeding to livestock.

143 On the Hoe Promenade, near the Naval War Memorial, there is a cross on the pathway that marks the site of the last public and appallingly botched execution of three 'mutinous' marines, attended by 10,000 naval men and the citizens of Plymouth in 1797.

144 The fine perpendicular gothic style Grammar School that still stands at Seymour Road, Plympton St Maurice, was built in 1664. Famous artist and founder of the Royal Academy, Joshua Reynolds, attended it, now called Hele's School, with his father as one of the masters.

CROWDFUNDED CONTENT

URBAN SPLASH – ROYAL WILLIAM YARD'S SECRET GEMS

145 The giant boulder before the Royal William Yard's entrance is a fitting tribute to the ship's biscuit, whose recipe it details; designed for long sea voyages, it was double-baked, making it as hard as rock. It could be eaten safely for up to 20 years after it was baked.

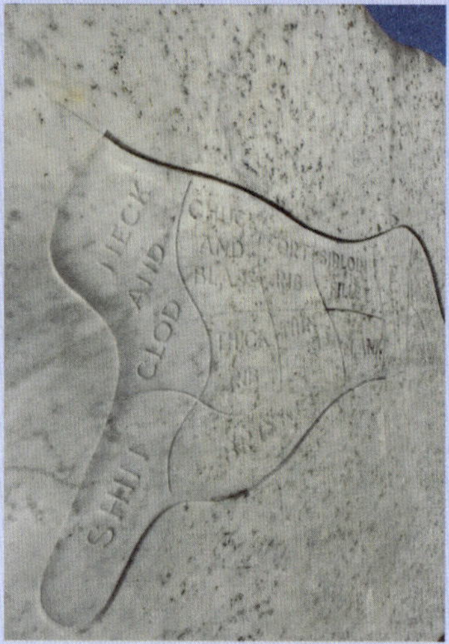

146 The same boulder shows, on the other side, the various butcher's cuts in an illustration of a side of beef. Today, only a few movable model cows remind us of the multiple uses of this former victualing yard.

147 The tourist gateway to the Yard, made from Penryn granite, with 13 foot tall King William IV's statue (AKA 'Silly Billy', owing to his penchant for eying up the ladies), is often mistaken for the main entrance to this historic naval victualing yard. In fact, the main way into the yard was from the sea and the second way from the Clarence steps. The tourist entrance also has four ox-heads that represent the meat victuals that were supplied to the navy, amongst many other goods, ranging from underpants to boiled tongue, the latter of which was considered a delicacy for the Officers.

148 On the right, as you enter the Yard, is the oldest post box (not in use) in England, which has remained, since 1825, inside the main gate of the Yard, where horses once pulled up for the postman to give the mail to the naval victualers.

149 Sited on 16 acres, much of the Yard was built from prehistoric rock, rich in fossils, with examples, dating back 15 million years, to be found in the walls of the liquid storehouse of the Clarence building. Darwin studied the quarry from which it was built.

150 On the left, as you enter the Yard, is the security detail, which was once 12 constables strong, back in the 1820s, demonstrating the importance of this majestic complex at that time. On the opposite side was 'the best looking slaughterhouse in Britain.'

151 The Yard's hidden and only house, is owned by Sally Proud, whose son, Ben Proud, is the world champion sprinter in 50m butterfly. Her amazing journey has taken her from her birthplace on the spice island of Zanzibar to Stone Town, a prestigious Sir John Rennie designed Georgian building, originally built for the Navy. Follow your nose, through the perfumed front garden of David Austen roses and the orchestra of birds, to her Orangery, with its stylish colonnade. She loves all the naval history, but, luckily for her guests, she does not serve ships' biscuits from the last bake-off in 1925.

To book Residence 3, the only private house in Royal William Yard, Plymouth, Devon, PL1 3RP. 07427 618696.

152 Bistrot Pierre, the gorgeous French restaurant, with toilets that would have impressed even Henry VIII, operates today, opposite Residence 1, the only boutique hotel in Plymouth. The grand design is a Grade II listed mansion, with 14 stylish rooms that overlook the expansive green in front that hosts the Good Food market on the first Sunday of every month, amongst other events. The likes of Lenny Henry have stayed here and it has been drawn by Plymouth artist, Sarah Smalldon. Room 1 was the original kitchen. The entrance to the hotel is tucked away next to an old chestnut tree that dates back to around 1830, which still produces nuts in September. Enjoyed by the squirrels today, over a hundred years ago they were used to nourish people on lengthy voyages.

158 Tim Burton, when directing the movie, Alice in Wonderland, stayed in the Mills bakery for three weeks. Some wonder if the ovens' ventilation openings inspired the design of the tiny door through which Alice passes to another world.

153 In its heyday, the Yard's 12 ovens were supplied with over 120 tons (270,000 lbs) of flour per week, ground from 27 millstones, powered by 2 steam engines.

159 In 1825, it cost £2 million to build the core of the Yard we see today, which was sold derelict to Urban Splash in 1999. The Brewhouse was built in 1830 to brew beer as a replacement for water for long voyages, since the water quickly acquired a green slime, while the alcohol ensured the beer remained bacteria-free and mould-free for much longer. Owing to the introduction of cast iron containers that enabled water to be stored for much longer, during the time the Brewhouse was under construction, the brewery was never actually used for beer making. Milk, being so perishable, could only be taken condensed in a tin, which had to be opened with a hammer and chisel.

154 In front of the opening to Firestone Bay, there are old holes in the granite where a wooden walkway once helped to corral the cattle as they were herded straight from boats into the yard.

155 During the war with Napoleon, he tried to cut off all food supplies to England, which made them more canny with production methods, like drying and preserving fruits and nuts, also useful for long ocean voyages.

156 Darwin, aged 22 years, departed on the Beagle for his five year voyage to the Galapagos Islands in 1831, from the back of the Yard. He spent as much time studying fossils in the quarried rock from Cornwall that was used to build the yard, as he did the islands, in coming up with his evolutionary theories and the Origin of Species.

157 Mills Bakery was where Ships' Biscuits were stamped with an arrow if they belonged to the king, a 'W' from the Royal William Yard, or 'C' from Clarence yard.

160 For more secrets, like where in the Yard the Churchill film was shot, and an in-depth history of the Yard, book a tour with Jane Dymock.

Jane Dymock +44 (0)7876402728
besttourguide.jd@gmail.com tourscornwall.com

CROWDFUNDED CONTENT

THE ROYAL WILLIAM YARD'S APARTMENT RENTALS

161 As you go through the arch, with King William IV looking out across the rooftops, there is a sense of magic that weaves a spell on all who visit the Royal William Yard. It's just as stunning when arriving by boat or descending the stairs from Devil's Point.

162 On a sunny summer's day, it's like entering a secret palace, hidden behind the Official Secrets Act for centuries, kept hushed up 007 style, until recently being converted into gorgeous contemporary apartments that still retain all the Georgian features.

163 Two apartments in Mills Bakery, owned by Beverley's family since 2015, are simply amazing spaces in which to stay, whether for work or holidays. Guests are wowed by the apartments' dynamic architectural features such as the thick iron columns and the strong wooden beams looking like they came off an old galleon.

164 These two elegant apartments are next to each other, so that groups of visitors can be close, but still private, and share their experiences in mirror image flats, both with the tranquility evoked by spectacular views over the water, and lovely window seats to read a book.

165 Whether it is blowing a force ten, or a gentle summer's day, it is an unforgettable, almost meditative experience, to sit on the apartment window seats, protected by solid walls a metre thick, and watch the boats and yachts bobbing on the water, as if dancing in the wind, with the clouds scudding past and the Cremyll Ferry going forever back and forth to Cornwall.

166 The stunning sunsets and twinkling lights of Plymouth, viewed across the water at dusk, have to be seen to be believed; a perfect place for a romantic getaway.

167 The apartments' floors, now carpeted to make them cosy, were originally for storing and preparing tobacco rations for sailors; one can almost feel the dust swirling around and smell the fragrant scent of leaves in the air. The milling and biscuit baking were done on the lower floors.

168 Families love to stay in these two excellently kitted-out apartments, any time of the year, whether toddlers or grown-up kids. It's a fantastic communal space for sharing time together that can be made quite discrete with the provided privacy screens. Families of 5 or more particularly like them as they make an excellent family environment with a kitchen and Netflix, children's television and more, to watch; much more comfortable and affordable than two hotel rooms.

169 Couples love it; especially two couples travelling together, staying side by side. The dining area makes it relaxing to cook at home or get a takeaway. People on business, in particular, specialists in the marine/naval/logistics side, medics and other fascinating professions, rebook regularly, owing to the efficient design of the space, and wonderful modern kitchen.

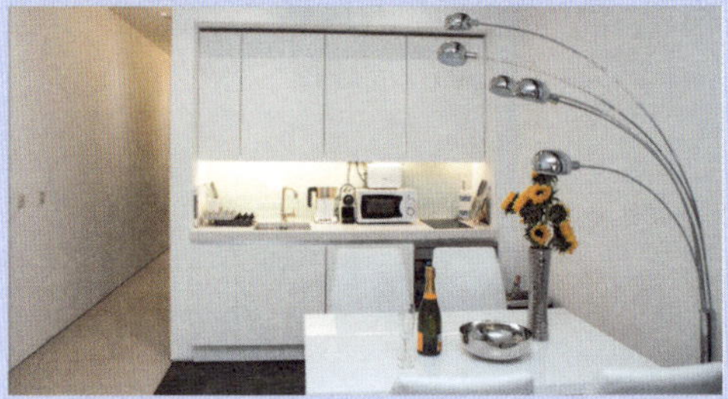

170 For relaxing on arrival and after a long day out, the apartments provide the latest espresso machine, with herbal teas and fresh coffee. So, treat yourself and make a booking.

07966 512507 mayflowerplymouth@outlook.com

CROWDFUNDED CONTENT

URBAN SPLASH – THE ROYAL WILLIAM YARD RESTORED

171 Melville, in the centre of the Yard, and the last building to be transformed, with striking clock tower and far-reaching views across the marina to Mount Wise, is truly iconic. It is soon to house more great work, retail and leisure spaces, including boutique cinema, Everyman, and independent restaurant, Hubbox. The grand open floor plates offer flexible options from 300 ft^2 to 100,000 ft^2.

173 Urban Splash, led by Commercial Director, Emily Handslip, has created an inclusive community at the Yard of which to be proud. The Yard boasts 215 award-winning homes and over 70 businesses; a vibrant mix of people. Urban Splash's respect and love for culture and creativity influences everything at the Yard.

174 The historic and grand Marina, focal point of the Yard, provides a gateway to coastal discovery, with a variety of coastal experiences on offer from 'cook your catch' events to lunchtime cruises.

> The potential of the Royal William Yard was already deep-rooted in its beautiful Georgian architecture, just crying out to be restored and appreciated once again.
>
> Urban Splash

175 Home to a bustling community, the Yard is a place where offices, apartments, restaurants, bars, leisure businesses and galleries rub shoulders, as waves lap the shore on three sides, and fascinating public spaces run through and around the Yard. This is a diverse community of business people and countless residents, to the hundreds of thousands of visitors who enjoy the calendar of year-round events, especially the annual stunning Illuminate festival, and daily experiences.

176 There are also over 12 outlets for dining in the Yard, the award winning Good Food market on the first Sunday of the month and amazing artisans and artists at Ocean Studios.

172 Devil's Point Swimming Pool

A walking tour of the Yard is a must, or climb the 'stairway to Devon' to explore Devil's Point peninsula, with its old defensive structures and rock staircases down to the sea, and the coastal path. Alternatively, go through the arch, like a secret doorway, in the seawall along from Residence One, to cool off in the Tidal Pool, try stand up paddle-boarding or kayaking from the rocks at Firestone Bay. Or take a ferry from the Marina, practice yoga on the green, or just enjoy a quiet drink at sunset.

GREAT PLACES TO STAY

179 It's hard to imagine a more beautiful panoramic view than that of the two hillside Shepherd Huts at Mount Edgcumbe, where you can get cosy in a gipsy-style wagon for a night of romantic bliss. Nestled by the woodburner or sitting outside overlooking the Sound, Plymouth City, the Tamar estuary and Dartmoor in the distance.
01752 822236 mountedgcumbe.gov.uk

177 The Duke of Cornwall Hotel oozes Victorian grandness and majesty as Plymouth's first luxury hotel, hosting a plethora of famous visitors over time.
01752 275850 thedukeofcornwall.co.uk

180 With the best sea view in Kingsand, and free parking, you won't do better for a fabulous getaway holiday than Storm Cottage, right by the sea.
homeaway.co.uk/p6934749

181 Boringdon Hall hotel – see Hotelier in 20 characters section.
01752 546196 boringdonhall.co.uk

182 Crowne Plaza Hotel See Crowdfunded spread on Page 202 for full description.
01752 639988 crowneplaza.com

183 Tom and Jeanette offer you a warm family feeling with a couple of lovely rooms in the attic of their Victorian house, 42 Prince Maurice Road in Mutley, where you can discover, in a 5 minute walk up the hill to Freedom Fields Park, how the road ironically got its name.
07717 214411

184 Rent any of a range of great value AirBnB apartments or rooms, like the Harlequin or Harbour Court A, ideally located 'yet very quiet' overlooking the Hoe.
airbnb.co.uk/rooms/16906914

185 Strathmore House Apartments at 13 Elliot St, round the corner from Nancy Astor's house, has 1 to 4-bedroom self-catering apartments from 2 to 365 nights a year.
01752 276797 strathmorehouse.co.uk

178 The Grade 1 listed architectural masterpiece, Residence One, is at the heart of the Royal William Yard, where you can enjoy the luxurious trappings of living like the Admiral of the Fleet and other officers of her majesty's Royal Navy, in one of their fabulous 14 luxury bedrooms. Steeped in mysteries of historic objects, smoking pipes, and golden ticket-like chocolate wrappers, each residence is two rooms wide, with every creature comfort. They either overlook the magnificent secret garden at the back, which is perfect for intimate wedding parties, or the green, where you can watch regular events that take place or play table tennis or interact with others from the Yard.
01752 262318 bistrotpierre.co.uk/rooms/residence-one/

186

Bovisand Holiday Park

When visiting Bovisand Lodge & Holiday Park, you will be utterly charmed by the location, such that you will highly likely want to buy one of the permanent caravans. Where else can couples and families alike enjoy a very quiet and peaceful location, complete with fluttering doves, curious chickens and naughty goats that share this wonderful valley by the sea. You can luxuriate for nine months of the year in a fabulous heated indoor pool with accompanying sauna and in the summer you can lie on the beach with glorious views across Plymouth Sound, knowing you are part of the Lodge's view over which engineer, Joseph Whidbey oversaw his, and Sir John Rennie's, mile long, 4 million ton Plymouth Breakwater. Rennie's son was the architect of the grand Royal William Yard. Your kids will love the wide open spaces, the amazing activities in the area, the spectacular beach-walks, and the playground, as well as the caravans themselves, which are fully kitted-out with modern kitchens and optional Wifi. Go rock hopping round the corner for delicious ice creams and awesome views.

01752 403554 bovisand.com

187 The magnificent Victorian 99-roomed New Continental Hotel, in the heart of Plymouth, has all the trappings of a fine hotel, including a leisure complex, swimming pool and enterprise grade wifi.

01752 276798 newcontinental.co.uk

188 You can now imagine living a couple of doors down from Nancy Astor, in the stunning apartments of the end-of-terrace, dual aspect 1 Elliot Terrace, with one of the most magnificent views in Plymouth.

0333 6669996
plumlocations.net/properties/elliot-terrace

189 Mount Batten Watersports & Activity Centre is not only a great place for all the family to indulge in all manner of water and land based activities, but also will provide you with hostel accommodation with great views at a great price.

01752 404567 mount-batten-centre.com

190 Bryony and Bertie give you the old Cider House at Buckland Abbey, with beautiful old gardens, and sumptuous and sympathetic accommodation, in the most peaceful secluded spot. They also host shepherd's huts, the getaway's getaway, blissfully isolated on a hill with stargazing luxury beds, charming décor, and amazing views, to which you get taken on a very cool converted military vehicle.

01822 259062 cider-house.co.uk

191 Number One, Windsor Villas, the Hoe, is an elegant, 1850 regency villa. Enjoy free parking, a full English breakfast, excellent facilities and a warm welcome.

01752 212 981 numberoneplymouth.co.uk

192 Be King of the Castle for a day and drive across Brunel's iconic Royal Albert Bridge to Cornwall, for a special afternoon tea or overnight break at luxury 5 star boutique B&B, Pentillie; a delightful setting, where Dawn French enjoyed the making of Sky 1's Delicious.

PLYMOUTH EXPERIENCES

193 'Run like a Local' is a neat little map, cleverly produced by the Crowne Plaza hotel, to promote three running routes of varying distances around the city that take in sensational sights.
01752 639988

194 The Cawsand Ferry, also known as 'The Red Pig', is a magnificent way to travel from the Barbican, along a truly beautiful stretch of coastline, to Cawsand and Kingsand, Cornwall.
plymouthboattrips.co.uk/ferries/cawsand-ferry

195 Papercutzglass is the answer to your dreams of putting a shine on your mosaic, fused or stained glass masterpiece, at Sheena's workshop at the Pannier Market in Plymouth.
07824 644962
papercutzglassdesignsbysheena.com

196 Treacherously slippery in winter, Devil's Point Tidal Pool becomes the best outdoor pool in the summer, rather like an au naturel infinity pool.
wildswim.com/devils-point-pool-plymouth

197 You can cycle from Plymouth's Central Park past Ford Park cemetery, down Pennycomequick, across to Victoria Park, along playing fields and down to the Scott Memorial in Mount Wise with very little time spent on busy roads. Hire bikes from the Barbican's Rockets & Rascals.
01752 927 555 rocketsandrascals.com

198 Kiss And Bite Letter Press, run by Ex-Western Morning News chief editor, is an innovative letterpress art & printing studio, where you can learn to print traditionally, but for modern impact.
Facebook.com/kissandbitepress

199 Craftspeople and software developers alike will love Kate Williams' weaving studio at Mt Edgcumbe, which is full of wild and whacky designs that will get you puzzlers working out how she does it, while others can select from a wide range of great gifts. Just looking at her complex weaving machines is enough to collapse any normal brain, let alone working out how to use them, but let your tactical brain try to crack the code.
katewilliamsweaving.com

200 Tinside Lido

Plymouth's Grade II listed Tinside Lido, luxuriating beneath Smeaton's Tower, was built in 1935, and recently judged 8th best in Europe. Wonderfully decked out in art-deco style, it is a fabulous place to swim while overlooking the iconic view of the Sound.

01752 261915 everyoneactive.com/centre/Tinside-Lido

201 For majestic examples of Regency architecture, visit the Devonport Guildhall and climb 137 steps to the top of the Devonport Column for a panoramic view of Devonport and beyond, and marvel at its commemoration as being a town in its own right in 1824.
01752 395028 devonportguildhall.org

202 Freestyle your way from Firestone Bay, on a gentle and safe 1.5 km swim to Drake's Island and back, seeing as you go, the full expanse of wonderful coastal sights from in the Sound.
wildswimming.co.uk/map/drakes-island-swim

203 The Mount Wise outdoor swimming pool complex in Devonport, with its three pools, is a lovely place for a hot day and, stunningly for this day and age, is free for all. Not only that, along one boundary, you can look out across the sea through the large openings in the wall and then take the children to the great playground next door, while you grab a delicious coffee from Café Roma. Also, the little known park, just above the swimming pools, is a little gem, where you can get a bit of peace, and marvel at the observation tower, Scott Memorial and views to Royal William Yard and Mt Edgcumbe.
0175 230 6265 everyoneactive.com

204 Try your hand at pitching and putting at the Putters on the Hoe, where you can also sit and eat the most delicious local award winning ice cream from Langage, in this beautiful corner of the Hoe leading up to the promenade.
visitplymouth.co.uk/things-to-do/putters-on-the-hoe-p2097113

205 Gorge walking from Mount Batten is an ecstasy of sliding down rivers, climbing up rocks, and diving into plunge pools of a natural gorge, with some rock scrambling thrown in.
01752 404567 mount-batten-centre.com

206 The Tamar Valley Scenic Railway takes you from Plymouth along all possible river delights, over viaducts, while hugging the meandering river with peaceful crossings galore, to Gunnislake, after passing through a plethora of picturesque villages.
01752 584777 greatscenicrailways.co.uk

207 Plymouth Bike Hire

Cycling is as big in Plymouth as anywhere and, owing to green spaces aplenty, you will never be short of places to visit around town or on big trips out of town. If you don't have your bike handy, The Bike Box at Coypool Park & Ride hire out a number of different bikes on a daily basis. A particular favourite is the glorious ride along the Plym Valley, all the way to Dartmoor, without traffic. The route is full of archeological bronze age ruins along the old route of the Great Western Railway, which would have been a key route in the industrial age but now, in great contrast, has been reclaimed by nature and those who appreciate the sight of nesting peregrine falcons, grand oak trees and suddenly appearing majestic viaducts.

07577 279928 plymouthbikehire.co.uk

> “Jayne kept our spirits high as the rain and high winds tried to dampen them.”
>
> Trip Advisor

208 Go out on a whim with Jayne Ashenbury, an expert Blue Badge Guide, on any tour around Plymouth, for micro adventures, involving a feast of facts and in-depth knowledge of the area. For a Mayflower treat, don't miss her double act with an accomplished Cornish Blue Badge Guide, Adrian Chapman.
07887 813143 whimsicaltours.com

CHILDREN'S ACTIVITIES

209 Dive into The National Marine Aquarium, where the whole family can connect with over 4,000 species of marine life, and learn about the amazing life of an octopus, in front of Britain's biggest marine tank. The daily events held in the deepest and largest aquarium tanks in the UK include meeting the twelve marine experts on different days and different times and learning first hand, from the likes of Charlie Preston, why the octopus is one of the sea's most intelligent creatures. As she shows you her arm covered in Octopus love bites, think of the Bond Film, Octopussy. Charlie is very much the action girl who arrives in the early morning, saying hello to all the fish, checking they are in a good mood and, most importantly, still alive and well.
0844 893 7938 national-aquarium.co.uk

210 Edward's Fudge Shop offers exquisitely delicious fudge in the bottom of a cone with ice cream on top. You can also have tasters, before making that important creamy choice.
edwardsfudgekitchen.co.uk

211 Climbing up Smeatons Tower not only exhausts some of that endless energy but also makes for a highly educational and uniquely visual experience to remember for a lifetime.
01752 304774
plymhearts.org/smeatons-tower/

213 Plymouth is very committed to developing its green spaces, with many visionary initiatives on the go. The City's lungs are at The Hoe, Central Park, Home Park, the People's Park, Mutley Park, Freedom Fields Park, Poole Farm and many more green spaces, where the kids can run around and you can learn some history, get active or just bask in the beauty of a vanguard of vistas.

214 For children up to 10 years, Jump is really exciting with its ball pools, fun inflatables, big climbing frames, slides, and toddler zones, amongst much more. You can also go wild with a themed party involving discos, dinosaurs or space. After all this you'll be be grateful for a break and refreshment at the chef's fresh food café. Drake's Den is also hard to beat with Festive Friday. Crafty Monday, after school meal deals, discos, music buses, coffee clubs, private parties, a trike area, a spiral slide, a rope bridge and a wave slide.
01752 782 415 123jump.co.uk
01752 794444 drakesden.co.uk

212 Treasure Island

Treasure Island is a trove of wonders for all children over two years old, especially lovers of pirates, gold, skeletons and skulls. At the West Hoe, watch them revel in the playground, and maybe join them, in a game of the craziest swashbuckling golf, or let them bounce off all that energy, like Tigger, in the trampolines enclosure. Let them imagine they are Lewis Hamilton on the go-carts, Agostini on the go-bikes, or the really young ones can set their sights on more likely careers with Bob the Builder. No pirate adventure would be complete without gold-digging, which is brilliantly set up round the pirate ship, Drake's Golden Hind. The awesome view of the Sound and buzz of the waterfront will keep parents energised.

215 Keep an eye on One Plymouth events, such as Treasure Hunts, Finding Elmer elephants and other delights and activities for children of all ages. There's always something going on!
oneplymouth.co.uk

216 Anyone in the family can get creative for half a day at Clayart and paint their own works of art from a range of great pieces of Bisque pottery, or have plaster casts or clay prints made of their hands, feet or paws!
01752 665565 clayart.co.uk

217 Plymouth Karting, for anyone above 7 years old, has got to be one of the most exciting, fast and furious experiences in the South West and also hosts the brilliant Laser Tag where you can be the harmless hunter or the hunted.
01752 651499 plymouthkarting.co.uk

218 At Devonport Naval Heritage Centre, children of any age can look into a periscope, see navy clothing and weapons, look at fantastic model ships, look up at giant figureheads, go around the submarine "Courageous", and take the blocks and pulley challenge.
01752 552326 devonportnhc.wordpress.com

219 Adrenalin & Super Tramp

Rush hour strikes at Adrenalin Leisure and they're on. Kids unleashed in The Ship, making space betwixt them and the ground. Curling, twirling, sidewinding, cartwheeling and vaulting. Jumping up, jumping out and jumping through. Combinations, bounces and rhythmic moves to musical beats. Slides, hops, bends and stretches. These are a few of the favourite moves as they run here, there, everywhere; powered on pure adrenaline. This great adventure playground is full of trampolines, inflatable slides, climbing frames and walls, bendy mushrooms, airbags galore, button swings, and more. It's similar at Super Tramp with 50 super trampolines, a slam dunk area, a big air bag plunge, dodgeball and "The Wall".

01752 717727 adrenalinleisure.co.uk
01752 710791 supertrampplymouth.co.uk

221 The Box is the cultural core of Plymouth with a wealth of wonderful stories and artefacts of the past and some seriously fascinating facts for inspiring children to explore Plymouth's extraordinary and unique past.
01752 304774 plymhearts.org/thebox/

222 Welcome to the greatest skate at Plymouth Pavilions ice rink, hosting skating lessons, ice discos, cheap sk8s, and chilly tots for any child with toddler foot size 6 or above. There's something for everyone.
01752 936363 plymouthpavilions.com

223 Let the kids, and you, if you like, act up at the Tripadvisor certified excellent Soapbox Children's Theatre for under 5's, and 5 to 15 year olds. Join the passionate staff, who are 'inspiring futures', in teaching kids drama, dance and art.
07754 177678 stiltskin.org.uk

224 Clip n Climb is the budding mountaineer's heaven, with high climbs of all shapes, colours and patterns, with an ingenious safety device for all.
01752 717567 plymouth.clipnclimb.co.uk

220 Mount Edgcumbe, as well as hosting the amazing native black bees, is a hive of activity, with Frisbee Golf, Adventure Segway, Baba Yaga's Circus School, Mountain Biking and Adventure Bay Surfing.
01752 822236 mountedgcumbe.gov.uk

FAMOUS PLYMOUTH PEOPLE

225 Imagine how you'd have felt if you had booked a ticket for Plymouth's Chamber of Commerce Christmas Ball in 1962, with the Beatles as the band, only to have it cancelled, owing to a lack of interest. Their next appearance in Plymouth was a sellout.

227 Sharron Davies, model and Olympic swimmer, struck a fine pose at Devonport Swimming Association where her meteoric career began, representing Britain at the Montreal Olympics, aged 13, and going on to win silver at the Moscow Olympics in 1980, aged 17.

226 Do you say transportation or transit? It's all the same to Plymouth boy, Andy Byford, who has now been a chief of it, to a greater or lesser extent, in four countries: London, NSW in Australia, Toronto in Canada and now New York, where he is the big chief in charge of some 7 million passenger journeys every day. As you probably can imagine, the Big Apple has the busiest transport system in North America, with its subways, rail and bus networks but Andy still likes to come home occasionally, is proud to be a Janner, and relishes the drama of The Pilgrims playing at the Theatre of Greens. Naturally, he would dearly love to see the airport at Plymouth reopened. Your city needs you, Andy!

229 Tom Daley launched his diving trajectory to stardom at seven years old, starting at the Plymouth Diving Club. Amongst other accolades, he won a bronze medal at the Olympics and was twice World Champion.

230 Heather Knight, educated at Plymstock, was fanatical about cricket and went on to Captain the Women's English Cricket team, which won the 2016 World Cup. She was later awarded her OBE in 2018.

231 Nicola Kavanagh provided the inspiration, during rehearsals of Othello, for Joseph Hillier's seven metre tall, over nine tons, bronze sculpture in dramatic pose, outside the Theatre Royal.

232 BBC Presenter, Philip Schofield, is famous for presenting This Morning and numerous other similar projects. However, he got his first break working for Plymouth Hospital Radio at 15 years old.

> I feel extremely lucky to compete openly as who I am, not worry about ramifications.

Tom Daley

228
The Rt Hon Michael Foot

A Plymothian commemorated at Freedom Fields Park, in Mutley, he was a true titan of the intellect. Secretary of State for Employment, Leader of the Opposition ('80 to '83), author, Social Democrat, journalist for the Evening Standard, great orator and more. Another irony for Plymouth, steeped in nuclear submarine history, is the fact that he was a campaigner for nuclear disarmament while being MP for Devonport. Also, MP for Ebbw Vale/Blaenau Gwent, he was a staunch advocate for sovereignty and withdrawal from the EEC.

233 One foot before another. The Rt Hon Isaac Foot was Lord Mayor of Plymouth, President of the Liberal Party, VP of the Methodist Conference, Privy Counsellor, MP for Bodmin, and father of four, including Michael.

234 Laurel & Hardy's final UK performance was to be at the Palace Theatre in Plymouth's Union Street in 1954, but due to Hardy's flu and heart problems, they never performed on stage again.

235 Dawn French

Comedian, Dawn French grew up in Plymouth and went to St Dunstan's Abbey School. Like Jennifer Saunders her father was in the RAF. One of her most famous roles was in Sky 1's Delicious, shot at Pentillie Castle and filming also took place at Royal William Yard.

236 What do Laurel and Hardy, Suzi Quatro, Charlie Chaplin, Anne Ziegler, Webster Booth, Lionel Blair, Hale and Pace, Dame Janet Fookes, Tommy Trinder, and Cameron Mackintosh have in common? They all stayed at the grand 150-year-old Duke of Cornwall Hotel, opened in 1865, and one of the most iconic landmarks in England, described by Sir John Betjeman as 'one of the finest examples of Victorian Gothic architecture'. It was the tallest building in the city until high rises started to fill the skyline, but its grandeur and timeless beauty remain, along with its impressive history and wonderful service. The interiors are also stunning with each room individually decorated with many a grand design, and upgrades boasting all kinds of trimmings like 4-poster beds, whirlpools and even a hidden room.

237 Legendary footballer Trevor Francis, with 52 England caps and 12 international goals, and the first English player to be sold for a million, spent much of his childhood in Plymouth.

238 What a nerve! Sir Andrew Fielding Huxley, half brother of Aldous (writer of the famous Brave New World), was an English physiologist and biophysicist, who worked with Alan Hodgkin, grandson of Thomas Hodgkin (discoverer of Hodgkin's lymphoma), at the Marine Biological Association laboratory in Plymouth, from 1935 to 1939. They studied how impulses travel along neurones, using the giant axon of the long-fin inshore squid; a genius of an idea, given the size and length of their neurones, some of the longest known to mankind. They were pulled off the work to have their nerves tested on warfighting challenges in WWII, but returned to Plymouth in 1946 for six years to define how nerve impulses travel. They both went on to win the 1963 Nobel Prize in Physiology.

239 Debra Searle, having never rowed before, and having been abandoned by her now ex husband early on in the race, rowed solo across the Atlantic in 2002, and went on to complete many other extreme adventures, be a motivational speaker and get an MBE.

240 Ben Proud, 50 metre butterfly World Champion in 2017 and Olympian, launched his career with a swimming scholarship at Plymouth College, before training in Turkey to compete in worldwide events.

FOOD AND DRINK

241 With grand vistas through grand floor-to-ceiling windows, Pier One is a bistro offering all kinds of delicious foods on the edge of the waterfront, looking directly out to the ocean, where the old pier used to be.
01752 251320 pieroneplymouth.co.uk

242 The Gog and Magog pub was so named after two ancient giants, who legendarily slugged it out on the Hoe, before one threw the other into the sea, commemorated for a time in chalk figures in the turf of the Hoe.
01752 264160 jdwetherspoon.com

243 The Boston Tea Party café, in Jamaica House, by the Barbican, was voted 'most ethical café in the UK', so treat yourself to a nice cuppa in your own cup, and feel better about the planet.
01752 267862 bostonteaparty.co.uk

244 The Fisherman's Arms in Castle Street, in about 1850, was one of many pubs formerly set up as a brothel and alehouse for a couple of guineas (just under £170 today).
01752 268243 fishermansarms.co.uk

245 Taste wines from across the world at HonkyTonk Wine Library, run by Fitz and Zoe who say, "We are a family of huggers, we embrace all who love to chill and make conversation".
01752 257968 honkytonkwinelibrary.com

246 Crowne Plaza's Steakhouse Bar & Grill, run by Marco Pierre White.
See Crowne Plaza section page 202

> "The sheer weight of water pulverised the pub but amazingly a year later, after dogged determination and a £1 million repair bill, we re-opened."

Waterfront Pub

248 Nearly destroyed by waves from the terrible storm of 2014, The Waterfront on the Grand Parade, rose again after a major refurbishment, and is decked out in wood, perfectly perched upon the water with exceptional food, drink, sailing decor and views.
01752 226961 waterfront-plymouth.co.uk

249 The Hook and Line in the Royal William Yard, would like to get you Hook, Line and Sinker, amongst other beers, cocktails, champagne, wine and especially rum at the Rum Bar, in this, the newest independent, seafood eatery and take-out in town, with its cool and rustic vibe.
thehookandlineplymouth.co.uk

250 At Column Bakehouse, the only social enterprise bakery, do your own bake off and learn first hand the secrets of artisan bread making with sourdough, au naturel, with no additives, from local sources.
01752 395137 columnbakehouse.org

247 Boringdon's Great Hall

Through the lion flanked stone archway, Boringdon's Great Hall has always been a great place to feast on food and fine wines from the time of Sir Francis Drake and his peers arriving after his singeing of the King of Spain's beard. What a party that must have been! The Àclèaf restaurant has captured the golden age of travel with their exceptional five star fine dining menu, and from here, you can view paintings of Plymouth's greatest sea faring heroes of old and other characters from the Tudor period. However bowled over you are by the hall, the waiters will tell you that the majestic bedrooms are a knock-out, with their four-poster, king size beds, and luxurious freestanding baths.

Boringdon Hall Plymouth PL7 4DP 01752 344455 boringdonhall.co.uk

251 Try the Barbican's Tudor Rose Tea Rooms in New Street or The Flower Café in Southside Street, to indulge in a traditional Devonshire cream tea with jam on the top!

01752 659087 tudorrosetearooms.com

252 The Good Food and Craft Market in Royal William Yard, holds monthly markets selling the freshest of produce and most artisanal of arts and crafts in Melville, one of its oldest buildings.

royalwilliamyard.com

253 The Hutong Café, at the entrance of The Royal William Yard, is a fun and environmentally friendly place to enjoy the views and have a delicious snack. Everyone knows everyone here and, as soon as you step through the door, George, Jack or Emma, of the Harman family, will greet you like a long lost friend. They make consistently delicious coffee, superb breakfasts, and a yummy fresh seasonal menu, including roasties, which is a popular snack for the Devil's Point paddle boarders. The brilliantly curated menus are inspirations from their travels and working in other exciting foodie cities like Berlin, Beijing, Sydney and Singapore. The delightful front terrace, with Parisian style seating, gazes over the waters of the harbour, where you can watch the world, while enjoying the latest Princess super-yacht cruise past, as they frequently do!

07455 376377 facebook.com/TheHutongCafe

254 The Jacka bakery has created a special Mayflower biscuit for 2020, to commemorate four hundred years since the boat sailed.

01752 262187 facebook.com/JackaBakery

255 The fine dining Greedy Goose restaurant, since 2014, has served excellent dining experiences in one of the oldest surviving houses in Plymouth, Prysten House on Finewell Street, built c.1498, from local Plymouth limestone and Dartmoor granite by a rich Cornish merchant, Thomas Yogge. It's a wonderful place to step back in time and eat, especially great value from 5pm to 6.30pm or anytime on a Tuesday. It has often been called 'the house by the churchyard' and has many doors to nowhere and a large well that sits as a centrepiece in one of the dining areas – a good place to lose your phone forever if you fumble while using the torch function to illuminate the well.

01752 252001 thegreedygoose.co.uk

256

The Duke of Cornwall

'Tea at the Top' is a unique experience offered by The Duke Of Cornwall Hotel. The hexagonal Reynolds Tower suite gives you unprecedented 360 degree views from on high, of Plymouth. To get there, you must reach through a hidden door and go up a wonderful wooden spiral staircase. There are amazing exhibits of memorabilia at each level, of bygone eras, and even an old accounts book to flick through, showing you just how much the cost of living has changed. The classic English cream tea is, of course, to die for, another day.

The Duke of Cornwall Plymouth PL7 400
01752 275850 thedukeofcornwall.co.uk

RETAIL THERAPY & COOL SHOPS

257 Sarah Pelly's Home Revival Interiors is a goldmine for those looking to bring their beloved but flaky furniture pieces back to life, using all kinds of methods, preparations and paints for an amazing array of beautiful finishes.
01752 975039 homerevivalinteriors.co.uk

258 The Upcycled Home Co. based at The Old Coach House at Mt Edgcumbe, takes you on a wonderful journey of rediscovery, that gives new life to hundreds of old things in ingenious ways, like turning forks into fancy eggcups.
07875 756311 theupcycledhomeco.co.uk

259 The Red Brick Cycle Shop is funky and fun for bike enthusiasts who need all kinds of bikes needing all kinds of repairs, for all sorts of experiences.
01752 6035268 redbrickcycles.co.uk

260 Michael Spiers, founded in 1957, is the South West's leading jeweller, and creator of fine jewellery for stars, such as Elton John. As well as leading the field, they stock nearly all the best brands, and exquisitely designed high end elegant watches. The Spiers family have also sold and crafted exclusive custom made jewellery, like Ben Proud's Olympic ring, and stunning eternity rings for the city's movers and shakers of all kinds.
01752 661981 michaelspiers.co.uk

261 Annterior combines timeless elegance and beauty with high quality retro, vintage, contemporary, or traditional antiques and furnishings.
01752 558277 annterior-plymouth.co.uk

262 Parisian Sweets Designer and Vintage Clothing is owned by a Plymouth born fashion expert who also styles stars, such as Jonathan Ross, in his spare time. Come here to talk Chanel.
07508 285668 facebook.com/ParisianSweetVintageClothing

263 Shopping for an expertly guided Plymouth tour? Devon and Cornwall Tour Guides provide regular walking tours that cover the city centre and the amazing Barbican in the old quarter, which shows sites most likely visited by the Mayflower Pilgrims; as well as wonderful views and historic landmarks along the Waterfront and up on the Hoe. The most iconic sites of Plymouth are brought to life with the Aquila qualified guides.
01752 290341
devonandcornwalltourguides.com

264 Plymouth Market is over 60 years old and is hard to beat for retail therapy at its 140 stalls selling all kinds of things, with great eateries interspersed amongst them.
01752 306551 plymouthmarket.co.uk

265 Sloggett and Son, set up recently, are an old Union Street family that sell interesting things, vintage and antique, skandi, and cool.
01752 665763 sloggettandson.co.uk

"My family loves Union Street, it has a great history and so much potential. We wanted to invest to make that happen."

Roland Sloggett

266 Make at 140

Make time to visit 'Make at 140' in Ocean Studios of the Royal William Yard, to make something special; pick from the biggest selection of buttons in the South West, with loads of vibrant zing, and the makers can bring any dull outfit to life, and make it sing. The shop is a dress-maker's dream with beautiful fabrics ranging from Organic Jersey to Atelier Brunette. Open from Wed to Saturday 10am to 5pm. You can follow them on social media @makeat140 to hear about their latest creative workshops from beginners' sewing courses to sew-your-own sexy underwear offerings.

07776 757300 makeat140.co.uk

For another great fashion shop in the Yard, see Identity Fashion, page 145.

267 **KW Brothers is the best Asian supermarket in the South West and supplies everything you could ever want in the way of the oriental food shopping experience.**

01752 208899

268 **There's so much going on at Artmill Galleries, where you can have your masterpiece beautifully framed, admire some of the most creative and innovative artwork in the South West and wander into the truly inspiring Sculpture Courtyard.**

01752 255020 artmillgalleries.co.uk

269 **Celebrations Cakes By Kelly sets her cake making at the highest and most important level possible; baking and decorating bespoke cakes for that special wedding day.**

07530 747828 celebrationscakesbykelly.co.uk

270 **Nicola Hurst Designer Jewellery will wow your future spouse forever, and inspire the hands-on among us, with her jewellery making courses.**

01752 228000
nicolahurst.co.uk

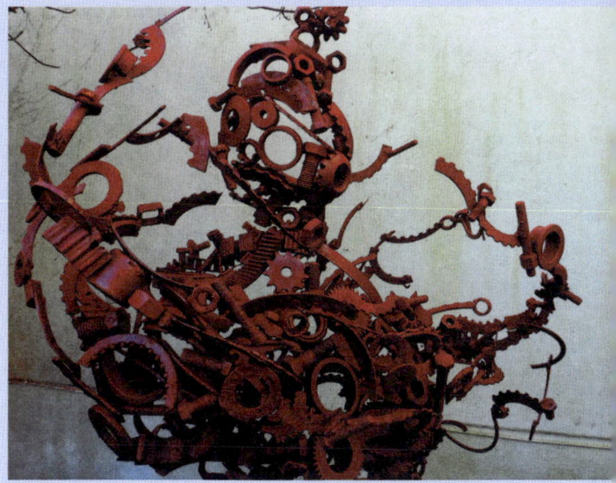

272 **The Clipper Inn is not what it seems. It is actually what you get when a community of people, by the name of Nudge, don't give up in an area and let buildings go to 'rack and ruin'; rather they band together to come up with great creative ideas that engage people of all ages and talents, getting them to realise dreams and engage in healthy social projects that benefit the community as a whole, and provide a leading example of what communities everywhere can achieve if they work together. The former all night drinking establishment has been turned, from drowning its sorrows, into accommodation, let mini market space and craft stalls, run as a social enterprise, part of the regeneration of Union Street.**

01752 229608 nudge.community

271 Vessel Craft Beer Shop is a hipster hangout that has interesting events, such as the bizarre sounding Verdant Putty launch and other such beverage bonanzas, in an unlikely part of town.

07796 667449 vesselbeer.co.uk

MUTLEY & THE BURBS

274 Not a dead end, the 34-acre Ford Park cemetery, west of Mutley, describes itself as 'a working cemetery in the heart of Plymouth' and is often full of life with many a social event, such as the odd coffee morning, bustling bric-a-brac sales, and guided walks about Devonport's people and heritage, all being organised within its peaceful grounds, surrounded by wonderful trees and flowers, with ornate graves and angel statues. Established by 1848, it reached its zenith, in the burial count stakes, in 1900, after which the popularity of cremations increased. You can get a real sense of the devastation and horrors of war when you see holes in gravestones made by shrapnel.
01752 665442 ford-park-cemetery.org

273 Mutley Plain is one of the oldest roads in Plymouth. Built during the Bronze Age (anywhere between 2,000BC to 650BC), it used to link Sutton Pool with the North. At the time of the Domesday Book (1086) it was just a few farms, worth a few shillings, within Judhael of Totnes' overlordship and consisted largely of open countryside until around the 1850s, when everything expanded with the Victorian era. Since then, it has always been a thriving centre of trade and shopping, and during WW2, the only place to shop. It is now home to large numbers of students and boasts many pubs, bars, clubs, cafés, small supermarkets and takeaway outlets. With students there comes the need for looking good and attracting mates, so it's not surprising the area is full of barbers and beauty salons, where you can get your bangs and other bits looking bang on.

275 Mutley Park, once part of the Mutley House estate, is a much understated peaceful place, with some wonderful trees. Secluded away, there are many places to sit and relax, marvel at the beauty of the copper beech, Monterrey cypress and redwood, walk your dog or watch your children playing in the park that includes swings, climbing frames and a basketball hoop.
plymouth.gov.uk/findpark/mutleypark

278 Mutley Park and its neighbour, Thorn park are pretty much the southernmost part of the amazing 15-mile Co-operative Way, which winds it way through some of the most breathtaking natural sites to the north of Plymouth.
plymouth.gov.uk/parkingandtravel

276 Go and spend a penny in the bushes of Thorn Park and discover a cast-iron one-man Victorian urinal that George Jennings created for the Great Exhibition of 1851 in London, where he coined the phrase by making 827,000 people pay for the pleasure.
plymouth.gov.uk/findpark/thornpark

277 For the 'trainspotters' now also known as 'gricers', Mutley railway station is a 'line-bashers' dream. All that remains of this once posh 'station of the gentry', financed by the local people in exchange for shares in the event of profits being generated, is a barely discernible platform on the Plymouth bound side, which can be found along the stretch of railway south of Apsley Road. Opened in 1871 as Plymouth's second permanent railway station, it was in competition with horse-drawn trams and later on, electric ones. It was finally closed just before World War II.

279 Freedom Fields Park is home to the Siege of Plymouth War Memorial 1643. Go and feel the history of the "Sabbath Day Fight", recorded as the "The Great Deliverance" of the Parliamentarians, against the King, after great hardships, having been under siege for more than three years.' Go and contemplate freedom with a snack at the rustic café and relax.
07914 238372 parklodgecafe.co.uk

280 Whether you want to be the best looking filly in town or the conquering romantic heroine of a wealthy bon vivant's heart, GG's Hair & Beauty Salon, the Plymouth Herald readers' champion out of 112 salons in 2018, will give you all the class you need in your quest for the ultimate prize.
01752 220609 ggssalon.com

281 Mutley Baptist Church, built in 1867, stands majestically and magnificently at the south end of Mutley Plain. The imposing Venetian-Italian Palladian style belies the feeling one gets when joining the 'family' or congregation inside. "I feel loved and am able to develop my faith," says one.
01752 203346 mutleybaptistchurch.co.uk

282 Sir Francis Drake seems ubiquitous in Plymouth and even lived at Thornhill House, Mutley in 1592, the site of which is now the fine looking Hyde Park Junior School.
01752 225314 hydeparkjuniorschool.co.uk

283 Drake's Leat, a 17-mile channel, 6 feet wide and 2 feet deep, started from the Burrator dam on Dartmoor, and passed through Mutley Plain on its way to supplying water to Drake's Manor Mill in Mill Bay.

284 The Fortescue Pub on Mutley Plain is a local favourite, which keeps alive old world charms, with great real ales and food for all the family.
01752 660673 greeneking-pubs.co.uk/pubs/devon/fortescue

287 Another gem saved by the people of Plymouth, The Hyde Park Inn is a riot of colour and memorabilia, chips in pint glasses, vibrant reds and greens, pizza specialties, dancing lions, 007, a Bentley sign, a gin club, and an upper class upstairs for hire. Drink some Dartmoor IPA and eat the locally sourced gourmet food from farm-to-table in this 150 year old, pure gold establishment.
01752 601446 thehydepark.co.uk

285 Dat Deus Incrementum (God gives growth) is a fitting motto for the coeducational Plymouth College on Hyde Park Road, for educating your 3 to 18 year old 'pride and joys'.
01752 505100 plymouthcollege.com

286 Head for the Buddhist Kadampa Meditation Centre, and learn how to achieve true, lasting happiness by discovering the secret of inner peace through meditation, with the deeply spiritual, founder of the centre, Venerable Geshe Kelsang Gyatso Rinpoche.
meditationinplymouth.org

288 The peacocks are finally in season in Mutley, where the trend in men's hairdressing and getting those diva hens to notice you, has truly taken off. There are now 8 Mutley barbers providing a dizzying array of treatments formerly thought only suitable for women.
yell.com/s/barbers-mutley.html

QUIRKY PLYMOUTH

289 Think Nelson wasn't afraid of anything? "You've been stitched up!" Back then, if you died at sea, you would have been sewn up in canvas, with the final stitch in your nose; and if you didn't respond to the piercing pain, you were considered dead. Nelson didn't want a burial at sea, some say because he feared being stitched up in a bag. He was instead, after being shot in 1805 at the Battle of Trafalgar, preserved at sea, brought back in HMS Victory to the mortuary of the Old Naval Hospital in Stonehouse, and then buried at St Paul's Cathedral in the grandest five day state occasion of its time.

290 Cannons to the back of them. Charles II, remembering how Plymouth sided with parliament against his pop, ordered some of the cannons mounted on the Royal Citadel walls to point into the city, to stop anyone having ideas about his head.

291 Sir Walter Raleigh is not responsible for 'living the life of Reilly'. The saying comes from Willy Reilly, who ran off with a rich maiden, was caught, tried and acquitted, to lead a blessed life with her and her wealth forever after.

292 A 'square meal' was not actually anything to do with a healthy meal but simply the shape of a ship's meal trays.

293 Not enough room to swing a cat in' is not to do with abusing cats, but a naval expression for when whipping errant sailors with a cat-o-nine-tails was considered the best way to keep order.

295 The busiest and arguably most iconic street in Plymouth, and cornerstone of the grand post war plan to build a truly 'state of the art' modern city, is Armada Way, which crosses Notte Street, where you see a statue of Drake uncharacteristically loitering on the right hand corner, above La Roux. What he would have made of the English adoption of the admittedly fine sounding Spanish word for a naval fleet is anyone's guess, having spent much of his life staunchly defending Queen and country against it.

294 Is history always written by the victors? Sir Francis Drake's most famous moment of cool-headedness, some of us were led to believe, came when he was playing bowls as the invading Spanish Armada of 130 ships, the biggest fleet ever to have been launched, sailed past Plymouth up the channel in crescent formation. "There's time to finish this game and thrash the Spaniards, too," he is believed to have said, but he would also have known, as a sailor, that it was low tide and the English fleet grounded. The waters then rose sufficiently to chase the Armada up to Gravelines. The rest is history.

296 The oldest Ashkenazi synagogue in the English speaking world does not hide among other buildings along Catherine Street. Rather, it remembers the heady days when it was sited in a commanding position over the main market square, a long time since, filled in with other buildings.

297 Despite Sutton Harbour appearing in many places as the official name of the water beside the Barbican, Sutton Pool is still regarded by the locals as its real name; the former is also the name of a 150 year old development company, focused on growing annual returns through creative asset enhancement.

298 A full scale replica of the Golden Hind, Drake's circumnavigation ship, could be floating as a wonderful tourist attraction in Sutton Pool, if Plymothian procrastination hadn't resulted in its being snapped up by a more enthusiastic London borough.

> "I'm so well assured of the strength of the building, that I'd like to be in it during the greatest storm that ever blew under the face of heaven."

Henry Winstanley

299 While the defeated Napoleon waited to hear his fate, aboard the Bellerophon in 1815, his clothes were being laundered in the Barbican, and people charged to touch or even wear them.

300 Some cafés in the City have hit upon the curious idea that if you have a rubbish bin that looks like an animal, kids will be more keen to throw their rubbish into its mouth. How's that for a lesson in environmental care?!

301 Sir Richard Grenville – machismo itself – was reputed to have crunched in his teeth and eaten wine glasses to impress the enemy, and singly taken on 53 Spanish ships, in the navy's finest ship, before being captured and perishing in a storm, having damaged 15 Spanish galleons.

302 Pitifully late to counter the blitz, RAF Harrowbeer, Yelverton, was built from the rubble of Plymouth's bombed buildings, to act as an airstrip from which to launch fighter planes to defend the city.

303 In a similar spirit of hubris suffered by the ill-fated Winstanley, the boastful architect of the elaborate original Eddystone lighthouse, the Titanic met with a similar fate in 1912 when a crew member said to embarking passenger, Sylvia Caldwell, "God himself could not sink this ship!" On her maiden voyage, she struck an iceberg, taking over 1,500 of the ship's passengers, mostly men, to a watery grave. Besides Cosmo Duff-Gordon, who famously saved himself on a lifeboat only a quarter filled, there were a number of surviving crew members who were secretly conveyed to Plymouth to avoid a lynching.

304 Walk around Plymouth Guildhall and imagine how it could have happened that it was saved from demolition after WWII by only one vote.

CONFLICT

308 Plymouth Castle played its part in a very dark episode of England's history, the Prayer Book Rebellion of 1549. Cornwall and Devon identified very closely with their Catholic heritage and were particularly upset by the Dissolution of the Monasteries and removal of religious relics from their churches. The translation of the Book of Common Prayer into English but not into Cornish was a tipping point. During the rebellion, a Cornish contingent took over Plymouth, except for some royalists and protestants, who took refuge in the Castle. The rebellion was eventually defeated through much bloodshed, betrayal and barbarity, with the leaders being grimly hung, drawn and quartered.

305 Plymouth Castle's swansong, while Drake finished his game of bowls, was in providing shelter for the Navy before they successfully defeated the Spanish Armada in 1588.

306 Bretonside is a street that marks how close the Breton raiders of 1403 got, in their arson spree, to Plymouth's heart, before its citizens descended upon them from Plymouth Castle.

307 Plymouth's motto, 'the name of Jehovah is the strongest tower' from Solomon's proverbs, was adopted during the Civil War, reminding us of how Plymouth fought valiantly against royal tyranny, under the aegis of biblical quotes.

309 The Armada Dial (sundial) by artist and sculptor Carole Vincent was erected in 1987 to commemorate the defeating of The Armada 400 years earlier.

> "Whosoever commands the sea commands the trade; whosoever commands the trade of the world commands the riches of the world, and consequently the world itself."
>
> Sir Walter Raleigh

311 Barabary slavers, for the Arab Slave Trade, were a regular terror to the coastal towns of Cornwall and Devon, and as far north as Iceland, from the 1500s, when they stole men, women and children, over a million Europeans in total, before they were defeated by the US, Swedish, English, Dutch and French in the early 1800s. Plymouth parliamentary records of 1628 detail complaints that the Navy were not doing enough to deter the raiders.

312 The well-preserved 1860s Crownhill Fort, just off Tavistock Road, is a brilliant example of cutting edge fortress design from that time period, and runs fascinating two-hour tours and open days.

01752 793754 landmarktrust.org.uk

310 Book a fascinating tour of the dramatic 1665 built Royal Citadel, one of the largest in Western Europe, and still well used today by 29th Commando Regiment.

english-heritage.org.uk/visit/places/royal-citadel-plymouth

313 Plymouth's night time economy was run by women. Sailors would book a 'wife' when they came into port and she would hire a room for them to live as man and wife for 6 weeks or whatever was requested. This was how Lady Astor, by sorting out the slums and engaging the women of Plymouth, got voted in by one of Plymouth's most powerful communities. It's also what famous artist, Beryl Cook's paintings are actually about.

314 Charles Street Church, built in 1641, was gutted during the blitz in 1941. Its striking shell has been preserved as a memorial to those who died in air raids on Plymouth during WWII.

317 Both St Andrews in Plymouth and St Pauls Cathedral in London were raised from the ashes and each one had RESURGAM – 'I will Rise Again', written across their porches. In the case of St Andrews, Margaret Smith nailed up a painted wooden board in March 1941 after the second air raid destroyed St Andrews' interior. The sign remains as a reminder to all, whether it be the Great Fire of London in 1666, which devoured the interior of St Pauls or the blitz in Plymouth, that such sacred places will rise again like phoenixes out of the ashes.

315 Even today, the blitz of Plymouth is often overlooked, because of the lack of publicity at the time. Yet, per head of population, it was the most bombed city in the UK in WWII.

316 The last raid on Plymouth was on 30 April 1944. In 4 years, it suffered 59 bombing raids, over 500,000 incendiary bombs, and thousands of high explosive bombs, killing 1,172 civilians.

318 Refusing to be a has-been, Marine Ben McBean, has been deservedly memorialised with a statue in Plymouth, after losing an arm and a leg in Afghanistan, but rising again to complete the London Marathon as an inspiration to all, highlighted by Prince Harry.

319 Sir Francis Drake's Drum, a key part of his military strategy, was used for ship's discipline, calls to action such as burials at sea, and as a strategy to intimidate the enemy, all well reported in Cynthia Gaskell Brown's excellent, The Battle's Sound. Sir Henry Newbolt's poem, in 1896, warned that if England is in peril Drake will return to drum the enemy 'up the channel, as he drummed them long ago'.

ARTISTS & MAKERS OF PLYMOUTH

321 Except for London, Plymouth boasts the most 1950s listed buildings in the country, owing to the grand plan of Lord Abercrombie and masterpieces like the mosaics on the Bank building at the top of the Parade.

322 Made in Plymouth is the place to discover Plymouth's creative and cultural scene, featuring artists, designers, writers and theatre; there is a wealth of talent to explore and patronise.
madeinplymouth.co.uk

323 Gosh! & Absolutely's Rachel creates original, up cycled, quirky hand made artistic lampshades, using vintage fabrics, ranging from mythical mermaids to old fashioned wooden sailing boats, entwined with mythical dragons. Beautify your living room with one of her vibrant colourful creations.
07906 599541 goshandabsolutely.com

324 Kaya Gallery resides in a 1658 building, showcasing artists like Brian Pollard. Beth Warne, the owners daughter, is a model and professional boxer, who talks art and how to combat bullying.
01752 267474 kayagallery.co.uk

325 Rock Pool Trading create locally made, sourced and generally fabulous artistic gifts and artisan art works as well as supporting other like-minded businesses.
01752 200312 rockpooltrading.co.uk

326 Laura is 'Gosh!' And doesn't waste any fabric as she creates everything from pin cushions to magical hair bands, buttons, broaches and rings. She loves all kinds of drawing and painting in many mediums.
01752 200312 goshandabsolutely.com

327 Martin Bush, in his Royal William Yard studio, paints vivid abstract contemporary artworks, inspired from his many travels to Asia and love of Buddhism with its wonderful philosophy.
07703 231150 martinbush.co.uk

328 Dominic Sanchez-Cabello's gallery is an unassuming setup, located in the Barbican arcade with no more than ten paintings, a filing cabinet, a 1970s desk, an Egyptian granite head and a show-stopping death mask of the philosopher Friedrich Nietzsche. On entry, you will be greeted by the ghostly face of Charles I that once, temporarily had another pair of lips painted on it, to conceal its identity after the Civil War, which were later removed. Oliver Cromwell, his usurper, hangs beside him. The selected paintings are a disparate crew of historical figures including the contemptuous gaze of a young Lord Byron lookalike. The William Tylney Long-Pole Wellesley portrait is of a man widely regarded as one of the best-looking but most contemptible of his time.
07969 074879

329 Armada Framing, whether you are a Marvel Superhero or Elvis fan, is the place to have your special moments framed, whether with glitter or in wood, by cool craftsman, Graham Bright.
01752 263031 twitter.com/armadaframing

> "Creativity takes courage"

Henri Matisse

330 Ocean Studios

Book a workshop or commission a maker at Ocean Studios, The Royal William Yard, a hub of artists working in thirty two rooms and workshops, covering ceramics, photography, film, print, pottery and more.

0330 223 4158 oceanstudios.org.uk

332 Artist Sue Wills, in The White Lane Gallery, Barbican, paints beautifully on slate, paper and canvas, capturing the human soul and spirit of Plymouth's buildings, people and animals. She loves teaching art as much as she enjoys painting.
01752 263727 suewills-artist.co.uk

333 Toby Gorniak MBE, the inspiration for Street Factory graffiti arts and hiphop dance, uses elements of Hip Hop to transform young people's lives, to exceed their potential and fall in love with what they do. *07527 887893 streetfactorystudios@hotmail.com*

336 St Saviours CIC (Community Interest Company) is all about community organisation, visual arts and education. The original building was opened in 1886 as the Sunday School of the Anglican Church of St Saviours, but was destroyed in the blitz during WWII. Used as a chapel up until the 1950s it was left to Plymouth City Council who let Robert Lenkiewicz use the whole building as a library for his substantial book collection. After his death in 2002, the books remained until it became David Partner's portrait studio in 2019, part of St Saviours Trust for community and artistic use.
facebook.com/stsaviourscic

334 See why Councillor, Tudor Evans says, "The figureheads will give visitors to The Box a real 'wow' factor as they step through the doors, and a great insight into how its maritime location and military connections have shaped Plymouth over the course of time". There are 14 of these giants of which King Billy is the largest at 13ft and 2 tons.

331 David Partner is an extraordinary portrait photographer who objectively captures the spirit of ordinary people in such an artistic and exciting way that he is one of only 22 living photographers, including Bailey, Snowdon, Testino, McCullin & Liebovitz, who have had solo exhibitions at the Gallery in the last decade. The curator said, "We at the National Portrait Gallery know about portraits; Partner's are some of the best we've seen".
davidpartner.co.uk

335 Robert Oscar Lenkiewicz (1941 – 2002) is famous for faking his own death in 1981 as a publicity stunt, announcing his demise to the local newspapers to publicise his exhibition 'Death', held the following year in 1982. He justified his crazy actions, explaining, "I could not know what it was like to be dead, but I could discover what it was like to be thought to be dead." He actually died, broke, in 2002, and when clearing out his building, an embalmed corpse of a tramp was found hidden behind panels of his bookcase. A controversial artist, he had a studio in the Barbican, where vagrants and addicts hung out, who he painted for free. Today, these images of underworld characters are worth a fortune and are considered some of his finest work; a selection can be bought from Michael Wood Fine Art where they incorporate art appreciation at the highest level.
01752 225533 michaelwoodfineart.com

SHIPS & SHIPWRECKS

337 An excellent scale model of the Mayflower ship can be found in the Mayflower Museum above the Tourist Information Centre in the Barbican. The beautifully reconstructed wooden boat, is the closest Plymouth has to how it would have looked in 1620, and demonstrates clearly the cramped conditions aboard the c.90' long by 25' wide vessel with 5' high living quarters, partitioned only by hanging canvases.
01752 306330
plymouth.gov.uk/visitorsandtourism

338 In 1621, the Mayflower returned from Cape Cod to Rotherhithe in London, where it lay for 3 years before being scrapped, near The Mayflower Pub that dates back to 1550.
020 72374088 mayflowerpub.co.uk

339 Sailing Tectona makes tectonic shifts in people's lives. Ever wondered if the 'devil has claimed your soul', and you want it back? Then join Sailing Tectona's mission to be the Sea Change in people's lives. People like Darren, who got out of a life on the streets and today is the lead singer of Black Tar Roses, meaning rebirth. Another life changing Tectona story is Rachel's, one of hundreds of people who have benefited from the incredible Tall Ship challenge. She explains that her life wasn't worth living; she lost her husband and her job and couldn't get out of bed to look after her daughters. She would self-harm by scratching them and writing HATE, with a knife. She became critically ill and could see no way out. Then, Rachel encountered Mind and took a chance to join an inspirational Tectona voyage, recounting, 'The laughs we had that week! I had forgotten what it's like to feel happy, confident and be myself.' The voyage gave her the confidence to rebuild her life, study and give her daughters their mum back.

341 Sailing Tectona Be the Sea Change: Whether you want to donate money, time or skills to help hundreds more people recover from the horrors of substance misuse or mental health issues, go to Sailing Tectona's website to see jobs for which they need support. Sailing Tectona aims to build a boat with former crew members and sail off on the adventure of a lifetime, across the Atlantic or around the World!
07595 908336 sailingtectona.co.uk

340 The Box has displayed 14 giant Navy figureheads (that mariners of old felt were the souls of ships they sailed) that tower over you as you enter the museum and eat in the café; a fitting welcome for a city, and museum, steeped in the history of 100 epic voyages of discovery and defence. Don't miss Mayflower 400: Legend and Legacy and the woolly mammoth.
01752 304774 plymhearts.org/thebox

342 One of the oldest and best established community archaeology projects in the world, SHIPS (Shipwrecks and History in the Plymouth Sound), has a database of about 600 shipwrecks in waters around Plymouth; 700 when including historical records and unidentified targets. The team do excellent school presentations, and public talks throughout Plymouth and present their fascinating findings at international conferences worldwide.
pete@3HConsulting.com promare.co.uk

343 Plymouth is teeming with great pubs, many have naval and marine connections and amazing stories to tell. The Navy Inn on the Barbican waterfront, originally the Navy Hotel is a proper pub frequented by Service personnel, amongst others.
01752 301812

344 Unlucky for some, on November 13th, 1941, HMS Ark Royal, formerly known as a lucky ship, was sunk. All that remains above the waves, of this giant ruler of the waves, is its anchor, north of the Hoe.

345 The Coronation Wreck is Plymouth's only diveable wreck site protected as an English Heritage Designation. If you want to visit a designated shipwreck site anywhere in the UK, contact Peter McBride and Peter Holt.
coronationwreck.org

346 Wreck diving is very popular in and around Plymouth Sound, where there are dozens of wrecks that do not need any special permissions.
promare.co.uk/ships/Wrecks/ListDiveSites

347 A Bronze Age trading vessel, which sank in 900BC while carrying tin, copper ingots, a bronze leaf sword and gold wrist torcs from Plymouth, among the 295 found artefacts, is the oldest shipwreck ever found in British waters.

348 During James I's reign (1603 – 1625), there were, amazingly, 26 ships recorded as being called the Mayflower.

349 Plymouth City language has been shaped by sailors' slang, which is now part of everyday speech, such as 'is everything above board?', 'show your true colours', 'we are at loggerheads', 'don't let the cat out of the bag', 'pipe down' and so many other salty sayings. 'Pull your finger out' refers to firing cannons, making it happen. 'Over a barrel' refers to being tied to a barrel and flogged. 'Feeling groggy', being 'three sheets to the wind' and many other coded sayings explain inebriation in a coded way that even posh people can understand.

350 Parade Antiques sell all kinds of fascinating nautical instruments. All the shipwreck items have important historical stories to tell.
01752 221443
paradeantiques.co.uk

351 The brigantine, Metta Catharina, which sank in 1786 off the coast of south east Cornwall, was discovered by divers in 1973, almost totally buried and wonderfully conserved in silt. The wreck contained staggeringly well-preserved top quality Russian leather, known to have been sold to Massachusetts colonists as early as 1650. Also found were hemp, glassware, pottery, clay pipes and a host of other fascinating artefacts, which now have pride of place at Mount Edgcumbe House. The leather was so well preserved that it has been used to make luxury goods and sold on the American market to fund further wreck dives.

352 Aquanauts run SCUBA diving courses and are very helpful to archaeologists with shipwreck dives. Further specialist courses are run several times a year by the Nautical Archaeology Society (NAS)

nauticalarchaeologysociety.org
aquanauts.co.uk

FAMOUS VOYAGES

353 From 1768 – 1771, HMS Endeavour, skippered by Captain James Cook, sailed from Plymouth to the other side of the world, via the Pacific, to map Australia, New Zealand and Tahiti.

354 From 1772 – 75, HMS Resolution, also captained by Cook along with HMS Adventure, captained by Plymothian, Tobias Furneaux, crossed the Antarctic Circle, visiting South Georgia, New Caledonia and the Easter Islands.

355 From 1776 – 1779, on HMS Resolution, Cook mapped very accurately the West Coast of the USA and Canada while in search of the North West Passage. He also discovered Hawaii, where he was killed by natives in 1779.

356 Since 2019, the eXXpedition team, sailing in a 73ft vessel S.V. TravelEdge, have embarked on a two-year, 38,000 nautical mile round the world voyage from Plymouth's Marine Station, to investigate the extent of plastic pollution and how we might address it.

357 Imagine a voyage, in the company of petty criminals, from Plymouth to Australia for 7 years of exile, for swearing an oath of secrecy to combat a third wage cut down to 30p/week for you and fellow farm workers of your village, Tolpuddle. Then, imagine your return, after serving 3 years, to Plymouth, as heroes of the first trade unionist action that saw the successful petitioning of 800,000 protesters. Interestingly, the Tolpuddle Martyrs decided to emigrate to Canada after this harrowing experience and who can blame them.

358 In 1577, Francis Drake made history, yet again, by being the first skipper (in his Golden Hind) to circumnavigate the globe; Magellan, before him, died en route, but his crew completed the feat.

359 Scott of the Antarctic, born into a long standing military family in Devonport, is best known for his ill-fated journey on the SS Terra Nova, being narrowly beaten to the South Pole in 1911, and tragically perishing on the return journey.

360 Sir Francis Drake

Drake's singeing of the King of Spain's beard in 1587 was arguably the most successful naval campaign in history, conducted with 4 galleons, including his Elizabeth Bonaventure, pinnaces and 20 merchantmen ships to stop an imminent invasion. The English fleet sailed from Plymouth and showed extraordinary courage in the face of one of the most powerful empires of the time and continued to wreak havoc and pillage Spanish ships all the way down their coast, for some time, after decimating its navy in Cadiz. Over 30 Spanish ships were destroyed, while a heavily laden treasure ship and the means to store supplies were seized, which depleted Spanish provisions, delaying their attack by a year, and compromising the 1588 campaign.

361 The Sea Venture, Grenville's flagship from a fleet of 7 supply ships, bound for the desperate Jamestown colony in 1609, was wrecked by a hurricane on Bermuda, but formed the basis of its colonisation and Shakespeare's The Tempest, where it takes a storm to put things right.

362 Spanish Armada

The English fleet based in Plymouth, with Drake as Vice Admiral, were caught somewhat by surprise as the 130 ships of the Spanish Armada sailed past them, up the English Channel, in crescent formation. They finally caught up with them to fight the Battle of Gravelines, where the lighter weight and superior agility of the smaller sized English ships enabled them to outmanoeuvre the Spanish, after breaking the crescent formation with the help of high winds and fire ships. With the wind behind them, they chased the Spanish all the way up the east coast of England, who were further battered by storms and even higher seas around Scotland.

363 Sir Walter Raleigh's final search for El Dorado ended in catastrophe, when he fell ill, leaving Kemys and his son, against his orders, free to attack the Spanish. Raleigh's son was killed in the attack, Kemys killed himself later in shame and Raleigh was beheaded for it in 1616 at the Palace of Westminster.

364 Sir Francis Chichester, the first to solo circumnavigate the globe, on his 50 foot Gipsy Moth IV, arrived back in Plymouth in 1967. Queen Elizabeth II knighted him with the same sword Queen Elizabeth I knighted Drake.

365 HMS Plymouth was among the first fleet of ships to get to the Falklands War that earned Maggie the name Iron Lady, so called by the Soviet Union, who at the time appreciated that NATO was a formidable force if one such member could project such power over 6,000 miles away. The USSR collapsed soon afterwards. In 1982, in Operation Paraquet, the frigate helped recapture South Georgia through bombardment and the launching of its helicopter.

366 The Second Voyage of the Beagle, from 1831 to 1836, was supposed to be a mere two year expedition, a first for Robert Fitzroy as Captain, who had some demons to quell; the former Captain Stokes had committed suicide under stress and loneliness, as had Fitzroy's uncle. The 22 year old Darwin, a recent Arts graduate and trainee pastor, who studied geology more as a hobby than a career, was almost an afterthought for the trip. Fitzroy cast around for a naturalist, more for company than for a specific purpose, and a few were offered the job before Darwin. But the final match was clearly an excellent one and the voyage became a five year spectacular with mind blowing revelations and the discovery of unequalled natural beauty, and both men achieving great successes.

367 In 1815, the Bellerophon, pride of the English navy and victorious in the Battle of Trafalgar, sailed to Plymouth Sound with the captive Napoleon aboard.

368 Remembered for saving all 27 lives of his team in a two year epic battle against a seemingly eternal winter, Sir Ernest Shackleton set sail in the Endurance to cross the Antarctic in August 1914, only for the ship to be crushed by the ice.

FURTHER AFIELD

369 You probably know the fastest cat on the planet but not necessarily which has the toughest bite. At Dartmoor Zoo, Sparkwell, you can see both in action and much more.
01752 837645 dartmoorzoo.org.uk

370 Crockern Tor, Dartmoor, is where the Stannary Convocation of local tin miners convened until the mid 1700s. Exempt from Westminster laws – don't be thinking you won't get punished – you were treated as a traitor if you tainted your tin.
legendarydartmoor.co.uk/crockern_tor

371 The stunningly beautiful house of Antony, lived in for over 600 years by the Carew Pole family, sits upon the Lynher estuary, and offers an enormous range of creative activities.
01752 812191 nationaltrust.org.uk/antony

372 Seamlessly segue your way around tracks that take you to houses, a pool, a temple, a village and even an amphitheatre, with Adventure Segway, based in Mt Edgcumbe Park.
0371 789 1024 adventuresegway.com

373 A kaleidoscope of wonderful colours, the Garden House is a stunning estate north of the city at Buckland Monachorum and forget it, you won't.
01822 854769 thegardenhouse.org.uk

374 Along one of Cornwall's most beautiful stretches of coastline, you will find the delightful village of Kingsand, once in Devon with a house called Devon Corn that straddles the former boundary. Stay at Storm Cottage to experience the sea up close with amazing views.
homeaway.co.uk

375 The ancient monastic Buckland Abbey, Drake's home away from it all, basks in some of the most peaceful countryside in the land. You can just sit there, meditating for hours and feeling the ancient calming spirits, or there's the huge cider barn with its mammoth apple press, wonderfully preserved at one end. The Abbey is an enthralling labyrinth of rooms, corridors and staircases, exquisitely laid out for the visitor's journey through history, with a wide range of fascinating exhibits, period props and clothes to really get you in the swing of it. The Ox Yard restaurant serves great food, too.
01822 853607
nationaltrust.org.uk/buckland-abbey

376 Pillars of the community, the Woollcombe family have been Devonians since the 1100s, Plymptonians since the 1500s and owners of the grand Hemerdon House since 1792. The house is full of art, original furnishings and fittings, and collections of a family prominent in naval and military service, local government, clergy, business, law, and medicine. Go and see all this, the parkland landscaped in 1802, the walled garden, the pond, the fireplaces, and feel the sense of history and community.
07704 708416 historichouses.org

377 Take Mt Edgcumbe's awesome 'Illustrated Tree Trail', which leads you through two miles of the most beautiful woods, to learn about 17 of the park's grandest and most enduring living beings.
mountedgcumbe.gov.uk

378 Ark Royal

Buckland Abbey is home to some great art like Knighting the Captains on board the Ark Royal. Some paintings are so valuable it is pointless trying to steal them, as you will get caught selling them, like the Rembrandt self portrait worth £30 million, which was discovered by chance. Go there and ponder how Rembrandt grew up with Pilgrim children.

379 The Nare, Cornwall's top 5-star hotel at Carne beach, past which the Mayflower would have sailed, organises coastal tours to Newlyn, allegedly the Mayflower's last stop before America. This trip is for truly adventurous guests, on the 38' classic gentleman's motor launch, Alice Rose. For stylish guests, you can be driven to Plymouth in the luxurious Range Rover for an exclusive Mayflower tour or go by helicopter, which lands next to the hotel. The Nare's visionary proprietor, Toby Ashworth also offers espionage missions around John Stock's To Snare a Spy, a novel revolving around the area. Will you be able to crack the code to uncover the identity of the Russian mole at the hotel and get away undetected in the Nare's motor launch, which is required for dropping agents at key locations on the Fal and Helford rivers? Only successful agents will be duly rewarded.
01872 501111 narehotel.co.uk

380 Eminent Plymothian historian, Cynthia Gaskell Brown reveals a lovely story about Lady Drake who asked J Passmore to fix Drake's drum in 1909. After killing the woodworm with paraffin oil and cleaning it, he discovered Drake's coat of arms underneath the centuries of dirt.

381 Cotehele House, near Saltash, gives you a great insight to Tudor England with amazing exhibits of armour and tapestries, but also beautiful gardens and woods, and even a mill and quay. Take a walk through the miles of wooded paths in 1300 acres of land.
01579 351346 nationaltrust.org.uk/cotehele

382 Explore the 1650s Mount Batten Tower, built on the site of a 1588 Elizabethan gunnery to protect the east side of the Plymouth estuary before the Citadel was built.

383 Pentillie Castle, near Saltash, built in 1698, although large now, was absolutely gigantic before demolition work started in 1966. The Coryton family host teas, talks, theatre and garden days. Look out for upcoming events and plan your visit accordingly. This is also a delightful place for an overnight stay.
01579 350044 pentillie.co.uk

384 Saltram House, near Plympton, built in 1614 by the infamous 'Bottomless' Bagg, a dishonest Head of Customs, was ideal for snooping on incoming ships, from the Prospect Tower. Nearly 100 years later, the Parkers of Boringdon fame brought respectability to the place and with them, pleasure grounds, 250 year old landscaped gardens, follies, a stable block, an orangery, coach house, a 3,000 book library, and a castle, which they filled with art, especially that of Joshua Reynolds. Most striking are the Robert Adam's Saloon for extravagant parties, and the four types of Chinese wallpaper. The place is so magnificent that George III and his extended family stayed for two weeks in 1789.
01752 333500 nationaltrust.org.uk/saltram

MOOR ON DARTMOOR

388 Dartmoor is a fascinating national park of immense natural beauty and cultural value, with 10,000 years of history and fantastic visitor centres for you to discover at Princetown, Haytor and Postbridge.
01822 890414
dartmoor.gov.uk

385 In 1809, Sir Thomas Tyrwhitt turned his hand to building a maximum security prison in which were housed up to 10,000 prisoners of the Napoleonic wars, formerly held in hulks (prison ships) in Plymouth harbour. Nowadays, it only houses 600 prisoners.

391 Dartmoor farmers conduct annual 'drifts' in late September, which involve rounding up their ponies to sell them at Chagford and Tavistock markets.

386 Author, Sir Arthur Conan Doyle, inspired by things vanishing in terrifying mists that appear from nowhere, and stories from the villagers about a phantom hound, wrote his most famous book, The Hound of The Baskervilles. The hound's bone-chilling howl can sometimes be heard in the wind and its terrifying gigantic footprints, are allegedly seen by early morning walkers, appearing out of nowhere and vanishing into impossibly boggy places. It's a place known for its darkness, black magic and superstitions. Even Doyle's brilliant detective Holmes comes to recognise the power of demons and bad spirits, conjured up to create havoc. Trying to track down this ghoulish hound, he quickly realises this is no playground for the faint hearted or foolish disbeliever.

387 Hidden in the Dartmoor grasses are broken ancestral gravestones, standing stones and, in one place, 300 metres of a stone road. Protruding granite tors appear, like giant spears of stone age giants, where the overlying sedimentary rock has eroded away.

389 Don't get caught taking sneaky photos at the Dartmoor Prison Museum or you'llend up as an inmate in the most feared prison of Victorian times.
01822322130 dartmoor-prison.co.uk

392 Princetown, Dartmoor's chief town, was set up in 1785 by Sir Thomas Tyrwhitt, in his attempt to tame the moorlands; but the moors were not for taming, as the soil is so poor.

390 Dartmoor's landscape is peppered with c.5,000 Bronze Age stone circles, built c.1,500BC, when people cleared land and burned wood to keep their homes warm, making it semi-barren.

393 60 years ago, owing to tin mining and agricultural needs, there were 20,000 of the mischievous but sweet iconic Dartmoor ponies, but now, with modern practices, number only 2,000.

394 Random stone crosses between scattered religious abbeys, act as boundary markers, from when the church owned much of the land. The Bennet's Cross, near the Warren House Inn pub,

takes you to a stunning 800 year old clapper bridge at Postbridge, made from big slabs of local granite. This unique national park is not just about the preservation of the landscape, but also the livelihoods of the people who live on the moor. The Postbridge Visitors Centre has self guided archaeological walks around Bellever forest and also covers the story of Whitehorse Hill. As a visitor, you are encouraged to become a Bronze Age History Hunter and learn how to build your own round house and conserve the area.

01822 880272 dartmoor.gov.uk

395 For atmospheric nights in Dartmoor and a truly unforgettable foodie experience, book Prince Hall, a boutique 8-room mansion, built in 1443, and rebuilt in 1787 by Justice Buller, the youngest ever British High Court judge, at 32. In 1945, the Astors bought it as a summer home. It's a unique place with up-cycled furniture, covered with wonderful hand-thrown pottery by owner Chris Daly, also a fantastic cook, who uses the best local farm produce. Mrs Simpson stabled 42 Arab horses in the barn, now used for pottery, and Yoga retreats in winter.

01822 8904043 princehall.co.uk

396 Wistman's Wood is genuinely spooky and not one to get lost in at dusk. A mile and a half walk from Two Bridges, it combines low growing twisting moss-covered oaks with a hundred lichens, to make for a really creepy effect, and you might find one of Dartmoor's giant Ash Black slugs, the world's largest at over 20cm long.

397 As you explore this devilishly beautiful and haunting spot with its 368 square miles of amazing landscape, remember that creativity also abounds with Dartmoor ice cream, honey, sparkling wine and Papillon, Black Dog, and Dartmoor Beast gin, just being a few of the products you can take home from the Visitor Centres.

398 High Willhays at 621 metres, is Dartmoor's highest point. All tors, wonderful for stargazing, are named, with fascinating stories, such as the Sphinx-like Vixen Tor, said to be controlled by a wicked witch who made many people vanish in the mist.

visitdartmoor.co.uk

399 Granite quarries on the moor at Merrivale provided jobs for building the prison in 1809, and supplying construction projects in London, most famously London Bridge in 1831 and Nelson's Column in 1843.

400 For award winning guided tours of Plymouth, Dartmoor and the South West check out chauffeur guide James Coulton of Select South West Tours

01752 290341 07470 022933

selectsouthwesttours.com

"The Mayflower voyage was one of the most influential journeys in global history. It changed the world and became a defining moment in the shared history of Britain, the USA and the Netherlands. The Mayflower 400 programme not only stands to strengthen our transatlantic links yet further but, through a fantastic range of arts and cultural events, will promote widespread awareness and education about the voyage and its enduring legacy."

Adrian Vinken, OBE, CEO Theatre Royal, Chairman of Mayflower 400

CONCLUSION

by Adrian Vinken

Messenger

Adrian Vinken, OBE, Chief Executive of the Theatre Royal, Chairman of Mayflower 400 & Destination Plymouth Limited has been the driving force behind Plymouth's cultural evolution, from a city that was once called a 'cultural wasteland' to the lead host of Mayflower 400 and 2nd in Condé Naste's Top 20 places to visit in the world in 2020. Here, in his own words, he talks about what he loves most about Britain's Ocean City.

If you know where to look, Plymouth is a kaleidoscope of fascinating gems. But it's a city that tragically vanished from the world map for several decades, after the Second World War prior to which it had been a must-visit destination for transatlantic cruise liners, and a frequent subject for GWR posters. Somewhere along the way, some of the city's identity and sense of itself seemed to have got lost. It was still rightly proud of its long association with the Armed Forces, especially the Royal Navy, but their presence was diminishing as a consequence of 'Peace Dividend' defence cuts and her dockyard at Devonport was rapidly shrinking. The only reason Plymouth grew so substantially over four hundred years to become the major city it is today, was that it became a vital strategic military asset, essential to Britain's role as a global naval power. It therefore benefited, over centuries, from a 'command economy', with its core economic activity being directly funded, first by the Crown and later the state. Basically, most of its jobs had been funded from the 'public sector' and, in consequence, it didn't have a strong entrepreneurial job-creating or industrial tradition. So, as government military spending reduced, Plymouth needed to forge a new future and identity for itself; one with a different economic focus to create new jobs to replace those lost in the docks and the Forces. Even as recently as 1982, when the Theatre Royal opened, Plymouth was only just emerging from the terrible impact of the Blitz, with the wholesale loss of its original city centre and replacement by Abercrombie's futuristic architectural vision. But just over a decade ago, things started to change, through a shared vision of a forward-looking, modern, culturally and economically vibrant waterfront city...Britain's Ocean City. An early version of that vision was captured in a cultural strategy called 'Vital Sparks'. Critically, City Council were encouraged to get behind that vision.

That then attracted funding bodies like the Arts Council, the Heritage Lottery Fund and Visit Britain to start to take Plymouth seriously and give their support. This, in turn, gave Plymouth City Council the confidence to start partnering and investing in new, world class facilities, alongside a raft of large bold economic development initiatives.

The Box, Plymouth's new arts, history and culture space, will be a game-changer for the city. Already recognised as the UK's most important museum development in 2020, it will make Plymouth the home of its largest contemporary art gallery west of Tate Modern.

> A mind blowing fusion of giant figureheads, revelations about Plymouth, its people and its pasties, woolly mammoths and stunning art.
>
> *Adrian Vinken, OBE, CEO Theatre Royal, Chairman of Mayflower 400*

Devonport Market Hall provides a new digital enterprise hub for creative industries and the Elizabethan House is being opened up to the public, with new heritage trails taking people on fascinating journeys into the city's rich historic past. Together, with 2020's broad and extensive cultural programme, they will constitute a step change in what the city has to offer to visitors and Plymothians alike. The Mayflower 400 commemoration has acted as a new cultural catalyst for the City. New public art is arriving in the City: The Messenger statue, in front of the Theatre Royal, created by Joseph Hillier, in a way captures the spirit of now.

Adrian's hidden gems

1 For me it is the Scott Memorial – powerful, moving and tragic – that stands out. Extraordinarily, it's also in one of the most beautiful and breathtaking locations in the city, yet largely unknown and rarely visited.

2 The '3 Ferries Trail' offers a world class experience for a few pounds. Catch the Cawsand Ferry from the Barbican, walk through Kingsand village and Mount Edgecumbe before catching the Cremyll Ferry and strolling to the Royal William Yard and the final boat trip back to the Barbican. A brilliant day out for the whole family with a huge variety of great places to eat and drink along the way.

Adrian's hidden gems

3 There's a very special surf break in Plymouth Sound. It's little known because those who surf it keep it secret. When there's a decent swell and a west-south-westerly wind, you can take your board mid-tide, on a 10 minute ferry from the city and ride some really serious surf against the backdrop of The Hoe, Mount Edgecumbe and Drake's Island. Name me another UK city that offers that!

4 The Dolphin (and its Bass Ale!) should be listed and have a very strict preservation order placed on it. It's a truly rare and precious thing in this day and age…a PROPER no frills pub! The foodie equivalent of The Dolphin for me is Supha's. You won't find its like anywhere else in the country. On the waterfront with a unique atmosphere, great Vietnamese food and wonderful fresh fish all at affordable prices. What's not to like?!

Messenger being brought in by the Royal Navy

It's a figure of a young girl in a dynamic crouching position, caught in a split second of composure and alertness, latent with explosive energy. It is a perfect metaphor for where the city is right now – poised, ready to propel itself into action for all the great things to come.

The sculpture has given rise to many conflicting interpretations and reactions from "the Incredible Hulk's sister" to a prostitute depicted in Othello. Love it or hate it, the 23-foot statue has made a huge impact on the city and is a message to the world. As one of the newest high-profile residents of Plymouth it was symbolically important that Messenger should arrive by water. This involved all sorts of logistical challenges but luckily Plymouth is blessed with an abundance of world class maritime expertise. So, with the help of the Royal Navy, the Queen's Harbour Master, Sutton Harbour Company and Associated British Ports, Messenger's precarious journey from the Royal Naval Base, out into deep water and back onto dry land in Millbay, went without a hitch, demonstrating the exceptional knowhow of the city.

Such innovation, creativity and spirit have been part of Plymothians' DNA for centuries. A major new piece of public art by Anthony Gormley has also been created. Named LOOK II, the "anthropomorphic" cast iron sculpture, weighing in at 2,700kg, was erected on the West Hoe Pier in May 2020. It comprises 22 individual iron blocks that have been cast as one single element to create a twice life-size figure, and will be sited at the very point where Sir Francis Chichester landed his Gipsy Moth IV in 1967 after becoming the first solo person to circumnavigate the globe by the clipper route.

A major performance and event programme, involving participation from communities throughout Plymouth, will be rolled out across the city over the next few years. This Land is possibly the most ambitious community theatre project ever undertaken: over 100 people from two communities either side of the Atlantic…one from the Wampanoag native people in Massachusetts nation in Massachusetts and the other from our inner-city Plymouth area. They are coming together to create a large-scale dramatic telling of the epic Mayflower story, warts and all. The show's songs are all written and played by local and nationally respected musician, Seth Lakeman, and his band. Most importantly, this anniversary is forcing us to honestly reassess, with the benefit of four centuries of historic hindsight, the overall impact of the 1620 voyage of the Mayflower and the world-changing mass colonisation that came after it. Previous tellings of the 'Pilgrims' narrative were largely rose-tinted accounts of a group of principled Christians driven by conviction to courageously forge a new community in the wilderness, supported by local Native Peoples. The principles of self-government they adopted, encapsulating democratic

> "Seth played the Boston Arena with Robert Plant, came straight off stage and was driven to the Mashpee library to share pizza with members of the Wampanoag tribe…within a year he had created *A Pilgrim's Tale*."
>
> *Adrian Vinken, OBE, CEO Theatre Royal*

A Wetu, the traditional home of the Wampanoags.

values and individual freedom under the law, went on to influence all future American constitutions through to the Declaration of Independence. What was missing from such narratives was the impact of the explosion in migration that followed and the grabbing of ever more land that the Wampanoag tribes amongst others had previously tended for 25,000 years before the arrival of the Mayflower. The growing tension between indigenous and migrant populations inevitably led to conflict in 1670 and, along with European diseases, the 'War of King Philip' in 1675, led to the near genocide of the Wampanoag nation.

Right from the outset, the Mayflower 400 team realised that, in order to do justice to the global significance of the Mayflower voyage, any cultural programme had to speak as truthfully to the Wampanoag aspect of the story as it did to the 'birth of a nation' narrative. We clearly weren't in a position to speak for the Wampanoag people. If the programme was to be both radical and authentic it had to be co-authored by their community. Over seven years, the Mayflower 400 team regularly visited Massachusetts and hosted reciprocal visits to Devon from representatives of our sister Plymouth 'across the pond'. This has helped develop many fruitful relationships between our communities; particularly, in recent years, with members of the Wampanoag Tribal Council and leaders of the Mashpee and Aquinnah Wampanoag tribes. As a result of these relationships and the trust they've promoted, many of the larger cornerstone projects of Plymouth's 2020 programme have been co-created with the Wampanoag community. The Box's landmark opening exhibition from May 16th 'Mayflower 400 – Legends and Legacy', the Theatre Royal's epic This Land community production, the amazing Wampum Belt craft project and the visual arts Settlement project in Central Park are either led or co-created by our Native American colleagues from Massachusetts and the wider USA.

In the process of assembling all these ground-breaking projects we have brought many new first-time visitors to the city and their reaction has served to remind us all of something we're often in danger of taking for granted: just how truly exceptional a city, Plymouth is.

The simple combination of its breath-taking coastal location, with Dartmoor and Cornwall on its doorstep, and the view of Plymouth Sound from The Hoe, parallels that of Sydney Harbour in Australia. Layer on top of that, the city's world-changing maritime heritage of Drake, the Mayflower, Cook and Darwin, as still captured in the bricks and mortar of the old quarter of The Barbican and The Royal William Yard. Making the most of these incredible world-class attributes has helped put the city firmly back on the world map. Its creative industries are burgeoning. Business start-ups are growing and a concept like The National Marine Park is readily embraced and supported. Because the 'Britain's Ocean City' brand and vision are not just cheap marketing slogans, but encapsulate a genuine truth about Plymouth's pioneering spirit, its equally stunning surroundings and the quality of life it offers, that vision has gathered momentum and become self-perpetuating. So, now we have a whole new generation of visionaries who believe in the city and want to build their future here, providing an ideal positive starting point for Plymouth's next 400 year adventure.

"Plymouth was once a city of swashbuckling venturers, sailors and pioneers, so vibrant that it spawned 51 other 'Plymouths' across the world to cement its global reputation. It now stands ready to reinvent itself for the next sea change."

> "Plymouth has got its mojo back and the wider world has been forced to take notice."
>
> *Adrian Vinken, OBE, CEO Theatre Royal*

Adrian's hidden gems

5 **Neolithic Dartmoor...drive 25 minutes from the city centre and head north on the ridge from Two Bridges. Cross the upper reaches of the West Dart river to Rough Tor and head west for half a mile and introduce yourself to the Beardown Man. He's a magnificent standing stone that's stood proudly on that lonely wild moor for nearly 5,000 years. It always feels to me like a rather spiritual encounter and I guarantee there'll be nobody else there to spoil your moment.**

Go prepared with water, food, map and all-round wet weather gear as this is a ten mile round trip from Two Bridges into the back of beyond. Interestingly, Dartmoor has one square mile for every day of the year.

Epilogue: The Vision Within
Connor McIntyre

Artist and actor Connor McIntyre has long since shed the mask of a heartless killer in Coronation Street, to create powerful abstract paintings in his Alamo studio, Plymouth, exploring the idea that the key to our future is understanding our DNA. Connor believes our history as a species, and our possible futures, are moving into sharper focus by the day, through understanding how our DNA affects us and the coded way we have repetitively behaved over cyclical events such as plague-like pandemics, which have recurred throughout history from the Great Dying of the 1600s, to the latest killer Coronavirus. By understanding more about who we are and where we have come from, through studying our DNA, we can recalibrate our approach for future events so such catastrophic outcomes can be avoided. His painting 'Dreaming Gilgamesh' (right), ingeniously encapsulates this concept. Through the complex layers of imagery he illustrates the inner thanataphobic quest for immortality; the many layers of paint show who and what we are in 'bits and bytes' of 'codes and codices'. Connor's paintings are both a great cautionary tale and also a hint at a possible coming together and reconciliation of society as a global community, where social barriers like racial prejudice and isolationism melt away. Re-unification of humanity can be achieved through the respecting of different cultural knowledge, like that of the Wampanoag's, the Pilgrims and the amazing people featured in this book, who ultimately, by understanding how DNA has shaped our past, can recode our future.

> When people take the journey into their ancestral pasts, their genealogies, and have their DNA tested and analyzed, they soon understand that there is no place for bigotry or prejudice, and that we are all connected. When you think about it, we are all made up of multiple strands and cultures, and yet ultimately are all one.
>
> *Lea Sinclair Filson, Director of Tourism, Massachusetts USA*

Acknowledgements

Thank you to these amazing people, without whom this book would not have happened:

In particular Adrian Vinken OBE and the first Plymouth Culture Board, musician Seth Lakeman and Plymouth artist and actor Connor McIntyre. The Wampanoag tribe, especially Cheryl Andrews-Maltais and Linda Coombs for her eye opening films on the lives of Wampanoag women being screened daily in The Pilgrims Hall Museum in Plymouth, Massachusetts. Lea Sinclair Filson, Director of Tourism, Plymouth, Massachusetts and Chris Messier. James and Josh at James Edgar Studio, Charlie Keeler, Sarah Smalldon for her wonderful illustrations, Photographer Guy Harris, Dominic Husband, Jodie Lidstone and Jasmine Butler. NatWest, Plymouth City Council, Visit Plymouth. The twenty amazing characters: Lord Mayor Richard Ball, John Cabello, Chris Robinson, Jessica Sneyd, Vicki Rowan, Sean Harrison, Jerry Sibley, Rt Rev'd Nick McKinnel, Catherine Hamilton, Ruth Mitchell, Jo Martin QC, Richard Pyshorn, Commander Steve Ward Royal Navy, Dr Jason Smith, Ayse and Brett Phaneuf, Jackie Gillespie, Deni Avramova Bastable, James Brent, Ashley Tod, Diane Nettleton, and Candice Hart. Also Emily Handslip Urban Splash, Lauren Rodgers Crowne Plaza. Lisa Brammer Business Development Manager at Bistrot Pierre and Residence One Boutique B&B, Royal William Yard, Beverley Priest The Royal William Yard Mill's Bakery Apartments, Jill Arnold, and Cherokee Mahoney. The team at The Box, Mount Edgcumbe, Boringdon Hotel, Theatre Royal, The Duke Of Cornwall, Bovisand Lodge Holiday Park, Aquanauts, Ben Squire & all his amazing team at Plymouth Boat Trips, Mount Batten Watersports, Sammie Coryton at Pentillie Castle, Phillippa Giles - the executive producer of Delicious, Toby Ashworth & Jamie Moore at The Nare, Dom Moore, Dominic Sanchez-Cabello, James Coulton, Sue Kay, David Coslett. Amanda Lee, Alice Pope, Jane Dymock and all the lovely people at Nash & Co solicitors. Ocean Studios, The Illuminate team in particular Jenny Bishop and Claire Honey.

The Crowdfunder Team, especially Bertie, Natalie and Christine. Kathryn Gray, University of Plymouth. One Plymouth, especially Scott Grenney. Deltor and Lee Doney. Marine Conservation Trust, especially Olly Reed. Erin, Shea and Paul Williams. Samad and Amzar Careem, Leo, Jennie and Johnny Keeler, Sharon Davies, Beth Warne, Brian and Karen Sanderson, Joe Dent. With extra special thanks to Sally Proud for all her help and support with the book from its infancy to completion.

With special thanks to: Holly Kellam, Euan Rellie, James Hill-Walker and the 176 others who backed our crowdfunding campaign.

And, finally, the 102 brave souls, who on Sept 16th, 1620 stepped on board a small ship called The Mayflower and set off from Plymouth.

Image Credits

Many thanks to the photographers, artists and illustrators and everyone in Plymouth, America and Holland.

PREFACE
4 (Pilgrim Hall Museum, Plymouth, Mass.) Foreword: 5,6,7,8 (Juliet Coombe).

THE MAYFLOWER
10, 21, 22, 24, 25, 26 (Juliet Coombe); 10/map (Sarah Smalldon); 11, 12, 13 (US Library of Congress); 17, 18 (Sutro Library, California); 19 (The Box, Plymouth); 23 (Charlie Keeler).

20 – 20 PLMOUTH PEOPLE
All character pictures and 54, 63, 110, 119, 167 by Guy Harris; all historic drawings and location maps by Sarah Smalldon; 30, 38, 95, 135 (Visit Plymouth); 47 (One Plymouth, Scott Grenney); 71, 75A, 87, 159, 171 (Juliet Coombe); 79, 82 (Theatre Royal); 91, 151, 154 (Charlie Keeler – 151, 154 thanks to Green Taverners); 103 (Mount Edgcumbe); 127, 143 (Urban Splash); 175 (Boringdon Hall); 183, 187 (Bovisand Lodge).

400 HIDDEN GEMS by gem number
3, 4, 10, 13, 31, 49, 51, 54, 55, 58, 64, 66, 67, 72, 73, 80, 81, 85, 93, 96, 103, 104, 118, 119, 120, 124, 126, 145, 147, 151, 154, 158, 160, 177, 179, 190, 207, 209, 213, 215, 250, 251, 256, 258, 265, 266, 268, 270, 273, 282, 283, 295, 303, 304, 329, 330, 335, 343, 350, 358, 359, 362, 366, 373, 377, 383, 385, 388, 391, 392, 394, 398, 400 (Juliet Coombe); 18, 21, 25, 57, 79, 86, 131, 135, 138, 139, 143, 201, 203, 210, 247, 274, 277, 287, 289, 309, 310, 314, 344, 360, 375, 378 (Charlie Keeler); 28, 104, 229 (Visit Plymouth); 127, 296 (Guy Harris); 33, 38, 39, 41, 44, 46, 47 (Plymouth Boat Trips); 61, 212 (One Plymouth, Scott Grenney); 90, (Theatre Royal); 171, 172, 174, 176 (Urban Splash); 186 (Bovisand Lodge); 97, 99, 100, 107, 112 (Crowne Plaza); 132 (Barbican Theatre); 152, 178 (Residence One); 163, 164, 168, 169 (Anita Benjamin); 173, 264 (Dom Moore); 189 (Mount Batten Watersports & Activity Centre); 192, 384 (Pentillie); 198 (Kiss & Bite); 200 (Andy Fox); 219 (Adrenalin); 227 (Sharron Davies); 234 (Sky 1's Delicious & many thanks to Pentillie for organsing this); 240 (Sally Proud); 252 (Greedy Goose); 294 (Devonport Naval Base); 316, 334, 340 (The Box); 320 (Nash and Co.); 322 (Holly Cumbers); 324 (Dave Crocker); 328 (Dominic Sanchez-Cabello); 339, 341 (Sailing Tectona); 352 (Aquanauts); 379 (Nare Hotel).

CONCLUSION
242, 244 (Theatre Royal); 243 (Charlie Keeler); 244.3, 246 (Juliet Coombe); 245 (Tom Griffiths); 248 (Connor McIntyre).

THE LIFE CENTRE
PLYMOUTH LIFE CENTRE
TAMAR BRIDGE
ROYAL ALBERT BRIDGE
P A F C
PLYMOUTH ARGYLE FOOTBALL STADIUM
CENTRAL PARK
MEADOW CAFE
DOCKYARD
DEVONPORT TOWERS
UNION STREET
DUKE OF CORNWALL HOTEL
TORPOINT FERRY
THE RED SCHOOL
CATHEDRAL
DEVONPORT GUILDHALL & TOWER
KING BILLY
SCOTT MEMORIAL
THE DOCK
CONTINENTAL FERRY PORT
CREMYLL FERRY
MUTTON COVE
PRINCESS YACHTS
STONEHOUSE TENNIS CLUB
KING POINT MARINA
DURNFORD ST.
ROYAL WILLIAM YARD
DEVIL'S POINT
FIRESTONE BAY
CONTINENTAL FERRY
HMS
MOUNT EDGCUMBE
DRAKE'S ISLAND
CORNWALL